Light in August

15-13

WADSWORTH GUIDES TO LITERARY STUDY

Maurice Beebe, General Editor

Light in August

and the
critical spectrum

edited by
John B. Vickery
University of California, Riverside

Olga W. Vickery

Wadsworth Publishing Company, Inc.
Belmont, California

L. C. Cat. Card No.: 79–142148
Printed in the United States of America
by American Book–Stratford Press, Inc.

1 2 3 4 5 6 7 8 9 10–75 74 73 72 71

Acknowledgments

Boston University: Darrel Abel, "Frozen Movement in *Light in August*," *Boston University Studies in English*, III (Spring 1957), pp. 32–44. Reprinted by permission.

Cornell University Press: Selection reprinted from Walter J. Slatoff, *Quest for Failure: A Study of William Faulkner.* © 1960 by Cornell University. Used by permission of Cornell University Press.

Louisiana State University Press: Olga Vickery, "The Shadow and the Mirror," from *The Novels of William Faulkner* (1964). Reprinted by permission.

Modern Language Association of America: Reprinted by permission of the Modern Language Association of America from C. Hugh Holman, "The Unity of Faulkner's *Light in August*," *PMLA*, 73 (March 1958), 155–166.

New England Quarterly: Ilse Dusoir Lind, "The Calvinistic Burden of *Light in August*," *New England Quarterly*, XXX (September 1957), 307–329. Reprinted by permission.

Princeton University Press: From "Light in August," in *Faulkner: Myth and Motion*, by Richard P. Adams (Copyright © 1968 by Princeton University Press), pp. 84–95. Reprinted by permission of Princeton University Press.

Random House, Inc.: Excerpts from *Light in August*, by William Faulkner. Copyright 1932 and renewed 1960 by William Faulkner; "Confrontations and Scenes," from *William Faulkner: A Critical Study*, 2nd edition (published 1962), by Irving Howe. Copyright 1952 by Irving Howe; selection from *The Achievement of William Faulkner*, by Michael Millgate. Copyright © 1963, 1964, 1966 by Michael Millgate. All reprinted by permission of Random House, Inc.

University of Kentucky Press: Hyatt H. Waggoner, "Outrage and Compassion," from *William Faulkner: From Jefferson to the World* (1959). Reprinted by permission.

University of Minnesota Press: William Van O'Connor, "A Part of the Southern Mores: Protestantism," from *The Tangled Fire of William Faulk-*

ner, University of Minnesota Press, Minneapolis. © Copyright 1954 University of Minnesota.

University of North Carolina Press: John B. Cullen and Floyd C. Watkins, "Joe Christmas and Nelse Patton," from *Old Times in Faulkner Country* (1961); John L. Longley, "Joe Christmas: The Hero in the Modern World," from *The Tragic Mask: A Study of Faulkner's Heroes* (1963). Reprinted by permission.

University Press of Virginia: Frederick L. Gwynn and Joseph P. Blotner, "Faulkner on *Light in August*" from *Faulkner in the University* (1959). Reprinted by permission.

University of Texas Press: Peter Swiggart, "The Puritan Sinner," from *The Art of Faulkner's Novels* (1962). Reprinted by permission.

Wayne State University Press: Alfred Kazin, "The Stillness of *Light in August,*" reprinted from *Twelve Original Essays on Great American Novels* edited by Charles Shapiro, copyright 1958 Wayne State University Press; "A Demonic World," reprinted from *Faulkner's Olympian Laugh: Myth in the Novels* by Walter Brylowski, copyright © 1968 by Wayne State University Press. Reprinted by permission of Wayne State University Press.

Yale University Press: "The Community and the Pariah," from *William Faulkner: The Yoknapatawpha Country,* by Cleanth Brooks. Copyright © 1963 by Yale University. Reprinted by permission.

Preface

Light in August was published in 1932, when William Faulkner was at the pinnacle of his creative powers. With *The Sound and the Fury, As I Lay Dying,* and *Absalom, Absalom!* it represents one of the most amazing concentrations of imaginative energy in American literature. By these works Faulkner established his claim as one of the twentieth century's finest and most distinctive writers. *Light in August* has played a unique role in the growth of Faulkner's reputation. Unlike his other major works, its structure and narrative are not so experimental as to confuse or alienate the reader making his first acquaintance with Faulkner. At the same time, it movingly develops many of the central themes both in Faulkner's mind and in the sensibilities of modern men. Violence, both individual and communal, race relations, the subtle and not so subtle influence of religion and Southern mores, and the struggles for identity and survival are all rendered powerfully. Faulkner's gift for stylistic shadings and graphic scenes and the spiritual and sociological intricacy of his characters give a profound sense of what it means to be alive in the twentieth century. The result is a novel that speaks to the contemporary scene in terms of universal significance. At the same time it deals with some of the major questions modern critics have been asking about the potential and the limits of tradition and innovation in the novel.

The above and other issues are carefully explored in the critical selections assembled here. As Faulkner is one of the most discussed American writers, only a fraction of the criticism available has been used. Yet, within that limitation, these pieces provide a sound and illuminating overview of what has been said about *Light in August.* Most of the critics have been careful to do justice to the novel by taking up all or nearly all of the issues it raises. As a result, a thematic or topical organization promised more distortion than illumination, since not every pertinent essay could be included in each section. Therefore, selections have been organized chronologically. The relationships between various essays are probed by the study questions at the end of the volume. They seek to suggest points of emphasis in individual selections as well as connections between essays on specific issues. The articles were chosen to provide, if possible, full statements of the critic's ideas concerning *Light in August.* To facilitate use of the collection for the controlled research paper, the original pagination of books and articles is indicated by boldface numbers in square brackets. The location of the bracketed number indicates the end of the page in the original.

Both editors wish to express their gratitude to the authors and publishers for their cooperation in granting permission to reprint the essays assembled here. They are also indebted to Anne Elizabeth Vickery, who labored with uncomplaining efficiency far beyond her years in the assembling and ordering of the materials for this collection.

Contents

τοῖσι λάμπει μὲν μένος ἀελίου τὰν
ἐνθάδε νύκτα κάτω

ἀστρα τε καὶ ποταμοὶ καὶ κύματα πόντου

Pindar

Faulkner on *Light in August*

FREDERICK L. GWYNN AND JOSEPH P. BLOTNER

Q. This is a question about *Light in August*. Could you tell me your purpose in placing the chapter about Hightower's early life in the end of the novel, that is, rather than when Hightower first appears?

A. It may be this. Unless a book follows a simple direct line such as a story of adventure, it becomes a series of pieces. It's a good deal like dressing a showcase window. It takes a certain amount of judgment and taste to arrange the different pieces in the most effective place in juxtaposition to one another. That was the reason. It seemed to me that was the most effective place to put that, to underline the tragedy of Christmas's story by the tragedy of his antithesis, a man who—Hightower was a man who wanted to be better than he was afraid he would. He had failed his wife. Here was another chance he had, and he failed his Christian oath as a man of God, and he escaped into his past where some member of his family was brave enough to match the moment. But it was put at that point in the book, I think, because I thought that was the most effective place for it. . . . [45]

Q. Sir, in *Light in August* the central character Joe Christmas had most of his troubles and persecutions and in his search to find himself was based on his belief that he was part Negro and yet it's never made really clear that he is. Was he supposed to be part Negro, or was this supposed to add to the tragic irony of the story?

A. I think that was his tragedy—he didn't know what he was, and so he was nothing. He deliberately evicted himself from the human race because he didn't know which he was. That was his tragedy, that to me was the tragic, central idea of the story—that he didn't know what he was, and there was no way possible in life for him to find out. Which to me is the most tragic condition a man could find himself in— not to know what he is and to know that he will never know.

Q. Sir, if he is not—does not definitely have Negro blood, well, what is the significance of Gavin Stevens's surmise there at the end when he explains that there's a conflict of blood? That is only a guess that stands for a guess and not a final knowledge of—?

A. Yes, that is an assumption, a rationalization which Stevens made. That is, the people that destroyed him made rationalizations about what he was. They decided what he was. But Christmas himself didn't know and he evicted himself from mankind.

Q. Mr. Faulkner, in working out the situation of Joe Christmas, did you deliberately have in mind a correspondence between his situation and Oedipus, for example, as has recently been brought out in an essay published in the *Virginia Quarterly* magazine?

A. No, not deliberately and not consciously. That's another matter of the writer reaching back into the lumber room of his memory for whatever he needs to create the character or the situation, and the similarity is there but it was not by deliberate intent. It was by coincidence—not accident but by coincidence. [72]

. . . that story began with Lena Grove, the idea of the young girl with nothing, pregnant, determined to find her sweetheart. It was—that was out of my admiration for women, for the courage and endurance of women. As I told that story I had to get more and more into it, but that was mainly the story of Lena Grove. . . .

Q. Sir, I've been told that the title *Light in August* came from a colloquialism for the completion of a pregnancy. Is that true?

A. No, I used it because in my country in August there's a peculiar quality of light and that's what that title means. It has in a sense nothing to do with the book at all, the story at all. . . .[74]

Q. In *Light in August* do you feel that Rev. Hightower dies feeling that he has achieved a certain kind of salvation—some sort of salvation?

A. He didn't die. He had wrecked his life. He had failed his wife. He had failed himself, but there was one thing that he still had—which was the brave grandfather that galloped into the town to burn the Yankee stores, and at least he had that. Everything else was gone, but since he had been a man of God he still tried to be a man of God and he could not destroy himself. But he had destroyed himself but he still couldn't take his own life. He had to endure, to live, but that was one thing that was pure and fine that he had—was the memory of his grandfather, who had been brave. . . . [75]

Q. Mr. Faulkner, most people are very struck by your change in style in *Light in August*. For example, you use the present tense to tell the story rather than the past. Did you mean something by that or were you just using a new form for dramatic import?

A. No, that just seemed to me the best way to tell the story. It wasn't a deliberate change of style. I don't know anything about style. I don't—I think a writer with a lot to—pushing inside him to get out hasn't got time to bother with style. If he just likes to write and hasn't got anything urging him, then he can become a stylist, but the ones with a great deal pushing to get out don't have time to be anything but clumsy, like Balzac, for instance. . . . [77]

Q. Referring to an earlier question, did you say that *Light in August* argues . . . for the acceptance of an inevitably tragic view of life? [96]

A. I wouldn't think so. That the only person in that book that accepted a tragic view of life was Christmas because he didn't know what he was and so he deliberately repudiated man. He didn't belong to man any longer, he deliberately repudiated man. The others seemed to me to have had a very fine belief in life, in the basic possibility for happiness and goodness—Byron Bunch and Lena Grove, to have gone to all that trouble. . . .

Q. Some of your names in your books are very suggestive, very highly suggestive. I wonder if that was pure coincidence or did you intend to make names like Gail Hightower, Joanna Burden . . . ?

A. Well, that is out of the tradition of the pre-Elizabethans, who named their characters according to what they looked like or what they did. . . . Of course, it seems to me that those people named themselves, but I can see where that came from—it came from the—my memory of the old miracle plays, the morality plays in early English literature. Chaucer. . . . [97]

Q. Mr. Faulkner, did you intend any Christ symbolism in *Light in August* in Joe Christmas?

A. No, that's a matter of reaching into the lumber room to get out something which seems to the writer the most effective way to tell what he is trying to tell. And that comes back to the notion that there are so few plots to use that sooner or later any writer is going to use something that has been used. And that Christ story is one of the best stories that man has invented, assuming that he did invent that story, and of course it will recur. Everyone that has had the story of Christ and the Passion as a part of his Christian background will in time draw from that. There was no deliberate intent to repeat it. That the people to me come first. The symbolism comes second.

Q. Well, I was just wondering why [for] such a sort of bad man as Joe Christmas you would use Christ, whether . . . [117]

A. Well, Joe Christmas—I think that you really can't say that any man is good or bad. I grant you there are some exceptions, but man is the victim of himself, or his fellows, or his own nature, or his environment, but no man is good or bad either. He tries to do the best he can within his rights. Now with Christmas, for instance, he didn't know what he was. He knew that he would never know what he was, and his only salvation in order to live with himself was to repudiate mankind, to live outside the human race. And he tried to do that but nobody would let him, the human race itself wouldn't let him. And I don't think he was bad, I think he was tragic. And his tragedy was that he didn't know what he was and would never know, and that to me is the most tragic condition that an individual can have—to not know who he was. . . . [118]

Q. Mr. Faulkner, could you tell me in your writing which character is most nearly perfectly tragic?

A. It would be between Sutpen and Christmas, Dilsey. I don't think I have a choice. It would probably be between those three. . . . [119]

Q. You spoke of titles before, Mr. Faulkner. I'd like to ask you about the origin of *Light in August*.

A. Oh that was—in August in Mississippi there's a few days somewhere about the middle of the month when suddenly there's a fore-taste of fall, it's cool, there's a lambence, a luminous quality to the light, as though it came not from just today but from back in the old classic times. It might have fauns and satyrs and the gods and—from Greece, from Olympus in it somewhere. It lasts just for a day or two, then it's gone, but every year in August that occurs in my country, and that's all that title meant, it was just to me a pleasant evocative title because it reminded me of that time, of a luminosity older than our Christian civilization. Maybe the connection was with Lena Grove, who had something of that pagan quality of being able to assume everything, that's—the desire for that child, she was never ashamed of that child whether it had any father or not, she was simply going to follow the conventional laws of the time in which she was and find its father. But as far as she was concerned, she didn't especially need any father for it, any more than the women that—on whom Jupiter begot children were anxious for a home and a father. It was enough to have had the child. And that was all that meant, just that luminous lambent quality of an older light than ours. [199]

Joe Christmas and Nelse Patton

JOHN B. CULLEN AND FLOYD C. WATKINS

AT NOON ONE DAY LATE IN AUGUST, WHEN I WAS A BOY FOURTEEN OR fifteen, my father Linburn Cullen, who was then a deputy sheriff, was called by telephone and told that a Negro had just killed a woman out north of Oxford and that he should come to join a posse at once. Before leaving, my father instructed me and my older brother to stay at home and keep out of trouble. But as soon as he had gone, we picked up our shotguns and headed to the place where we thought the killer would travel as he fled to the nearest big thicket from the location of his crime.

As we drew near this place, we heard gunfire and saw a big Negro run across the railroad at Saddler's Crossing about two hundred yards ahead of us. At that time I could run like a foxhound and I never lost sight of him until he jumped into a vine-covered ditch leading into Toby Tubby Bottom. He was running along a valley between two hills, and my brother ran down one of them and I the other. In the valley there was one clear place which the criminal would have to cross before he reached the big thicket in Toby Tubby Bottom. I kept my eyes on this opening, and when I reached it, I knew that he was hiding somewhere back up the valley. The posse was coming [89] on, so I knew that soon we would have him. When the Negro, Nelse Patton, saw that I knew he was hiding in the thicket, he attempted to come by me. I yelled for him to halt and when he kept on running, I shot at him with squirrel shot from both barrels of my shotgun. This stopped him. But that was about the first time I had ever shot anything bigger than a cottontail rabbit, and my squirrel shot were far too small to do much damage at that distance.

I reloaded and ran up close to him and told him to put up his hands. He said to my brother, "Mr. Jenks, you knows I'se a good nigger."

"I know you're a good nigger," my brother said, "but get your hands up." But Nelse never did put his hands up.

He was still standing up, and I believe he was trying to get a chance to grab my gun. If he had tried this, I was ready to shoot him between the eyes. Mr. Curt Hartsfield, the sheriff, and his deputy, Mr. Guy Taylor, rode up. When Mr. Taylor searched him, he found in his pocket a bloody razor with one corner broken off. I probably would have been killed if my father had not accidentally shot a big forty-five Colt out of Nelse's hand with a long-distance rifle shot as he went over a high hill north of Oxford.

After turning Nelse over to the sheriff, I went to the scene of the crime. Mrs. Mattie McMillan was lying in the dusty road about seventy-five yards from her home. How she had run that far I do not know. Her head had been severed from her body, all but the neck bone. Dr. Young, who was examining her, found sticking in her neck bone a piece of steel which fitted the gap missing from Nelse's razor. [90]

The news spread over the county like wildfire, and that night at least two thousand people gathered around the jail. Judge Roan came out on the porch and made a plea to the crowd that they let the law take its course. Then Senator W. V. Sullivan made a fiery speech, telling the mob that they would be weaklings and cowards to let such a vicious beast live until morning. Mr. Hartsfield, the sheriff, had left town with the keys to the jail, because he knew people would take them away from him. My father was deputized to guard the jail. Had he had the slightest doubt of Nelse's guilt, he would have talked to the mob. If this had not proved successful, they would have entered the jail over his dead body. After Senator Sullivan's speech, the mob began pitching us boys through the jail windows, and no guard in that jail would have dared shoot one of us. Soon a mob was inside. My brother and I held my father, and the sons of the other guards held theirs. They weren't hard to hold anyway. In this way we took over the lower floor of the jail.

From eight o'clock that night until two in the morning the mob worked to cut through the jail walls into the cells with sledge hammers and crowbars. In the walls were one-by-eight boards placed on top of one another and bolted together. The walls were brick on the outside and steel-lined on the inside. When the mob finally got through and broke the lock off the murderer's cell, Nelse had armed himself with a heavy iron coal-shovel handle. From a corner near the door, he fought like a tiger, seriously wounding three men. He was then shot to death and thrown out of the jail. Someone (I don't know who) cut his ears off, scalped him, cut his testicles out, tied a rope around his neck, [91] tied him to a car, and dragged his body around the streets. Then they hanged him to a walnut-tree limb just outside the south entrance to the courthouse. They had torn his clothes off dragging him around, and my father bought a new pair of overalls and put them on him before the next morning.

Nelse Patton's crime and the lynching of Nelse are more widely known than anything else of this kind that ever happened in Lafayette County. William Faulkner was eleven years old at the time, and since he has spent most of his life in this community, he must have heard numerous stories about the Patton case. Faulkner has written about many lynchings in his books, and I believe that several of them are generally based on the story of Nelse Patton.

In some ways, the entire book of *Light in August* is centered around the lynching of Joe Christmas, and it seems to me that Faulkner used the stories he had heard about the Nelse Patton case. There are a number of parallels between the stories of Nelse and Joe. Joanna Burden and Mrs. McMillan both lived outside of town, and each of them had her throat cut from ear to ear by a Negro man using a razor. Nelse and Joe both attempted to escape in a similar way over similar terrain. Both of the Negro men were lynched: Nelse was shot in the jail, and Joe was shot in the kitchen of the Reverend Hightower. Senator Sullivan, who incited the mob to riot in Oxford, reminds me a little of Percy Grimm, who led the lynchers in *Light in August*. Both bodies were mutilated, though in slightly different ways. These likenesses seem more important because Faulkner knew more about Nelse Patton's lynching than about any other single episode of that kind. [92]

. . . Southern newspapers of that period published full-length stories about the lynching of Nelse Patton. *The Lafayette County Press* of September 9, 1908, printed the most complete and accurate account. This story, reprinted below, shows how Southern reporters wrote about such crimes in those old days. This is a colorful (perhaps too much so) and factual version of a story that was of great interest to William Faulkner. The mistakes are in the original.

NEGRO BRUTE CUTS WOMAN'S THROAT

Mrs. Mattie McMullen, A White Woman The Victim—Lived But Ten Minutes After The Tragedy. Sheriff Hartsfield And Posse of Citizens Give Chase and Land Negro in Jail

Mob Storms Jail and Kills Desperado

Officers and Guards Overpowered, and Failing to Find the Keys the Orderly
Mob Quietly and Deliberately Took Matters in Their Own Hands, Forced
Entrance to Cell Where Negro Was Confined Negro Armed with Poker
Puts Up Desperate Fight and is Killed. [93]

One of the coldest blooded murders and most brutal crimes known to
the criminal calendar was perputrated one mile north of town yesterday
morning about ten oclock, when a black brute of unsavory reputation by the
name of Nelse Patton attacked Mrs. Mattie McMullen,[1] a respected white
woman, with a razor, cutting her throat from ear to ear and causing almost
instant death. Reports as to the cause of the tragedy vary, but as near as
can be learned the partic- are these:

Mrs. McMullen, whose husband was confined at the time in the county
jail at this place, was a hard working woman living alone with her 17-year-
old daughter and two other very small children. It seems that Mr. McMullen
wanted to communicate with his wife, and as was his custom as such occasions, he called the murderer, who was a "trusty" prisoner at the jail, to
carry the missive. Arriving at the house, the negro, who was in an intoxi-
cated condition, walked into the house without knocking and took a seat.
Seeing the woman apparently alone and without protection, his animal passion was aroused and he made insulting remarks to her. He was ordered
from the house and some angry words passed between them, when the
woman started toward the bureau drawer to get her pistol, The brute seeing
her design made a rush at the woman from behind and drawing the razor
cut her throat from ear to ear, almost severing the head from the body.
The dying woman rushed out of the house, and the daughter hearing the
confusion rushed in, and was instantly grabbed by the negro. Jerking herself
from the brutes grasp, she followed her mother who had fallen dead a few
yards from the house. The daughter's screams alarmed the neighbors who
quickly responded to call and immediately sent in a hurried telephone message to the Press office to summons officers and a physician, who in [94] less
than twenty minutes were on the way to the scene of the murder. The news
spread like wild fire and it was but a short while until the sheriff was joined
by a posse of citizens all in hot and close pursuit of the brute. After chasing
the negro three or four miles over fences, through briars and fields he suddenly ran amuck of Johnny Cullen, the 14-year-old son of Lin Cullen, who
was out with a double-barreled shotgun. Seeing the negro coming towards
him, he called a halt, but the negro paid no attention to the command and
the boy let him have a load of No. 5 shot in the chest, which slackened his
speed but did not stop him. The boy gave him another charge in the left
arm and side which stopped him. The negro was at once surrounded by his
pursuers and gladly gave up. Over a hundred shots were fired from all kinds
of weapons but the negro was out of range. Being weak from loss of blood,
the brute was put on a horse and hurried to jail.

As soon as the news spread of the capture, hundreds of people began
to gather around the jail and in small groups about the street. They were
not indulging in idle threats, but from the seriousness of their expression one
could see the negro's fate was sealed.

Between nine and ten o'clock the crowd began swelling to large propor-

---

[1] The name was spelled in various ways by the newspapers of the time, and
it is also pronounced several ways. As nearly as I can determine, it is McMillan.

tions about the jail. Speeches were made advocating letting the law take its course and vice-versa, but patience had fallen far short of being a virtue ih a crowd like that. One wild shout went up, with a rush the crowd advanced on the jail, pushing open doors. and jumping through windows. Officers and guards were overpowered and disarmed. The keys could not be found, but the hardware stores and blacksmith shops were made to furnish the necessary tools and a set of quiet and determined men plied them. Four and one-half hours of hard and persistent work it took to break through the thick walls of steel and masonry. The hall was at last reached, and a search of the cell occupied by that black [95] fiend incarnate was made. It was at last found and broken into. Crouched and cringing in a dark corner of the cell, with the gleam of murder in his eye stood the miserable wretch armed with an iron poker awaiting the advance. In one, two, thee order the mob entered the cell, and in the same order the iron decended upon their heads, blood flew, the negro having all the advantage in his dark corner, held the crowd at bay and refused to come out. Only one thing was left to do. It was done. 26 pistol shots vibrated throughout the corridors of the solid old jail, and when the smoke cleared away the limp and lifeless body of the brute told the story.

The body was hustled down stairs to terra-firma, the rope was produced, the hangmans noose properly adjusted about the neck, and the drag to the court house yard began.

This morning the passerby saw the lifeless body of a negro suspended from a tree—it told the tale, that the murder of a white woman had been avenged—the public had done their duty. Following is the verdict of the Corners Jury:

We the Coroners Jury of inquest impaneled and sworn to investigate the death of Nelse Patton, colored find after inspecting the body and examining necessary witnesses that to the best of our knowledge and belief, the said Nelse Patton came to his death from gunshot or pistol wounds inflicted by parties to us unknown. That any one of a number of wounds would have been sufficient to cause death. We find further that Sheriff J. C. Hartsfield and his deputies were dilllgent in their efforts to protect said Nelse Patton from the time of his arrest until they were overpowered by a mob of several hundred men who stormed the jail and dug their way through the walls until they reached the cell in which said Nelse Patton was confined and that said officers never surrendered the keys of jail or cells but that the locks were forced by some party or parties to us unknown and that the said Nelse Patton [96] was shot with pistols or guns while in his cell and while attempting to protect himself with an iron rod. We further find that the said Nelse Patton was dead before being brought from the jail and being hung.

Respectfully submitted,

E. O. Davidson
R. S. Adams
P. E. Matthews
B. P. Gray
A. F. Calloway
F. Wood

The papers gave special attention to Senator Sullivan's role in the lynching. This is a quotation from the Jackson *Daily Clarion-Ledger,* of Thursday morning, September 10, 1908. Errors are again reproduced from the original.

SULLIVAN'S HOT TALK ON OXFORD LYNCHING

Former United States Senator from Mississippi Led The Mob

(Associated Press Report)

Memphis, Tenn., Sept. 9.—A special from Oxford, Miss., quotes former U. S. Senator W. V. Sullivan as follows, with reference to the lynching of last night:

"I led the mob which lynched Nelse Patton and I am proud of it.

"I directed every movement of the mob, and I did everything I could tto see that he was lynched.

"Cut a white woman's throat? and a negro? Of course I wanted him lynched.

"I saw his body dangling from a tree this morning and I am glad of it. [97]

"When I heard of the horrible crime, I started to work immediately to get a mob. I did all I could to raise one. I was at the jail last night and I heard Judge Roane advise against lynching. I got up immediately after and urged the mob to lynch Patton.

"I aroused the mob and directed them to storm the jail.

"I had my revolver, but did not use it. I gave it to a deputy sheriff and told him: 'Shoot Patton and shoot to kill.'

"He used the revolver and shot. I suppose the bullets from my gun were some of those that killed the negro.

"I don't care what investigation is made, or what are the consequences. I am willing to stand them.

"I wouldn't mind standing the consequences any time for lynching a man who cut a white woman's throat. I will lead a mob in such a case any time." [98]

Confrontations and Scenes

IRVING HOWE

MODERN CRITICISM IS TOO READY TO ASSUME A DEEP CONGRUENCE BETWEEN form and content in a work of fiction, thereby neglecting to ask whether the sheer persistence of these terms may indicate that they point to necessary distinctions. There is, to be sure, something valuable in a stress upon the intimacy between form and content in a successful work of literature—provided one bears in mind that this unity is never complete and the relation among its elements is somewhat less than perfect. But modern criticism, in its passion for "structural analysis," too often forgets this qualification. Too often it proposes *ad hoc* rationalizations for adjusting mishaps of form to supposed needs of content, or indulgence of content to presumed requirements of form. And in practice this means to ignore the fact that in the novel, that most impure of literary genres, the actual relation between form and content is almost always unfinished and improvisatory, rarely as neat as critics like to suppose. Accepting this fact may at least allow us to trace the varying relationships between thematic content and embodying form: where the two really fuse, [200] where they draw apart, and where a clash breaks out between them.

In *Light in August* a central concern is with the relation between a man's social role and private being: Hightower as a failed minister who rots in quiet neglect and Hightower as a ruminative observer of human folly, Joe Christmas as a harried mulatto who starts life without even a name and Joe Christmas as a bewildered man struggling toward the rudiments of consciousness. The one character, Lena Grove, in whom the distance between social role and private being is slight, necessarily emerges as a comic figure. She stands for the outrageous possibility that the assumption shared by Faulkner and his cultivated readers may be false:—the assumption that suffering finds a justification in the growth of human consciousness. For Lena is and does "right" with a remarkably small amount of consciousness or suffering, neither of which she apparently needs very much; she is Faulkner's wry tribute to his own fallibility, a tribute both persuasive and not meant completely to persuade.

The split between social role and private being wounds us in ourselves, but we feel the pain most sharply when facing other people. It is in moments of confrontation that one is most troubled by a sense of self-estrangement, as in moments of loneliness that one learns to reckon the exhaustion that comes from human relationships. These are the facts—so, for the purposes of the novel, Faulkner invites us to regard them—which shape the design of *Light in August*.

The book is focused on a series of confrontations: Lena-Burch, Lena-Bunch, Lena-Christmas, and then another series: Bunch-Hightower, Christmas-Hightower, Grimm-Christmas. These meetings, mostly between strangers and some of them mere suggestions of possibility, form the spinal column of the book. If, as I have been saying, Faulkner means to dramatize both the terrors of isolation and the erosion of relationships, [201] it is appropriate that several characters, each breaking out of his own obscurity, should collide, cause pain and then part. There are large possibilities for drama in such a pattern, if only because it virtually insures strong climaxes; and Faulkner has mined these possibilities to their limits. There are also troublesome

problems of organization—for one, how to avoid a split of the narrative into several divergent lines. It would be excessive to claim that
Faulkner has quite solved these problems.

The necessary meetings take place: the chords of dissonance are
struck. A link is established between each of the three major characters, though a rather tenuous one between Lena and Christmas, forced
upon them more by Faulkner's desire to weight the book with symbolic richness than by an inherent necessity of the action. For we
cannot assume that a relationship in a novel has been established
simply because an author indicates his wish that it be there or a critic
obligingly infers its necessity. The problem is not how to rationalize in
one's mind the several strands of action, but what Faulkner makes of
them in the book. Put another way, it is a problem in economy and
waste: How much is gained for Christmas by his juxtaposition to
Lena? How bright an illumination does the mind of Hightower cast on
the conduct of the other characters? What value follows from the
contrast between the stillness of Lena and the restlessness of everyone
else?

Light in August moves on two levels of time: the dramatic
present, shaped almost entirely into terse and powerful scenes, and the
recalled past, worked up through discursive summaries and flashbacks.
In the main, those sections of the novel set in the present command
greater vividness and authority than those falling back into the past.
The sections set in the present are there because we must see them;
the sections set in the past are there because we need the information
they provide. The numerous cinematic flashbacks come to appear too
conspicuously "functional," several of [202] them occurring whenever the
source or meaning of a scene requires more material than Faulkner can
provide within it. Between the requirements of the theme and the
rhythm of the action there is thus a certain conflict, and it is not always
happily resolved. Two of the flashbacks, those for Joanna Burden and
Doc Hines, are in excess of what the narrative requires or their intrin-
sic value might justify; the grotesque Hines episode, coming at a point
where the reader's emotional resources have already been engaged by
the tragedy of Christmas, has a distracting rather than intensifying
effect. Faulkner solicits too wide a variety of emotions, and the reader,
to conserve his powers of response for the climax he knows is yet to
come, must begrudge the flashbacks the attention they might deserve.
This is especially true in the second half of the novel, where there is a
wasteful scattering of effects among subordinate characters.

So rich a novel as *Light in August* might easily absorb this waste
were it not a symptom of a more important weakness. The novel
proposes a triad of actions: Christmas carries the burden of the book,
Lena a sub-plot idyllic in itself but significantly ironic in regard to
Christmas, and Hightower, as participant and observer, has a dual
function. He must fail Christmas in his moment of crisis and must

provide a reflective consciousness upon which the conduct of the surrounding characters, most notably Lena and Christmas, can register. Necessarily, these actions involve a complex shifting in point of view. No single character can comprehend all that is happening; the meanings must beat against each other as do the actions themselves—when, that is, they beat in time.

Like all of Faulkner's Negroes, Christmas is seen mainly from the outside, but he is so graphic a figure that for a good portion of the book this limitation is entirely satisfactory. Observed in moments of characteristic conduct—reading a pulp magazine from cover to cover "as though it were a novel," somberly shaving [203] during his flight—Christmas seems immediately and indisputably real. We know about him all that we need to know, and perhaps more than we can fully absorb. But midway through the book, in the chapter where he murders Joanna Burden, one comes to feel that an interior view, an intimate record of what his experience signifies to him, may now be necessary. For the development of the novel leads one to expect that we will now see directly and fully what it is—the "it" is in his mind—that leads him to kill his mistress. My criticism is based not on any general notions about novels or Negroes, but on the inner logic of *Light in August* itself. Like a camera sighting its object from a distance and then edging its way toward close-up, the book moves in, warily, toward Christmas—but not to the point of entering his inner life, not to the point of providing the "flash-in" that we are led to desire. As a result, the murder of Joanna Burden, while explicable through several hints placed by Faulkner, does not acquire the tragic scope and intensity it should have. It remains too much an event in the story, not enough an experience of Joe Christmas. In the final reckoning, to be sure, the failure to work into Christmas' mind does not seriously detract from his total impact; nothing could. But it does cause the novel's weight of consciousness to be lowered upon another character—not, happily, upon Lena Grove.

Beyond a doubt Lena is the most harmoniously conceived and drawn figure in the book, reflecting one of Faulkner's most benign moods: a relaxed whimsical affection for simple life and a readiness to grant major virtues to passivity as a moral style. In writing about Lena, Faulkner never strains, as with Hightower, or becomes feverishly troubled, as with Christmas. Yet she is decidedly less interesting than Hightower or Christmas, and one should resist the desire of certain complex critics to romanticize her simplicity, for then she would be less interesting still. She is surely not to be compared, [204] as one Christian-minded critic has, to the primitive saints, if only because she has never known the life of trouble, the ordeal of surmounting, which is usually taken as a prerequisite for sainthood. She may indeed possess, as another critic writes, a "holistic" consciousness which shields her from the suffering of the other characters, but it necessarily remains a very limited sort of consciousness. So meager and self-contained an intelligence as Lena's must limit, though not eliminate, our feelings for her.

Those who see in Lena a triumph of healthy traditionalism and in Christmas the self-destructiveness of "modernism"—who see this and nothing else—do not really grant Faulkner's mind its due. They take an important step with him, but fail to follow his later turnings. It is true enough in a way that Lena is healthy (it is the health of pre-consciousness) and Christmas sick, but surely Faulkner has not written so troubled and complex a book merely to tell us that. Is he not rather suggesting that Christmas and Hightower are destroyed because each, in his own inadequate way, does try to accept the challenge of his humanity, the first by seeking selfhood and the second by a deluded immersion in history, while Lena, the good unruffled vegetable Lena, survives them all in her impervious detachment? Lena's story frames the agonies of the book, at the beginning as she walks, blithe and pregnant, toward Jefferson, and at the end as she and Byron Bunch go off, watching her child and seemingly unscarred by all that has happened. There is something utterly outrageous and infuriating in her capacity to move through and past this accumulation of miseries—so outrageous and infuriating that one must acknowledge the final effect of the novel to be perversely comic: a comedy that underscores the tragic incommensurability between the fates of Joe Christmas and herself. That, Faulkner seems to be saying, is the way things are: the Joe Christmases get lynched, the Lena Groveses get husbands, and anyone [205] who would seek moralities of reconciliation in all this must be a bit of a fool.

That the Lena I have been sketching should so completely triumph is something we do not find easy to accept, for it hardly assuages our self-esteem as cultivated persons; and so there is naturally an inclination to elevate her into a kind of moral heroine or earth goddess or even a putative saint. But for the sake of the novel, we should decline this temptation. The point and the power of it all rests on the fact that Lena is just a good healthy mindless country-girl, and to conclude anything else is not only to dissolve the tensions of the book but to transform Faulkner into the simple-minded moralist which in his inferior books he is.

The reading I have suggested here not only allows the novel a well-earned complication of irony, it also invokes an observable truth: the price of consciousness often is self-destruction, and equally often the reward for animal calm is safety. One may be fond of Lena, but one identifies with Hightower or, in a somewhat different way, with Christmas. To regard Lena as an agent of morality and let it go at that is to graze the notion that goodness is contingent upon a noble paucity of intelligence.

Because of Lena's inherent limitations and the failure to enter

Christmas's mind, a great burden falls upon Hightower. Although he moves us again and again, although he is unforgettable as the young minister preaching a kind of martial godliness and his characterization is poignant as the old man lacerating himself on the tasks Byron Bunch brings him, Hightower will not quite do. Alfred Kazin is right in saying that Hightower is "too vague, too drooping, too formless, in a word too much the creature of defeat and of obsession, to compel our interest or our belief. . . . Hightower, acting in various sections of the book as a foreground observer, brings to them not merely a stillness but a [206] deadness which intervenes between us and the other characters."

To register the full meaning of Christmas's tragedy, Hightower must command an active mind and fresh sensibility. Yet, insofar as he is an actor in the story rather than its somewhat detached observer, he must fail Christmas, and fail him because of his fear of human involvement and his need for protective routine. Here Hightower becomes what Sherwood Andersoon called a "grotesque," the shell of a once ardent man, reminiscent of the twisted creatures who wander through *Winesburg, Ohio*. This mustiness of character, though persuasive enough in its own right, seriously qualifies Hightower's usefulness as the moral "reverberator" of the novel. Fully to absorb the significance of all he sees, fully to grasp the meaning of Christmas's death, Hightower would have to be less delusional than in fact he is; and if less delusional he might more actively have tried to prevent Christmas's death. Yet the theme and working-out of the novel require that Christmas die and no one be able to prevent it.

Now, between the role of actor and the role of observer in a novel there is no necessary conflict; both can be performed by the same character. Nor is it difficult to see that such a character might have a large capacity for understanding and a small one for action. But some conflict is clearly present between the kind of behavior allotted Hightower and the qualities of observation he is presumed to possess. In a somewhat different way Richard Chase has noticed the same problem:

In the case of Hightower there seems to be a failure of consciousness precisely at the point where we should understand the quality of the association between Hightower and his own history. Hightower has projected his sexual and spiritual [207] impotence back upon a myth of his grandfather. Faulkner goes along with Hightower on this point, assuming too much that a fantasy projected from some center of real causation is the cause itself. He nearly allows Hightower to determine the quality of his [Faulkner's] consciousness.

Faulkner is almost always uncertain in his treatment of those characters who serve both as chorus and center of intelligence. The claims he makes for his intellectuals he can rarely validate; Hightower, Benbow, and Gavin Stevens are not nearly such impressive thinkers as he would have us suppose. And it is only occasionally that he has managed to solve—or skirt—this problem. In *The Hamlet* the sewing-machine agent, Ratliff, is credible in both roles simply because he performs them not as a sophisticated intellectual or what passes for one in Faulkner's mind, but as a Yoknapatawpha man completely at home in his world. In *The Sound and the Fury* the roles are split, Quentin Compson providing a center of intelligence and Dilsey a magnificent chorus.

Neither so flaccid as Benbow nor so pretentious as Stevens, Hightower is easier to accept than both of them; but he is still taken too much at his own valuation. One is reminded of T. S. Eliot's remark about a character in *Roderick Hudson:* "He [James] too much identi-fies himself with Rowland, does not see through the solemnity he has created in that character, commits the cardinal sin of failing to 'detect' one of his own characters." Faulkner's failure is more complex: he does "detect" Hightower's weakness and delusion, but tries to endow them with a tragic grandeur they cannot possibly sustain. Between Faulkner and Hightower, as between Faulkner and most of his reflective figures, there is insufficient distance. Exactly right in his relation to Lena and at one or two points perhaps a trifle remote from Christmas, Faulkner is certainly much too close to Hightower—too close, particularly, in his [208] fantasying about the Southern past, a fantasying Faulkner sometimes accepts and more often grows impatient and irritated with, but which nevertheless creates problems of involvement. It is a sign of this excessive involvement that while many fine passages are granted Hightower, few of these passages have the sustained scenic thickness, the absolute immersion in the flow of experience, that one finds in the chapters devoted to Christmas: notably the remarkable figure of the wheel rushing through his mind at the end of the novel ("As he sits in the window, leaning forward above his motionless hands, sweat begins to pour from him, springing out like blood, and pouring. Out of the instant the sandclutched wheel of thinking turns on. . . .").

That *Light in August* suffers a certain structural incoherence, an occasional imbalance between matter and form, seems clear; and this may be the reason it fails to achieve the classic economy of *The Sound and the Fury.* Yet one can only hope that such strictures, whatever their usefulness, will not be taken too solemnly. The "looseness" of representation which roused Henry James to severity is here an evident flaw; but surely this novel, if only because of its reliance on the scenic method and its enviable portion of creative energy, would have attracted the eye of the James who wrote the preface to *The Awkward Age.* Few American novels are so lavish in dramatic inci-dent, so infused with images of sensation, so precisely fixed in place and weather. The most stringent criticism—too stringent, I should think—to be made of *Light in August* is that Faulkner's clumsiness in transitional stitching and narrative preparation, particularly his lame summary of Christmas's young manhood, reduces the book to a series of brilliant tableaux. But even then, the tableaux remain in all their solidity, the rich scenic substance of the novel.

Obvious though it might seem, this point requires a kind of special presentation at the moment. American criticism, fascinated by mechanics and ingenuity, is [209] ready to honor everything in a novel—ingenuity of structure, schemes of imagery, deeply inlaid symbolism, weighty moral implications—everything but the immediate rendering of life, the picture itself, which *is* the novel and without which there would be little cause to read, let alone interpret, works of fiction. It is this abundance of representation, this copiousness of postures observed and manners poetically evoked, that makes *Light in August* so splendid a novel.

The picture, not the deliberate symbol, is the source of this excellence. In most of the instances in *Light in August* where Faulkner employs symbolic devices they are poorly and often half-heartedly done. Remove the several cloudy suggestions that Christmas is some sort of Christ figure, and it would hardly matter: Christmas affects us as a vulnerable man, not as a religious token. When the boy Christmas discovers that women are "victims of periodic filth," and soaks his hands in the warm blood of a sheep he has slaughtered, this symbolic incident adds little to what we already know about Christmas. A rather showy display of parallels, it merely raises a problem in credibility. By contrast, the symbol of the wheel of thought which turns in Hightower's mind "with the slow implacability of a medieval torture instrument, beneath the wrenched and broken sockets of his spirit," is a remarkable soaring of the imagination. Here the first requirement for a symbol is entirely satisfied: that it enlarge the meaning of the object to which it refers and enforce attention in its own right. No mere arbitrary sign or pale duplicate, the symbol acquires a color and momentum of its own, referring back to its object—the fate of Hightower—but also enriching the book with new associations. Seldom do the other symbols in *Light in August* fit so well, and none plays nearly so important a role in sustaining the book as do the dramatic scenes themselves. Finally, it is the sheer power of representation, the power of apprehending and then taking a full unflinching measure of an [210] experience, which makes *Light in August* so remarkable a book.

Power in a successful work of fiction is recognized easily enough; accounting for its sources is another matter. In *Light in August* one may point to Faulkner's absolute sureness of locale, equalled only in *As I Lay Dying* and *The Hamlet*. More than mere pleasant landscape or inert backdrop, the locale is quickened to a force visibly shaping and opposing the characters. As in Hardy, the locale becomes a "character," a sentient presence with qualities of its own. On the first page of the book Lena is placed through a few exact details: "six or eight times a year she went to town on Saturday, in the wagon, in a mail-order dress and her bare feet flat in the wagon bed and her shoes wrapped in a piece of paper beside her on the seat." Lifting the sentence to precise rightness are two details, evidence of intimate knowledge: the feet flat in the wagon bed and the shoes wrapped in a piece of paper.

The farmer, Armstid, who befriends Lena is defined by the words "humped" and "bleacheyed," the first noting his condition as a poor farmer and the second his mildness as a submissive man. In a few sentences describing Lena's offer to share food with another farmer, a distinctive style of behavior is perceived and rendered:

"I wouldn't care for none," he says.
"I'd take it kind for you to share."
"I wouldn't care to. You go ahead and eat."

Partly, too, the power of the novel derives from Faulkner's awareness of the recalcitrance of the social world. *Light in August* is the most socially inflected of Faulkner's novels, sensitive to the limitations and distortions society imposes on human conduct. In none of his other books is there such a full rendering of the force of dead institutions and dead matter as they exact their tyranny upon men. That men are not free to choose [211] their world and their selves, that past and present conspire to defeat the eager will, is a common notion in Faulkner's books, usually explained by references to a flaw in character or an arbitrary blow of fate. In *Light in August*, however, the limits of freedom are defined primarily through social co-ordinates, Christmas, in one important sense, being simply a function of his society, and Hightower a relic of his. The entire experience of Christmas is that of dashing himself blindly against a series of walls which contain his movements and frustrate his desires. He has no abstract conception of society whatever, but he learns through the most bitter of lessons that it confines and breaks the will. Aware of how refractory his environment can be, Christmas often reacts with a wry anticipation of suffering, an almost comic bewilderment before the terrors of social existence.

The power of the novel has other, perhaps deeper sources. Faulkner is never better, never more fully committed to the grandeur and misery of the human lot, than when showing the entanglements between men, their gift for draining one another of all strength, exhausting one another of all hope and yet thereby living out their destinies. Chapter twelve of the novel, in which the affair between Christmas and Joanna Burden reaches its climax, is surely one of the most powerful pieces of writing ever done by an American: a narrative which leaves one not so much with the sense of having witnessed an ordeal as having participated in it. All of the straining and heaving of Faulkner's prose, the reaching out after improbable tropes, the magnification of rhetorical effects, is justified here by the fury with which

Faulkner sets out to subject the reader to the full weight of a human experience, driving further and further, relentlessly, to its very marrow. One can quote almost at random, though never with anything like the power of the chapter as a whole: [212]

It was as if she knew somehow that time was short, that autumn was almost upon her, without knowing yet the exact significance of autumn. It seemed to be instinct alone: instinct physical and instinctive denial of the wasted years. Then the tide would ebb. Then they would be stranded as behind a dying mistral, upon a spent and satiate beach, looking at one another like strangers, with hopeless and reproachful (on his part with weary: on hers with despairing) eyes.

Or again:

At first the beginning of the night was always a flood, as if the hours of light and of separation had damned up enough of the wasting stream to simulate torrent for a moment at least. But after a while the stream became too thin for that: he would go to her now with reluctance, a stranger, already back-looking; a stranger he would leave her after having sat with her in the dark bedroom . . .

But it is in Faulkner's gift for rendering selective incident, for the isolation of that critical moment in experience which, once seen, lights up the wastes behind and the darkness ahead, that *Light in August* strikes its full power. Though Faulkner may be wasteful in disposing of incidents, most of them are constructed internally with a firm economy. I have remarked on the frequency of confrontations in *Light in August*, and it is the confrontation which, in this book as in others, is a major resource in the composition of scenes. There is the rending moment Byron Bunch asks Hightower to save Christmas, and the two men stand face to face, aware that an irrevocable choice has to be made. There is the meeting between Christmas and the "leatherhard woman"—is it not between Christmas and the entire alien world?—when he asks, "Can you tell me what day [213] this is?" There is the dialogue, nervous and amusing, between Armstid and his wife after she decides to give her egg money to Lena—a page of incomparable prose. There is the brush between Burch and the old Negro woman who is to send his message to the sheriff for "a dollar cash." And others: moments of climax, two human beings revealed in urgency.

Such incidents occur within a progression of scenes, some dramatic and others pictorial. The dramatic scenes, like Christmas himself, are all turbulence and motion. The pictorial scenes, forming compositions of contrast, are projected in static depth: Lena Grove on the road, a picture light-filled, airy, pastel; Percy Grimm over the body of Christmas, a picture stroked with darkness.

Finally, there is one other source of the novel's power: In *The*

Sound and the Fury and *As I Lay Dying* everything is subordinated to
the voices of the characters—the voices are the characters. But in *Light
in August* a new voice is heard, partly Faulkner's own and partly, as it
were, an over-voice speaking for the memories and conscience of a
people. Sounding again and again a characteristic note of anguish,
lingering over the spectacle of heroism and failure, this voice records
the entire Yoknapatawpha story. It will be heard again, in Faulkner's
later books. [214]

A Part of the Southern Mores:
Protestantism

WILLIAM VAN O'CONNOR

. . . THIS NOVEL AT CENTER IS A PROBING INTO THE TERRIBLE EXCESSES OF
the Calvinist spirit.[1]

If one does not perceive that the Calvinist spirit is the central [72]
issue in *Light in August*, the novel will of necessity seem confused in
theme. The Civil War and the black shadow of slavery, as some critics
insist, suffuse the novel. It is proper enough to relive with Hightower the
imagined scenes of galloping horses, burning buildings, the wounded

---

[1] It has been suggested that the novel is two separate stories, the Lena
Grove–Byron Bunch story and the Joe Christmas–Joanna Burden–Hightower–
Jefferson story. This probably is not so. There are three strands in the novel:
(1) Lena Grove–Byron Bunch, (2) Hightower, and (3) Joe Christmas, all of
which relate to the theme of rigidity of spirit as opposed to the need for acceptance of human frailty and fallibility and the need for pity and sympathy.
    Joe Christmas is also the victim of another kind of excess, the by-passing of
deserved punishment. When as a five-year-old he steals and eats toothpaste, he
expects to be punished, but the dietitian, who believes he has witnessed the intercourse between her and a young intern, tries to buy him off. Later Mrs. McEachern attempts to scheme with him to outwit the restrictions and rigidity of her
husband, but young Christmas is more at ease with the excesses of McEachern than
he is with the softness and weakness, as he sees it, of Mrs. McEachern. In other
words, he wants to live inside a system of rules and sanctions. He associates softness and blind devotion with women and is contemptuous of them.
    Hightower's relationship with Christmas is never made quite explicit, but
there seems to be at least a hint of homosexuality in it. However, in contrasting
the sexuality of Christmas with that of Joanna Burden, the author comments that
while she was terribly perverted Christmas was not: "Within six months she was
completely corrupted. It could not be said he corrupted her. His own life, for all
its anonymous promiscuity, had been conventional enough, as a life of healthy and
normal sin usually is."

and the dead of the Civil War; these do live on into the 1920s, even in the minds of those less crippled by such memories than the defrocked old minister. But the greater force, in which the War and the black shadow are caught up, is Calvinism, and, larger than it, rigidity of principle and harshness of spirit; and it is this force that menaces Joe Christmas, the putative Negro, and that persecutes Hightower. Byron Bunch and Lena Grove are more than comic relief; they are proof that one need not succumb to such a force.

The irony of the name Joe Christmas is noted by every reader of *Light in August*. (And it is equally obvious that other names in the novel have their appropriateness also: Gail Hightower, Percy Grimm, Calvin Burden, Bobbie [Barbara] Allen, Lena Grove, Byron Bunch, and Euphues Hines.) Certainly the major significance in the name is the irony of Joe Christmas' being pursued and harassed throughout his life by voices of Christian righteousness: Old Doc Hines, his mad grandfather, McEachern, his stern foster parent, and Joanna Burden, his guilt-haunted lover, and finally by [73] the society itself insofar as its religion, as Hightower claims, drives the community to *"Crucifixion of themselves and one another."*

Euphues Hines is certain he is doing God's will in killing the man who had seduced his daughter, in refusing to allow a doctor to assist his daughter in the birth of her illegitimate son (after which she dies), in getting a job at the orphanage where he has secretly put the boy, then taking up a position as a threatening presence at the edge of the boy's consciousness, in allowing the boy to be adopted by Simon McEachern, and, twenty-five years later when Joe Christmas, now a murderer, is captured in Mottstown, in screaming that he should be lynched. Through it all runs the assurance that he, Hines, is God's instrument. One of his mad speeches is a bitter parody of the doctrine of predestination:

It was the Lord. *He* was there. Old Doc Hines give God His chance too. The Lord told old Doc Hines what to do and old Doc Hines done it. Then the Lord said to old Doc Hines, "You watch now. Watch My will a-working." And old Doc Hines watched and heard the mouths of little children, of God's own fatherless and motherless, putting His words and knowledge into their mouths even when they couldn't know it since they were without sin yet, even the girl ones without sin and bitchery yet: Nigger! Nigger! in the innocent mouths of little children. "What did I tell you?" God said to old Doc Hines. "And now I've set My will to working and now I'm gone. There aint enough sin here to keep Me busy because what do I care for the fornications of a slut, since that is a part of My purpose too," and old Doc Hines said, "How is the fornications of a slut a part of Your purpose too?" and God said, "You wait and see. Do you think it is just chanceso that I sent that young doctor to be the one that found My abomination laying wrapped in that blanket on that doorstep that Christmas night? Do you think it was just chanceso that the Madam should have been away that night and give them young sluts the chance and call to name him Christmas in sacrilege of My Son? So I am gone now, because I have set My will a-working and I can leave you to watch it."

Twenty years after the event Joe Christmas knew that the most lasting mark from his boyhood had been made the Sunday McEachern whipped him for failing to learn his Presbyterian catechism. The punishment had been given in all righteousness. [74] McEachern's "voice was not unkind. It was not human, personal, at all. It was just cold, implacable, like written or printed words." Several times, always after the passage of a full hour, the boy was whipped again. McEachern sat stiffly watching the boy, "one hand on his knee and the silver watch in the other palm, his clean, bearded face as firm as carved stone, his eyes ruthless, cold, but not unkind." Later the man knelt with the boy to ask "that Almighty be as magnanimous as himself" in forgiving the boy's disobedience. That day Christmas learned silent resistance.

And that evening, in refusing food brought by Mrs. McEachern—dumping the dishes on the floor—he learned how to refuse sympathy, to harden himself against the feminine world. He felt she was trying to make him cry. "Then she thinks they would have had me."

Joe Christmas was almost eighteen before he learned how to outwit McEachern in his niggardly denials of the flesh. A waitress, Bobbie Allen, also a semi-professional whore, is the first person from whom he accepts any sympathy, and he does this at first because of sexual desire for her. But McEachern destroys this relationship by following them to a country dance, where, like the "representative of a wrathful and retributive Throne," he calls her "harlot" and "Jezebel." Joe strikes him down with a chair and after stealing a small amount of money from Mrs. McEachern runs away. But Bobbie Allen is offended at the treatment she has had (Faulkner makes high comedy of her indignation at being called "harlot"), screams at him that he is a nigger, and allows her friends to beat him up.

The climactic parts of Joe Christmas' life are lived in Jefferson, where he becomes the lover of Joanna Burden, the spinster descendant of an abolitionist family from New Hampshire. The family had been Unitarians with the "agonized conscience" described by George Santayana in the well-known passage in his "Genteel Traditions in American Philosophy." They believed

that sin exists, that sin is punished, and that it is beautiful that sin should exist to be punished. The heart of Calvinism is therefore divided between tragic concern at its own miserable condition, [75] and tragic exultation about the universe at large. . . . Human nature, it feels, is totally depraved: to have the instincts and motives that we necessarily have is a great scandal, and we must suffer for it; but that scandal is requisite, since otherwise the serious importance of being as we ought to be would not have been vindicated.

Joanna's grandfather and brother had been killed in Jefferson by Colonel Sartoris for "stirring up the Negroes." And she had heard such insistently held opinions as this of her grandfather's: "He got off on Lincoln and slavery and dared any man there to deny that Lincoln and the Negro and Moses and the children of Israel were the same, and that the Red Sea was just the blood that had to be spilled in order that the black race might cross into the Promised Land."

In conversations with Joe Christmas she rehearses the actions and long-held opinions in her family that establish their being outside the Latin desire to be at ease with the world. (In fact, there are passages in her story of the family history curiously similar to those in *Absalom, Absalom!* in which the two worlds, Protestant Mississippi and Catholic New Orleans are contrasted.) Joe Christmas knows that Joanna's helping the Negro is a duty undertaken, but that it is abstract and impersonal. She acts not out of sympathy for other human beings but out of an obligation to carry out God's design in a depraved world. It is a helpless world, and the Negro's plight finally is irremediable. Her father tells her: "You must struggle, rise. But in order to rise, you must raise the shadow with you. . . . You can never lift it to your level." The suffering of the Negro *and* the guilt over slavery are the outward signs of a terribly guilt-ridden world—and both are permanent.

Joe Christmas believes that the demonic quality of Joanna's sexual perversions are the excesses inevitable to one who believes in the New England biblical hell and who feeds her emotion-starved body in spite of it. Faulkner describes Joanna's corruption as it appears to Joe Christmas:

At first it shocked him: the abject fury of the New England glacier exposed suddenly to the fire of the New England biblical [76] hell. Perhaps he was aware of the abnegation in it: the imperious and fierce urgency that concealed an actual despair at frustrate and irrevocable years, which she appeared to attempt to compensate each night as if she believed that it would be the last night on earth by damning herself forever to the hell of her forefathers, by living not alone in sin but in filth. She had an avidity for the forbidden word symbols; an insatiable appetite for the sound of them on his tongue and on her own. She revealed the terrible and impersonal curiosity of a child about forbidden subjects and objects; that rapt and tireless and detached interest of a surgeon in the physical body and its possibilities. And by day he would see the calm, coldfaced, almost manlike, almost middle-aged woman who had lived for twenty years alone, without any feminine fears at all, in a lonely house in a neighborhood populated, when at all, by Negroes, who spent a certain portion of each day sitting tranquilly at a desk and writing tranquilly for the eyes of both youth and age the practical advice of a combined priest and banker and trained nurse.

Driven mad by a sense of lost youth and her fear of damnation, she none the less holds unquestioningly to her own beliefs. Like Euphues

Hines she sees herself as God's instrument—declares that it is God, not she, insisting that Joe Christmas pray:

> They looked at one another. "Joe," she said, "for the last time. I don't ask it. Remember that. Kneel with me."
> "No," he said. Then he saw her arms unfold and her right hand come forth from beneath the shawl. It held an old style, single action, cap-and-ball revolver almost as long and heavier than a small rifle. But the shadow of it and of her arm and hand on the wall did not waver at all, the shadow of both monstrous, the cocked hammer monstrous, back-hooked and viciously poised like the arched head of a snake; it did not waver at all. And her eyes did not waver at all. They were as still as the round black ring of the pistol muzzle. But there was no heat in them, no fury. They were calm and still as all pity and all despair and all conviction. But he was not watching them. He was watching the shadowed pistol on the wall; he was watching when the cocked shadow of the hammer flicked away.

The pistol misfired. Then he killed her, almost severing the head from her body. [77]

Following the murder, Christmas is hunted and finally caught. During the days he is a fugitive he is involved in a number of violent acts, but one in particular is appropriate to the theme the novel is dramatizing. It is the scene, reported by a member of the Negro congregation, in which Christmas breaks up a revival meeting:

> He [the member of the congregation] had come direct from a Negro church twenty miles away, where a revival meeting was in nightly progress. On the evening before, in the middle of a hymn, there had come a tremendous noise from the rear of the church, and turning the congregation saw a man standing in the door. The door had not been locked or even shut yet the man had apparently grasped it by the knob and hurled it back into the wall so that the sound crashed into the blended voices like a pistol shot. . . . a woman began to shriek . . . "It's the devil! It's Satan himself." Then she ran, quite blind. She ran straight toward him and he knocked her down without stopping and stepped over her and went on, with the faces gaped for screaming falling away before him, straight to the pulpit and put his hand on the minister. . . . "We could see Brother Bedenberry talking with him, trying to pacify him quiet, and him jerking at Brother Bedenberry and slapping his face with his hand. . . . And he began to curse, hollering it out, at the folks, and he cursed God louder than the women screeching . . ."

It is as though Christmas knows, and perhaps we are to infer that he does know, that the church, far from making his life easier, is one of the agents of his destruction.

The tragedy of Hightower is presented less directly than that of Christmas, mostly as remembered experiences. Hightower's speculations upon his own history and the character of Jefferson furnish most of the explicit commentary on the significance of the action. We learn that he was born to middle-aged parents, an invalid mother and a fifty-year-old father, a minister and doctor, who though strongly opposed to slavery served four years in the Confederate Army. A point is made about the father's character by stating that he would neither eat the food nor sleep in a bed prepared by a Negro.

Hence during the War and while he was absent from home, his [78] wife had no garden save what she could make herself or with the infrequent aid of neighbors. And this aid the husband would not allow her to accept for the reason that it could not be repaid in kind. "God will provide," he said.

> "Provide what? Dandelions and ditch weeds?"
> "Then He will give us the bowels to digest them."

Hightower was born after the War, inheriting organs which "required the unflagging care of a Swiss watch." As a child he was fascinated, bewitched by the War and lived with "those phantoms who loomed heroic and tremendous against a background of thunder and smoke and torn flags." Thinking of it caused him to "experience a kind of hushed and triumphant terror which left him a little sick."

Hightower's grandfather, a gruff man who smelled of whisky and cigars, had greeted his son's bride with this observation: " 'I reckon you'll do,' he said. His eyes were bluff and bold, but kind. 'All the sanctimonious cuss wants anyway is somebody that can sing alto out of a Presbyterian hymnbook, where even the good Lord himself could not squeeze any music.' " One of the grandfather's amusements was to turn church revivals held in a grove into "a week of amateur horse racing while to a dwindling congregation gaunt, fanaticfaced country preachers thundered anathema from the rustic pulpit at his oblivious and unregenerate head." The grandfather had been killed in "Van Dorn's cavalry raid to destroy Grant's stores in Jefferson." This too was one of young Hightower's torturing phantoms, causing him shudderings of delight. His own father, although alive, was also a kind of phantom to the boy. He and his invalid mother looked upon the father as foreign to them, almost an intruder. Hightower lived in a twilight vision of a cavalry troop galloping into Jefferson.

In the seminary, to which he was drawn by its promise of peace, he told himself repeatedly, "God must call me to Jefferson because my life died there, was shot from the saddle of a galloping horse in a Jefferson street one night twenty years before it was ever born." That the seminary had not proved to be the sanctuary [79] for the "garment-worried spirit" he had hoped for did not trouble Hightower greatly because it was merely a preparation for his getting to Jefferson. In the seminary he met his wife. She was the daughter of one of the ministers who was a member of the faculty. Hightower did not live in the everyday world and did not know that she could live there all her life and not be beautiful, nor did he know that for "three years her eyes had watched him with almost desperate calculation, like those of a harassed gambler." Once she spoke suddenly of marriage and escape:

> "Escape?" he said. "Escape from what?"
> "This!" she said. He saw her face for the first time as a living face, as a mask before desire and hatred; wrung blind, headlong with passion. Not stupid: just blind, reckless, desperate. "All of it! All! All!"

Hightower's congregation in Jefferson had thought him a little mad when from the pulpit in his rapt, eager voice he preached of God, salvation, his grandfather, and galloping horses. Looking back at his life, Hightower said he had failed his congregation because he had not preached to them of mercy, pity, and the forgiveness of human frailty. He knew too that he had failed his wife. Eventually she had scandalized Jefferson by not attending church, going away suspiciously for weekends, once screaming at her husband during his sermon, and finally jumping from a hotel room in Memphis where she had been registered under a fictitious name as someone else's wife. Hightower had refused to resign and for a time, before the parishioners locked him out, he had preached and prayed in an empty church. The congregation wanted him to leave Jefferson and gave him a sum of money, but he refused to leave and settled on a little side street. He remained even after he had been taken out of town by the Ku Klux Klan, tied to a tree, and beaten unconscious.

The last trial Hightower is subjected to is a request from Byron Bunch (who is scheming for his own purposes) and Christmas' grandmother, Mrs. Hines, for him to swear that Christmas could not have killed Miss Burden because he had spent the night of the murder and many other nights with Hightower. The old minister [80] refuses to suffer this last outrage, but when Percy Grimm pursues Christmas into Hightower's house he does try to prevent the murder by declaring that Christmas had spent that night with him.

Because Hightower, despite his many weaknesses, was capable of nobility of motive and action, his view of the church, stated shortly before his death, must be stressed:

It seems to him that he has seen it all the while: that that which is destroying the Church is not the outward groping of those within it nor the inward groping of those without, but the professionals who control it and who have removed the bells from its steeples. He seems to see them, endless, without order, empty, symbolical, bleak, skypointed not with ecstasy or passion but in adjuration, threat, and doom. He seems to see the churches of the world like a rampart, like one of those barricades of the middleages planted with dead and sharpened stakes, against truth and against that peace in which to sin and be forgiven which is the life of man.

Earlier in the story Hightower had singled out one service, that on Sunday evening, as the only one during which "there is something of that peace which is the promise and end of the church." It is an hour of faith and hope. Hightower looks forward to this hour in the week when from his darkened window he will watch the people move toward the church. On Sunday nights during the summer he loves to listen to the organ tones, rich and resonant. But on the Sunday before the lynching of Joe Christmas he thinks:

Yet even then the music has still a quality stern and implacable, deliberate and without passion so much as immolation, pleading, asking, for not love, not life, forbidding it to others, demanding in sonorous tones death, as though death were the boon, like all Protestant music. . . . Listening to it he seems to hear within it the apotheosis of his own history, his own land, his own environed blood: Pleasure, ecstasy they cannot seem to bear. Their escape from it is in violence, in drinking and fighting and praying; catastrophe too, the violence identical and apparently inescapable. *And so why should not their religion drive them to crucifixion of themselves and one another?*

Of the lynching, he says:

And they will do it gladly, gladly. . . . Since to pity him would be to admit self-doubt and to hope for and need pity themselves. [81] They will do it gladly, gladly. That's what is so terrible, terrible.

Hightower was right about how it would be done. Percy Grimm, another of the avatars of self-righteousness, is the town's instrument in the killing of Joe Christmas. He does not act in the name of deity, but he moves with the same aura of assured virtue. He sees himself the agent of pure patriotism—which in the context means the protection of each detail of the mores, whatever its source. Faulkner insists on the righteousness of Grimm: "There was nothing vengeful about him either, no fury, no outrage" as he pursued Joe Christmas across ditches, behind cabins, and finally into Hightower's house. And the righteousness is further insisted upon in the description of his voice when Hightower, lying to prevent the lynching, says Christmas had spent the night of the murder with him: " 'Jesus Christ,' Grimm cried, his young voice clear and outraged like that of a young priest." Then the outrage turns into an insane kind of fury (like that of Hines or Joanna Burden) and Grimm castrates Joe Christmas with a butcher knife.

Lena Grove and Byron Bunch are not merely the comic subplot, the relief from the terrible anguish of the lynching. They are a part of the complexity of the community, and by what they are and the way they act they insinuate powerfully what is wrong with the community. Only rarely does Faulkner allow them to comment explicitly on the other part of the action, as when Lena Grove sees in Hightower's face "that ruthlessness which she had seen in the face of a few good people, usually men." Neither she nor Byron Bunch is the intelligent refractor, in Henry James' terms, of the action; it is by being what they are that they imply a commentary.[2]

Lena is a creature of faith, humility, and endurance. Setting out from Alabama in her eighth month of pregnancy and with only thirty-five cents, she hopefully expects to find her seducer. In her trustfulness and willingness to be helped, she accepts the attentions and [82] assistance of many, including Bunch. Her manner causes the people she meets, or most of them, to treat her in kind, generously, courteously. But she is not without guile. She knows how to lead Byron about, taking an almost but not quite innocent advantage of his abject devotion. She belongs among those who are fallible but who live in "tranquil obedience . . . to the good earth." She is a minor earth goddess. Harshness of spirit and rigidity of principle are completely foreign to her.

Burch, the seducer of Lena, is characterless. He stands outside the two groups that dominate the novel, those with the religious beliefs that cause them to crucify their fellowman and those, like Lena and Byron, with the kind of belief that makes existence sufferable and even pleasant. He is a kind of Judas (and is called just that) in his willingness to sacrifice his friend Joe Christmas, but actually he is amoral and therefore hardly human at all. Byron says Burch "was just living on the country, like a locust." He has no pride in himself and he has no sense of responsibility. He is capable neither of loyalty nor love.

Byron Bunch, on the other hand, has committed himself to the moral life, to a Protestant orthodoxy. He is the friend of Hightower (who offers him the conventionally good man's advice to avoid Lena), and he is a choir leader. Obviously a product of the Protestant ethic, he is described as having "a still stubborn, ascetic face: the face of a hermit who has lived for a long time in an empty place where the sand blows." He believes in the sanctity of work, that a man gets into mischief when he is not working; therefore he works on Saturday afternoons and keeps a record of the hours he is not working. He attempts to search out the truth and he worries his conscience, but he is never self-righteous. Except that he has humor about himself, he belongs to the tradition of Piers Plowman and of Bunyan's Christian, a kind of Protestant Everyman. Faulkner identifies him as belonging to the hill people, the pine hill farmers, and describes him as "small, non-

---

[2] It is quite possible that Faulkner took from Shakespeare, or from his knowledge of Elizabethan drama, which he is said to know quite well, his use of episodic structure and free intermingling of characters from different levels. This structure undoubtedly contributes to the sense of multiple life that many of his stories give.

descript, whom no man ever turned to look at twice." He is the only significant character whose background is not explored.

But Byron is free from the excesses of the Protestant tradition. [83] He is not in search of martyrdom, but he endures the hardships that his sense of obligation tells him are his to accept. He can admit self-doubt, he can pity, and he is charitable. Faulkner describes him as acting kindly "as a reflex." He is fallible and, like Lena, capable of guile, but Byron Bunch believes in "that peace," as Hightower describes it, which results from sinning and being forgiven, "which is the life of man. [84]

. . . *Light in August* might also be examined in terms of the psychology of sex, especially in relation to the social or racial situation treated in it. Probably it is remaining closer to the main intention of the novel, however, to see it in terms of the Protestant mores, a subject with which Faulkner seems preoccupied. Certainly it is mark of his genius that Faulkner can develop the terrible irony that it is out of the religion itself that the lynching comes, without resting in it, and is able to introduce the complementary theme, that inside the religion one can also find direction, discipline, and consolation. . . . [86]

The Shadow and the Mirror

OLGA W. VICKERY

DESPITE FAULKNER'S USE OF A CLEARLY DEFINED PLOT, *Light in August* is by no means a return to the traditional novel. Rather it constitutes his attempt to integrate certain experimental features of his earlier novels into a conventional narrative frame, thereby carrying one step further his use of structure to clarify theme. In both *The Sound and the Fury* and *As I Lay Dying* the public world serves merely as a frame for events which the reader is engaged in seeing from different perspectives. In *Light in August*, however, we are no longer concerned with examining the particular nature and limits of the individual consciousness but rather with its relation to other minds and to the public world of events, statements, and mass responses.

Because of the interpenetration and interdependence of the private and public worlds, each character is multidimensional. He is at once subject and object, observer and observed, creator and created. Thus, Joe Christmas as well as the Reverend Hightower and Joanna Burden are both self-crucified and crucified by others, both villain and victim. The interplay of these polar aspects of the human being produces much of the dramatic tension and the grotesque quality in the novel. There is a continual movement from one world to another, each with its own kind and degree of distortion. Depending upon who is acting as observer, this distortion provides a mirror image of the particular world of the observer or of the public world as represented by the town of Jefferson. In a sense, the individual and the community are obverse reflections of each other. Yet because [66] the reflection is obverse, each fails to recognize himself, and so reacts with instinctive fear and anger which ultimately lead him to destroy his own image. In short, each is the victim of the other.

The nature of the private world and its relation to others is indicated by a threefold pattern of interlocking imagery—the circle, the shadow, and the mirror. All the main characters in *Light in August* are strangers to Jefferson and they remain strangers no matter how long their stay or how deep their roots. Their isolation is suggested by the image of the circle which achieves its clearest expression and greatest significance in the episode of Joe Christmas' flight and his sudden realization: "It had been a paved street, where going should be fast. It had made a circle and he is still inside of it. . . . 'And yet I have been farther in these seven days than in all the thirty years,' he thinks. 'But I have never got outside that circle.'" (296) * In the midst of that jostling, noisy intercourse which is society and to which all men contribute, each is alone, unable to break through the circumference of his own circle or to admit anyone into it. Because of the solipsistic quality of the private world, each individual sees others and is himself seen as a shadow, ghostlike and unreal. Walking the streets of Jefferson, Joe Christmas, for example, looks like "a phantom, a spirit, strayed out of its own world, and lost." (99) The images of the circle and the shadow are linked in the description of Byron Bunch and Brown, passing "one another as though on opposite orbits and with an effect as of phantoms or apparitions." (386) It is Hightower, however, who extends the insight provided by these images with his recognition that other people are simply "mirrors in which he watches himself." (427)

Yet no matter how isolated and impenetrable the private world of an individual, he still has a physical and social existence in the public world which makes its demands of him. His comfort, if not his life, depends on his accepting and exemplifying in his own life those stereotypes which represent society's vision of itself and its past. And since withdrawal or rebellion are as much public acts as is affirmation, no one can escape. Society has myths not only of the hero but also of the antagonist, and it has evolved rituals to deal with each. Collectively, Jefferson is Southern, White, and Elect, qualities which have meaning only within a context which recognizes something or someone as

---

* All quotations from *Light in August* are from the Modern Library edition (New York: Random House, 1950).

Northern or Black or Damned. This antithesis is periodically [67] affirmed through the sacrifice of a scapegoat who represents, in fact or popular conviction, those qualities which must be rejected if Jefferson is to maintain its self-defined character.

Miss Burden, Hightower, and Christmas serve as such scapegoats and serve willingly, almost eagerly, since they too have accepted the absolute necessity and validity of the dichotomies in whose name they are destroyed. Thus, Miss Burden, despite her birth in Jefferson, is a "Northerner" in the eyes of the town, and hence she is automatically aligned with the "Negro" and the "Damned." Hightower, on the other hand, offends not by being a Northerner but by refusing to play the role of "Reverend" in the manner established by custom and tradition. He becomes "Gail Hightower Done Damned in Jefferson." (52) This judgment is then in part justified and in part explained by the town's accusation of Hightower's unnatural relationship with a Negress. Out of this judgment his ritualistic punishment by masked men and his ostracism follow inevitably. Joe Christmas, of course, represents the third category, that of the Negro, and it is this assumption that pre-determines the manner of his pursuit and lynching. But at the same time he constitutes an omnipresent threat to all categories: he cannot say with certainty whether he is Negro or white; he is a Southerner with too many Northern ideas; and he seems quite indifferent to salvation or damnation.

Accordingly, Christmas has a dual function in the novel. As an individual, he explores his own relation to the myth of the Negro, while as a part of society, he is identified with the myth. Through his oscillation between repudiation and affirmation of his black blood, he reveals his own uncertainty and his need to resolve the dilemma posed to him by the old Negro gardener: "'You dont know what you are. And more than that, you wont never know. You'll live and you'll die and you wont never know.'" (336) He is obsessed with the idea that he must choose, yet his every action emphasizes his inability to do so. In the world of Jefferson, however, after Brown's accusation has taken root, he is treated as if he were in actual fact a Negro. The varying responses, ranging from Gavin Stevens' cool, impersonal analysis to Gail Hightower's anguished sympathy to the mob's violence, are directed at the concept of the Negro with which he is identified. Inescapably Joe is forced into the ritual of pursuit and lynching performed almost casually by a society which has been elaborating it for generations.

The basis of this pattern is Jefferson's conviction that the [68] in-dividual can only become a member of society by permitting himself to be classified according to race, color, geographic origin, and so on. Created by man, these categories become creators of man insofar as they establish social identification as the necessary prerequisite to human existence. The sheer weight of generations, each in its turn conforming to and therefore affirming this process of public labelling, establishes the labels not only as a matter of tradition but as a kind of revealed truth. What starts as a verbal pattern of classification thus becomes a social order not to be challenged or changed. And what starts as a category becomes a myth, for certainly the word "Negro" is a compressed myth just as the stock response to that word is a compressed ritual. The result is that men like Joe Christmas or Velery Bon, who can neither fit nor be fitted into these categories, are either sacrificed to or driven out of the society whose cherished beliefs they threaten.

Certainly there is no one set of categories which can claim Christmas or be claimed by him. He is indeed the "disaccommodated man," with "something definitely rootless about him, as though no town nor city was his, no street, no walls, no square of earth his home." (27) Yet he cannot ignore the concept of race which assigns men to one of two separate worlds, each with its traditions and modes of thinking and acting. The irony of Joe's position is that what seems to be a choice is in reality a delusion: Negro or white—to choose one is to affirm the existence of the other. His awareness of this dichotomy makes him take up the role of antagonist in all situations. In the presence of whites he becomes Negro; among Negroes he feels himself to be white. The result is that series of tensions and conflicts for which he himself is at least partly responsible. The Joe Christmas who is finally lynched as "Negro" is the joint creation of his private world and of the larger public universe.

In this respect Mrs. Hines's account of his birth becomes significant, for it reveals that Joe is born into a myth created for him by others. Since Millie's pregnancy is considered an unforgivable sin by Hines, he looks for a scapegoat who will bear the guilt and punishment. By calling her lover a "nigger," he can transform a commonplace seduction into the horror of miscegenation. That is his justification, moral and religious, for the brutally inhuman treatment of his daughter, her lover, and her child. His reasons for regarding Christmas with malevolence and hatred remain personal, but his actions and statements help [69] formulate that confused and violent myth which is Joe's particular agony. His brooding watchfulness having isolated Joe from the other children at the orphanage, Hines then provides the three year old with an explanation: "'Why dont you play with them other children like you used to? . . . Is it because they call you nigger?'" (335) The awareness of something strange or different about Joe is thus simultaneously impressed on Joe and on others.

The identification of Joe with Negro receives additional and unexpected support from the dietitian. Surprised in the midst of her clandestine love affair, she lashes out at Joe calling him a "little rat" and a "little nigger bastard." In the days of frenzied uncertainty and fear which follow, she links the carelessly spoken invective with

Hines's attitude and with the meaningless taunts of the children. Though she had never considered Joe to be a Negro, "she believed that she had, had known it all the while, because it seemed so right: he would not only be removed; he would be punished for having given her terror and worry." (113) At cross purposes, each speaking a strange, private language, and each motivated by personal reasons, the dietitian and Hines, nevertheless, combine to extend and intensify Joe's awareness of himself as a different kind of being and to force the matron to act on the assumption that he is indeed a Negro.

Although the "taint" of Negro blood is never revealed to Mc-Eachern, Joe himself is imbued with its possibility. For a time, however, it lies quiescent in his consciousness while he endeavors to assimilate yet another aspect of his life. To the social pattern of black and white, the implications of which he is yet to realize, is added the religious pattern of the elect and the damned. His vague, emotional response to God is replaced by the creed and discipline of a particular church. And the spiritual relationship of father and son is submerged in an intricate and deadly game of good and evil, reward and punishment. McEachern's religious discipline is accepted eagerly by Joe because it makes his life completely predictable, relieving him of the necessity for self-judgment and responsibility. Accordingly, he rejects Mrs. McEachern's awkward and uncertain attempts to establish a more purely human relationship with him.

Ultimately, however, he seeks and finds such a relationship in his love for Bobbie, the waitress. It is this love which prompts him to rebel against McEachern's Calvinistic ritual of confession and penance and to resist the customary punishment which [70] McEachern seeks to inflict on him at the dance. But this achievement is short-lived, for Bobbie's later shrieks of rage signal the destruction of the last of Joe's natural, spontaneous emotions. Her betrayal, which impels him into the long, lonely street of his life, is not only sexual but religious and racial, for all three are involved in the idea of miscegenation into which their affair is suddenly transformed. So long as their affair proves satisfactory and trouble free, Bobbie simply ignores Joe's confession the " 'I think I got some nigger blood in me.' " (171) In a moment of crisis, however, and in order to save herself, she, like the dietitian, finds it convenient not only to believe but to act upon that belief. All blame, all possible punishment is shifted to Joe as "Negro" who significantly enough has himself provided the material for this accusation. Suddenly conscious of her white blood, Bobbie has no compunctions about abandoning a "nigger" whom she had naïvely mistaken for a white man nor about watching that "nigger" beaten senseless by her friends.

The beating establishes the antithesis of black and white in Joe's own physical experience and thereby intensifies his awareness of it. His life becomes a series of episodes in which he provokes racial violence

from Negro and white alike, a violence which constitutes an almost
joyful affirmation of the Negro-white pattern in which both Joe and his
opponents are trapped. That someone could simply ignore that pattern
fills him with an indignant amazement and outrage. He beats the
prostitute who refuses to be horrified by his Negro blood, thus forcing
her to initiate that ritual of violence which he expects. His reaction is
understandable, for her indifference challenges the validity of the
premise on which he has built his whole life. Whether or not he himself is a Negro may remain in doubt, but that there is something called
Negro which demands certain attitudes and actions on the part of all
white people must not be denied.

During his relationship with Joanna Burden, Joe's preoccupation
with such categories becomes especially acute since he recognizes the
same obsession in her. In fact, her concern with racial, geographical,
and religious myths serves as a complement and antithesis to his own.
Not even their frenzied and insatiable love-making can destroy their
ingrained awareness of what each believes the other to represent.
While her body surrenders completely to his, Joanna still mutters
"Negro! Negro! Negro!" And Joe, on his way to her bedroom, still
pauses to smash the dishes of food prepared by the white woman and
left for him in the [71] kitchen. Thus, even miscegenation is powerless
to erase their concern with racial differences and indeed serves only to
intensify it.

Joe's wild hope, as he holds her letter in his hand, that they can
escape from their own preconceptions into a world where " 'She is still
she and I am still I' " (238) is doomed from its very inception. For
what he visualizes is a return to the natural world where the only
meaningful categories are male and female and the only meaningful
relationship is sexual. But Joanna, her physical need for him exhausted, demands of him that choice which he has spent his whole life
evading. She insists that he ignore his uncertainty and accept once and
for all the role of Negro as modified by the North together with that of
repentant sinner. The violence between them is inevitable, but significantly it is both impersonal and unimpassioned. Joanna's act of
raising the pistol and Joe's use of the razor are both projected as
shadows against the wall—phantom weapons directed at phantom
opponents. For each sees embodied in the other that racial myth which
has dominated their lives and which they must destroy if they are to
be free.

Yet in the very act of gaining his freedom, Joe loses it. The act of
murder leaves him vulnerable to society's judgments and actions. The
fire at Miss Burden's and her decapitated body generate a tension in
the milling crowd which needs only the proper spark to explode it into
violence. That spark is supplied by Brown, a man whose parentage is
as obscure as Joe's own. The pattern made familiar by Hines, the
dietitian, and Bobbie is repeated as the cry of "Negro" and the sugges-

tion of miscegenation channel the restless and undirected energy of the observers away from the accuser. Three times Brown repeats " 'Accuse the white man and let the nigger go free' " until the crowd grasps the significance of that contrast and prepares itself for action. Once he pronounces the word "Negro," the actual guilt of Joe Christmas, the circumstances, and the motivation, all become irrelevant, for the connection between "Negro" and "murder" is part of the public myth. At the same time Joanna Burden loses all individuality, becoming simply a white woman and hence an innocent victim who must be avenged. Accusation, conviction, and punishment constitute a single, simultaneous belief-act as "Joe, the son of Joe" becomes Joe, the son of a Negro.

The compelling nature of the pattern evoked by Brown is [72] indicated by the fact that no one thinks to question his premise. The mob is, of course, wholly absorbed in the idea of revenge, but even those who sympathize with Joe never doubt that he is a Negro. Though he has ample evidence of Brown's character, Byron still takes his word and in his turn convinces Hightower. The intense shock felt by the latter is occasioned by his sickening realization that a public myth is once more demanding its victim, that the ritualistic sequence of the chase, the pursuit, and the final immolation is now inevitable. Even the cosmopolitan Gavin Stevens, with his Harvard and Heidelberg studies behind him, is not able to see Joe Christmas except through a filter of preconceptions. Though he recognizes that Hines is quite mad, he, nevertheless, accepts his contention that Joe's father was actually a Negro. More important: despite his disinterested rationalism and objectivity, he assigns definite though arbitrary moral values to black and white blood, claiming that it was the former which made Joe strike Hightower and the latter which enabled him to die heroically.

As these stock reactions and attitudes crystallize in Jefferson, Joe Christmas himself is able if only temporarily to escape their coercive pressure. At the outset he is still sufficiently obsessed with the fictions he has spent his life affirming through endless challenges to pause in a Negro church. Standing in the pulpit and cursing God, he assumes, possibly in his own mind and certainly in the minds of the congregation, the terrifying form of anti-Christ. But the body's need for food and rest erases all the illusions that the mind creates and perpetuates. The stage beyond, where even food becomes unnecessary, gives to Christmas the human dignity all his violence could not seize. For the first time, he sees his life not in terms of "black" and "white" but simply of the human race. Inevitably his new found awareness of himself as man causes him to be rejected by both the Negroes and the whites. Negro fear is balanced by white outrage at the fact that " 'He never acted like either a nigger or a white man. That was it. That was what made the folks so mad.' " (306)

Ironically, as Christmas transcends the categories of black and white and of good and evil, thus resolving his own personal dilemma, he is once more forced to exemplify them in the sequence of flight and pursuit, capture and death, begun by his own act of murder but given shape by Brown's accusation of "nigger." Dazedly he half-comprehends that he has given himself up to the public world by his act and that he can no longer [73] refuse the role it has given him to play. Since he is a "nigger" murderer, each gesture, even each emotion which he is permitted to feel, is already established. Sardonically he reflects on his unsuccessful attempts to give himself up: " 'Like there is a rule to catch me by, and to capture me that way would not be like the rule says.' " (294) As Christmas recognizes the inevitability of this pattern and of his own part in it, he visualizes himself sinking "at last into the black abyss which had been waiting, trying, for thirty years to drown him and into which now and at last he had actually entered, bearing now upon his ankles the definite and ineradicable gauge of its upward moving." (289) Significantly, he becomes aware of the borrowed shoes as a symbol of his acceptance of "the black abyss" only when he is in the wagon on his way to Mottstown to give himself up and thus to assume the role of Negro which Jefferson has prepared for him.

It is, then, as "Negro" that Christmas is lynched in a scene that echoes and intensifies all the earlier acts of his life. In the "cloistral dimness" of Hightower's house Christmas resembles "a vengeful and furious god pronouncing a doom" (406) on the men whose "faces seemed to glare with bodiless suspension as though from haloes." (405) Saints and sinners, the elect and the damned, the victim and the persecutors become strangely confused with one another. Through Percy Grimm, the "young priest" of the occasion, the elect and white of Jefferson castrate and slay the Negro according to ancient custom, but instead of purification, they are left with a sense of their own guilt and self-doubt. Through his castration, Christmas finally does escape society's categories. Having made him a "Negro" in order to crucify him, society, by its own passion for affirming the reality of its myths in actual living experience, in the end explodes both those myths and the categories out of which they were evolved. It is no longer the Negro murderer or even Joe Christmas but simply "the man" who rises "soaring into their memories forever and ever." (407)

In the moment of Christmas' death, then, there occurs a final violent fusion of the public and private myths of the "Negro," a fusion developing out of the interaction of these myths as charted in the actual chronological sequence of the novel. Moreover, in the process of unfolding this interaction the chronological sequence has shown the gradual identification of the individual, Joe Christmas, with this public myth. Through Joanna Burden and Gail Hightower that identification is given historical [74] perspective, not only because they themselves are conscious of the historical origins of the particular myths which dominate Joe Christmas and themselves alike, but because they have virtually stopped living in the public world where their beliefs might be modified by further interaction. At the same time they represent the two remaining categories, one geographical and the other religious, in terms of which the South establishes its identity. The Negro, the Yankee, the Apostate—these are the key figures in a society which defines itself by exclusion.

Like Joe Christmas, Joanna Burden presents an obverse reflection of one aspect of the South. For though she is excluded from the community as a Northerner, she too is obsessed with the myth of the Negro. Despite the apparently irreconcilable opposition of their attitudes which led them to actual war, both North and South are concerned with the problem of the Negro, a concern which gives form and substance to a concept but which takes no cognizance of individuals as individuals. In both, this concept, bolstered by the legends of history as seen from their own particular perspective, engenders a set pattern of beliefs and actions. Eventually, these acts and beliefs involving the "Negro" are transformed into a kind of religion, a distorted version of Calvinism in which black and white replace or are identified with evil and good. Each holding this extreme view, Joanna Burden, the scion of New England, is scarcely distinguishable from McEachern or even Hines.

Joanna's increasing awareness of this myth parallels Joe's, though without his tormenting uncertainty as to his own relationship to it. As a child, she simply accepts the fact that certain people have darker skins than her own. But this innocence or naïveté is not permitted to continue. Her father, Nathaniel Burden, slowly transforms the physical black and white she sees into a moral and religious order. She is made aware of "Negro" " 'not as people, but as a thing, a shadow in which [she] lived, we lived, all white people, all other people.' " (221) The shadow becomes a "black cross" to which she is a martyr, a phantom priestess immolating herself on a phantom altar. Consequently, her whole life is devoted to perpetuating and giving substance to a metaphor: " 'You must struggle, rise. But in order to rise, you must raise the shadow with you.' " (222)

To this belief in her martyrdom, Joanna Burden sacrifices all her natural impulses, thereby creating a bifurcated individual. Thus, Joe sees her as "a dual personality: the one the woman at [75] first sight of whom in the lifted candle . . . there had opened before him, instantaneous as a landscape in a lightningflash, a horizon of physical security and adultery if not pleasure; the other the mantrained muscles and the mantrained habit of thinking born of heritage and environment with which he had to fight up to the final instant." (205) His entrance into her life signals an overt conflict between these two aspects of her being. The sex-starved body conquers for a time "the mantrained habit of thinking" and expresses itself in a desperate and imperious need to experience every possible sensation and every possible emotion that physical love can suggest. Acting out of a world of fantasies, she quickly passes "through every avatar of a woman in love": (226) the lover's pursuit, secret trysts, baseless accusations and jealousy, seduction, and even rape.

Yet even in the midst of these exaggerated manifestations of her long suppressed desires, she is not entirely free of her intellectual heritage. She can only seek to postpone its mastery over her: " 'Don't make me have to pray yet. Dear God, let me be damned a little longer, a little while.' " (231) The implicit identification of sex with sin prepares the way for the corruption of her relationship with Joe and for her own final perversion in which he ceases to be the means of satisfying her physical demands and comes to symbolize the sexual superstitions associated with the Negro. In this last phase, she is not having intercourse with a man but with an image of her own creation, with the idea of "Negro" for which she has given up her life. Accordingly, she emerges from the affair with her instincts once more subdued and with her obsessions once more crystallized and intensified.

No longer driven by her desire to sin, Joanna is left free to brood over the fact that she has sinned. In retrospect she naturally sees all the facets of her relationship with Christmas in the light of her old "mantrained habits of thinking" and the result is a reaffirmation of Calvinism and rededication of herself to the black cross. Nor can she leave Christmas alone, for he is the Negro, the symbol of her responsibility, her sin and damnation, and most important, her salvation. Her pleading, bribes, and threats are her attempt to make him translate into living flesh and act her concept of the Negro. He is to ignore his own uncertainty, admit his black blood, his sinfulness, and his dependence for salvation on her and her God. Joe's refusal to submit himself [76] to that formula threatens that myth for the sake of which she has continued to draw breath. She reacts to his recalcitrance, as the mob does later, by resorting to violence. Ironically the transformation of Joe Christmas into a Negro which she does not accomplish in her life is effected through her death.

Gail Hightower is, of course, rejected by Jefferson because he has proved himself unworthy of directing its religious, spiritual life. Like Joe Christmas and Joanna Burden, he is an impure element of which society must purge itself; and like them, he too mirrors yet another aspect of the South: its preoccupation with the legends of its own past. The exploits of the gallant Confederate forces are part of the inheritance of every Southern boy as well as an article in the belief of every Southern community. Such legends, provided they are accepted as legends, remain as valuable and harmless as the stories of Charlemagne. Hightower, however, sees a kind of revealed truth in the vision of his grandfather, compounded of an old Negress' storytelling and his own boyish imagination. The imagination is given full scope because there is nothing and no one to contradict his fictions. With an equal opportunity for deifying his father who also had a share in the glorious war, young Gail is unable to place the mantle of heroism on his shoulders. Thus, the dead grandfather becomes the symbol of "that fine shape of eternal youth and virginal desire which makes heroes," (423) while the living father evokes only the grim brutality and carnage of battle.

Eventually the legends of the past become the only truth and the only reality for Hightower, rendering his connection with the public world precarious at best. For unlike his father, he cannot function as "two separate and complete people, one of whom dwelled by serene rules in a world where reality did not exist." (415) And since nothing can compare with his vision, the people he meets and the tasks he is forced to perform become annoying interruptions of the commonplace and trivial. What destroys Hightower is not the fact that he has a dream, but that for the sake of the dream, he becomes insensitive and indifferent to the quality of his actual experience. Thus, he ignores his wife and her needs because the affection due her has already been pre-empted by her counterpart so that "when he did see her he did not see her at all because of the face which he had already created in his mind." (420) Dominated by his vision, he stands in the pulpit, fusing religion, the galloping cavalry, and his dead [77] grandfather into one incoherent rhapsody, while he remains sublimely indifferent to the growing uneasiness of his parish and to the suicide of his wife.

As if recognizing that he has no place in Jefferson, that indeed his dream-world is threatened by it, Hightower deliberately provokes the violence which will ensure his isolation. For he can only justify and safeguard his withdrawal by "making it appear that he was being driven, uncomplaining, into that which he did not even then admit had been his desire since before he entered the seminary." (428) Each of his actions becomes a defiance, a calculated incentive to public outrage and retribution. Thus he, like Christmas, is at least partially responsible for his own isolation and for the violence he suffers. In his self-chosen role of antagonist, he experiences a fierce exultation, momentarily revealed by his demonic grin hidden by the prayer book. As passive victim, he suffers the threats and beating by the K.K.K. "with that patient and voluptuous ego of the martyr," (429) since it merely confirms his contemptuous judgment of society.

Safe at last in his lonely house, unvisited and undisturbed, Hightower yet retains one tenuous connection with the external world in the person of Byron Bunch. And it is Byron who ultimately forces him to re-examine his world and his life. Compelled by Byron to attend the birth of Lena's child, he becomes for the occasion a participant in rather than a spectator of life. But more important, through the birth he is initiated into the world of nature and discovers that life itself is a source of human value. Reversing his former opinion of Lena, he sees her as a symbol of life and a new paradise: *"That will be her life, her destiny. The good stock peopling in tranquil obedience to it the good earth."* (356)

Byron's plea that he at least attempt to save Joe Christmas is much more difficult to deal with. For though Hightower is willing to accept the natural world, he is not prepared to re-enter the social world. From the moment he hears of Christmas' Negro blood and of the murder, he knows beyond any doubt the sequence of events which must culminate in violence and death. He knows because he himself had been caught in a similar pattern. And though he feels pity, compassion, even horror, he waits passively for the mob to turn once more "with insult and violence upon those who like them were created by the same God and were driven by them to do that which they now turn and rend them for having done it." (319–20) To interfere with the [78] beliefs and rituals of society would be to admit his responsibility for that society. It would, in effect, expose the futility of a life devoted solely to the worship of a dream and to a world "intact and on all sides complete and inviolable, like a classic and serene vase, where the spirit could be born anew sheltered from the harsh gale of living." (419)

Nevertheless, when the escaped and fleeing Christmas rushes into his house, Hightower does make the one gesture which could give substance to his vision. Ironically, this one fumbling but heroic attempt to save Christmas at the risk of his own life, this one act which so far transcends practical considerations that it contains the germ of another legend, is nullified by a younger version of himself. Percy Grimm, engrossed in his own vision of military gallantry which has been fostered by a more recent war, sees nothing in Hightower's words but another example of the degrading crudeness of the non-military world. Too much has happened to Hightower and to Jefferson since the day he abandoned his chosen calling for him to be able to sway or influence the lynch-mob in any way. The past is irremediable.

Jarred out of his complacency and self-righteousness by Joe's death, Hightower sees his past with a new clarity. The image of the great wheel, which gives form to his memories, echoes and passes judgment on all the other solitary circles that have collided violently without ever establishing contact with one another. What he finally comes to recognize is the interdependence of the individual and society, of the private and public worlds, and, more important, the interdependence of individuals within the public world. He, Joe Christmas, and Joanna Burden have all been self-created martyrs to an idea and to that idea they have sacrificed others beyond themselves. Society, no less deluded, attacks and sacrifices them in the name of the same ideas. Their personal histories, like the history of Jefferson, consist of a perpetual denial of life for the sake of empty rituals, each of which enshrines some abstraction. Hightower has the intelligence to attain this bitter self-knowledge and to realize that the responsibility rests with the individual, but he does not have the strength to live with it. As his head falls to the window sill, he hears once again the thunderous cavalry charge peopling Jefferson with the old insubstantial phantoms.

Compared with the embattled lives and specter-haunted thoughts of Hightower, Christmas, and Miss Burden, the calm journey of Lena Grove with a willing Byron Bunch in her wake [79] seems almost an impertinence. Yet it is through her presence that we achieve a final perspective on the action. Into the schematic world of Jefferson she introduces, by virtue of her own intellectual limitations and her pregnancy, the world of nature with its total indifference to both moral and social categories. This provides a significant contrast to Joe Christmas' painful initiation and absorption into society. Both are strangers to Jefferson; but while Joe comes bearing death for himself and others, Lena comes bearing life. The ritual in which she involves others is the natural one of pregnancy and birth. Thus, while the one crystallizes the obsessions of society, the other dispels them. The same almost anonymous figures who attach the label of Negro to Christmas in order to lynch him also forget the social stigma of Lena's pregnancy in order to help her.

Like Joe Christmas, Lena herself is a center for the actions and reactions of various characters and the object of a clearly defined public attitude. Each person she meets sees not her but an image of what he believes her to be, and that image is at least partly predetermined by the convention that identifies virginity with virtue. For Mrs. Armstid she is the fallen woman; for the men at the store, a foolish virgin to be treated with mingled pity and scorn; and for Byron, who loves her, she is the innocent victim of a scoundrel. Each of these images, grounded in a concern with Lena's unmarried state, conveys more information about the observers and their society than they do about her, for unlike Christmas, she does not mirror or share the preconceptions of the community. From the moment we see her delicately licking the sardine oil from her fingers, she is wholly absorbed in the new sensations with which her leisurely travels provide her. Even her search for a father for her child is more a matter of instinct than of morality. What she is looking for is security not respectability. Once Byron assumes this responsibility, she shows no great haste to marry and so to remove the social stigma from herself and her child.

Though Lena is judged harshly, she is consistently treated with kindness. The reason is that she offends against the mores of society without challenging its very foundations as Joe Christmas does. In a sense, the community's convictions and actions operate independently. Mrs. Armstid or the men who offer Lena a ride preserve the myth of virginity in which they share by revealing their contempt for the unmarried Lena, but at the same [80] time they respond to her needs as a woman about to give birth to a child. Here the pressing demands of nature take precedence over social convention.

Thus Lena's arrival signals the breaking up of the old compulsive patterns which match action to judgment. Mrs. Armstid's tight-lipped offer of food, shelter, and money prepares us for Byron's quick abandonment of his routine of overtime work and weekly trips to the country church when Lena appears. He too acts "contrary to all the tradition of his austere and jealous country raising which demands in the object physical inviolability." (42) It is not, however, until Mrs. Hines calls him to the cabin where Lena is in labor that he fully realizes and admits to himself that she is not a virgin. Hightower, despite his distrust of Lena and his fear for Byron, disrupts the pattern of his life and leaves his sanctuary to attend the birth of her child. The sheriff, momentarily overlooking the letter of the law, recognizes her need and therefore her right to use Miss Burden's cottage. Even the anonymous truck driver is trapped into kindness towards Lena and gives up his bed, though not the right to grumble about it.

In each of these cases, the separation of judgment and action is made possible by Lena's own indifference to the former. The relationship between society and the individual is reciprocal as the lives of Hightower, Miss Burden, and Christmas amply illustrate. But Lena refuses or rather is incapable of acting in the light of society's preconception of her. Accordingly, where Joe Christmas intensifies, she destroys the barriers between herself and 'others; where he forever threatens life with extinction, she becomes the means of its renewal and continuance. This difference is made explicit by the incidents involving food. Lena herself is indifferent to the spirit in which it is offered so long as it sustains her and her child. And her acceptance of it invariably fosters a more personal, human relationship with the giver. Christmas, on the other hand, is forever rejecting the food offered him because of his abnormal sensitivity to the thoughts and attitudes of the giver. He is able to share food with Bobbie, believing that she loves him, but he consistently rejects meals offered by Mrs. McEachern, Byron Bunch, or Miss Burden. The food which sustains Lena in her world of physical experience proves poisonous to Christmas, who lives largely in a world of obsessive ideas which he projects, rightly or wrongly, into every situation. Joe and Lena [81] thus present two contrasting attitudes to experience and to society, and these in turn evoke sharply different responses from society.

Both make a claim on Byron Bunch, the one uncommitted character in the novel, since he has isolated himself from both nature and society. But it is his love for Lena and his sudden and unexpected initiation into the world of nature which she represents that makes Byron willing and eager to help Christmas. Her needs destroy those protective barriers of meaningless routine which he has built around himself. As Hightower points out, Byron, by loving her, becomes vulnerable, for he has allowed himself to be caught up in a chain of events and circumstances over which he can exercise no control. At the same time, however, he has gained in some measure a self-respect, a dignity, and a courage which was lacking in his isolated safety and which gives promise of being a sufficient shield against whatever catastrophes he may encounter. His romantic desire to protect Lena, to convert Hightower, and to save Christmas appear, at first sight, exaggerated reactions to his former passivity and belief in noninterference. But the important thing is that he does not rest in these attitudes or treat his vision of Lena as immutable. He is still necessarily the creator of his own world, but now he is willing to recognize when he has built awry and to reshape it with an eye to reality.

His ability to do so is dependent, to a large extent, on his eventual discovery of the resources of humor. His love for Lena, itself an irrational act, makes him realize the comic aspect of his own behavior. By laughing at his own follies and gullibility, he is able to continue acting irrationally which, in this case, is also humanely; for laughter is one means of re-examining the shibboleths of society and of placing the individual and his world once more in perspective. Though Byron is still sustained by illusions, he is no longer blindly ruled by them. Instead he endeavors through them to establish his kinship with other men. Though he continues to believe in Lena's chastity, Hightower's wisdom, and Joe's black blood, nevertheless, he arranges for the confinement, argues for the first time with Hightower, and does what little he can to help Joe. His illusions are thus more nearly centered on humanity and grounded in the immediacy of living experience. It is man's nature to dream and dreams by their very essence are both distortions of reality and desires for a new shape to experience. [82]

Certainly, the real Lena, more than slightly stupid and more than slightly selfish, and the real Confederate Hightower, who found an inglorious death in a chickencoop, are both unworthy of the dreams and the devotion they inspire. The responsibility, however, lies not with them but with the Byron Bunches and Gail Hightowers who can be moved to save or to deny Joe Christmas because of their dreams. Reason and imagination can prove an integrative force, identifying the interests of the individual with those of the community and establishing a link between the private and public worlds. They can also be destructive insofar as they enable man to invent infinitely various excuses which permit him to live while ignoring life itself. Rationally conceived categories and myths may render morality simpler and clearer by providing formulas of universal applicability, but in the process they destroy those essential motives for morality which must be found by the individual in life itself. This is the truth that Hightower could only know; it is also the truth which Byron, in fumbling and often farcically inadequate fashion, seeks to live. [83]

Outrage and Compassion

HYATT WAGGONER

IN ONE OF GAIL HIGHTOWER'S FINAL MEDITATIONS HE PRONOUNCES AN often quoted judgment on Southern Protestant Christianity. The music he hears coming from the church seems to him to have "a [100] quality stern and implacable, deliberate and without passion so much as immolation, pleading, asking, for not love, not life, forbidding it to others, demanding in sonorous tones death, as though death were the boon, like all Protestant music." "Puritanism," or punitive religious moralism, is perhaps the chief intended antagonist in *Light in August,* as it is the immediate antagonist in *Sanctuary.*

"Pleasure, ecstasy," Hightower thinks, "they cannot seem to bear." Hines and McEachern could be his illustrations, the two most obviously pious people in the story and the two most responsible for the fate of Joe Christmas. He does not think of them because he does not know what we know about Christmas's past, but we, reading, supply them for him. And when we have finished the novel we feel that events have proved Hightower right when he pictures a crucifixion inflicted not despite but because of the religion of his fellow townsmen:

And so why should not their religion drive them to crucifixion of themselves and one another? . . . It seems to him that the past week has rushed like a torrent and that the week to come, which will begin tomorrow, is the abyss, and that now on the brink of the cataract the stream has raised a single blended and sonorous and austere cry, not for justification but as a dying salute before its own plunge, and not to any god but to the doomed man in the barred cell within hearing of them and of the two other churches, and in whose crucifixion they too will raise a cross. 'And they will do it gladly,' he says, in the dark window.

Hightower's thoughts constitute a terrible indictment of Southern Christianity, charging that it has become so distorted that it leads men toward hatred and destruction and death, crucifying Christ all over again, and "gladly." A great deal of the substance of the book has the effect of leading us to accept this judgment, and *Light in August* is Faulkner's most fully documented statement on what he sees as the religious errors and the racist guilt of his region. The grim fanatical fundamentalism of McEachern and the mad fundamentalist racism of Hines are judged in negative terms and without any shadow of qualification. [101]

But a recognition of this theme of the book, necessary as it is, will not alone take us to an understanding of the whole novel. We may get at a further meaning by going on with Hightower's meditation to a passage which, unlike the negative judgment of the Southern Protestant churches, has not been quoted by the critics. Hightower has thought that the people would crucify "gladly." Now he thinks why they will have to do it gladly:

'Since to pity him would be to admit self-doubt and to hope for and need pity themselves. They will do it gladly, gladly. That's why it is so terrible . . .'

They will do it as Percy Grimm commits his murder and mutilation, secure in the confidence that they are doing their duty, without the least shadow of self-doubt, with perfect confidence in their own rectitude; like Percy Grimm, whose face "above the blunt, cold rake of the automatic . . . had that serene, unearthly luminousness of angels in church windows."

But the whole strategy of the book is designed to prevent the reader not only from sharing their sense of their rectitude—this would be easy—but from resting confident in his sense of his own rectitude, his superiority to Joe Christmas, the warped sadist and murderer, and to Christmas's bigoted and cruel tormentors. Faulkner has said that a writer should be judged partly in terms of the difficulty of what he attempts, and that those writers who lack courage and so continue to do only what they know they can do well perhaps have earned less of our respect than those who attempt more and fail. In *Light in August* Faulkner attempts a task difficult enough to be a challenge to any novelist, too difficult perhaps to be perfectly accomplished. He attempts to make us pity, identify ourselves with and even, in the religious sense of the word, love, a man who would be rejected not only by Southern mores with their racial bias but by any humane standard. He tries to awaken compassion for "one of the least of these" based on a recognition of universal guilt and mutual responsibility, not so that we may suspend judgment entirely but so that we may judge with love. *Light in August* [102] is addressed not only to the conscience of the South but to the conscience of all readers anywhere. It has never to my knowledge been called a tract, but if it were not so powerful as a work of art it might well justify that designation. The moral feeling in it is intense. It demands nothing less than a withholding of self-righteous negative moral judgments and a substitution of unlimited compassion. If it shows us how and why "faith without deeds is dead," it shows us equally why we must "repent" before we "believe."

The novel moves toward this end the hard way, aesthetically and morally. It never makes Joe Christmas attractive. With the exception of a few passages on which I shall comment later, it does not picture him as "good at heart," forced into bad actions by circumstances. It shows us a man of whom we might say that it is surprising not that he commits one murder but that he has not committed more, a man apparently capable of any violent and repulsive deed, a man who hates not *even* those who love him but *especially* those who love him. It asks us to consider this man's death as parallel to the crucifixion of Christ.

The Joe Christmas–Jesus Christ analogy is prominent and consistent throughout the novel, and not simply, as the introduction to the Modern Library edition would have it, begun and then forgotten. It has nothing to do with any resemblance in character or outlook between Christmas and Jesus: indeed, this is precisely the point, that we are asked to see Christmas's death as a crucifixion despite the fact that Christmas is in every imaginable way different from Jesus. To make us pity a Christ-like figure would be easy, but the novel never attempts to do this. It asks pity for Christmas by making us see that the terrible things we do and become are all finally in self defense. We are asked to feel not that Christmas is really good or nice but that he epitomizes the human situation. To do this is difficult for precisely the reason given by Hightower: it must be preceded by a personal confession of sin and a felt need for pity, forgiveness.

When we first see Joe Christmas it is through Byron Bunch. [103] Bunch refuses to judge him but we are not likely to make the same refusal. Christmas's hat is "cocked at an angle arrogant and baleful above his still face." And there is nothing superficial or deceptive about the appearance of arrogance. All the men in the mill note his "air of cold and quiet contempt." The foreman speaks the general mind when he says "We ought to run him through the planer. Maybe that will take that look off his face." Christmas is later run through a planer of suffering, but "that look" comes off his face only at the moment of his death. The foreman is right, in a way, but his judgment is that of the reader at this point, lacking compassion.

After we have seen Christmas at his baleful and repellent worst we are taken back into the childhood that produced the man. The homicidal maniac who now thinks in fantasy "God loves me too" is the product of a complete absence of love in his earliest formative years. The experiences in the orphanage beyond present conscious memory were the formative ones in Christmas's life, and they all lead to one multiple impression: rejection, self-hatred, hatred of others.

Memory believes before knowing remembers. Believes longer than recollects, longer than knowing even wonders. Knows remembers believes a corridor in a big long garbled cold echoing building of dark red brick sootbleakened by more chimneys than its own . . . the bleak windows where in rain soot from the yearly adjacenting chimneys streaked like black tears.

By the time the McEacherns take the boy he is already shaped to reject love and respond only to hatred. It is unnecessary to qualify the description of McEachern as a "ruthless and bigoted man," a man cold, hard, and cruel, to recognize that he was faced with a virtually hopeless task in his efforts to transform Joe into an acceptable Presbyterian foster-son. We learn that though the man beat him and the wife attempted to be kind and was unfailingly sympathetic, the boy hated the woman more than the man:

It was the woman: that soft kindness which he believed himself doomed to be forever victim of and which he hated worse than he did the hard and ruthless justice of men. [104]

When we remember his response to Mrs. McEachern's attempts to befriend him and his kicking of the Negro girl in the shed, we see that his finally murdering the woman who had loved him and was trying to help him was predictable, in character, true to form psychologically. Unable to accept himself, Joe Christmas seeks punishment and death throughout his life as, earlier, he had forced McEachern to beat him. Psychologists might describe his character as "sado-masochistic." His aggressiveness is turned in upon himself as well as out toward others: he seeks to hurt and be hurt. Only when he has suffered the final pain and outrage inflicted by Percy Grimm does a look of peace come into his eyes. He had been waiting for this since the dietician offered him fifty cents instead of beating him.

Joe Christmas wants justice, not kindness—law, not mercy. The dietician should have punished him to preserve life's moral clarity. Christmas would be justified by keeping the Law, not by declaring himself a sinner and throwing himself on the Grace of God. To be able to accept kindness is implicitly to acknowledge one's self in need of it: Christmas is like his persecutors in having no humility, for all his "inferiority complex." He is like them too, even like mad old Doc Hines, in being an absolutist and a legalist. This is the quality which creates the curious kinship between him and McEachern even while they oppose each other with all their strength. For both of them right and wrong must be clear and definite; only so may a system of rewards and punishments ensure justice. McEachern seeks to enforce his, and God's, commandments, Christmas to violate them. The two are more alike than different.

All his life Christmas demands to know whether he is black or white. What he feels he cannot endure and will not accept is the not knowing, the ambiguity of his situation. Like many another Faulkner character, he is Ahab-like in his scorn of all petty satisfactions and his determination to "strike through the mask" to get at absolute truth, ultimate certainty and clarity, for good or for ill. He must know the truth, and for truth kindness is no substitute. In this sense his very "idealism" drives him to every degradation and finally to his destruction. [105]

But there is still another light in which we may look at him. We have seen him as doubly victimized, first by circumstance and a love-less society, which together have made him what he is, second by his own need for the kind of justice and certainty not to be found (the novel implies) in life. But now, as we think of the final events of his life, we see him becoming society's victim in still a further sense—its scapegoat. Society heaps on him all the sins which it cannot, will not, see in itself. Hightower has understood this too: "to pity him would be to admit self-doubt and to hope for and need pity themselves." A scapegoat is needed not by the innocent but by the guilty. Joe Christ-mas makes it possible for his persecutors never to recognize their guilt. Hines, McEachern, and Grimm are all, in their several ways, "be-lievers," but they have never repented and their actions are uncon-sciously calculated to protect them from the need to repent. To concentrate on this aspect of the portrait of Christmas leads one to feel the religious profundity of *Light in August,* and to realize that the work is deeply Christian in its meaning, despite its excoriation of the exemplars of piety.

This is the man, then—debased murderer, victim, scapegoat—whom we are forced, by the frequent symbolic pointers, to think of in terms of Christ. Readers have generally taken the parallel either as pure irony—everything so much the same, and yet the two figures so utterly different as to be quite incomparable—or as an ironically ex-pressed insight into a likeness that remains real despite the irony. For the latter reading, which seems much better able to account for all the facts of a highly complex portrait than the former, a passage of Scrip-ture is helpful:

Then shall they also answer him, saying, Lord, when saw we thee an hungered, or athirst, or a stranger, or naked, or sick, or in prison, and did not minister unto thee?
Then shall he answer them, saying, Verily I say unto you, Inasmuch as ye did it not to one of the least of these, ye did it not to me. (Matthew 25:44-45).

Joe Christmas is surely "one of the least of these." When the novel opens he is soon to be captured and put in prison; early in [106] the book we see him naked beside the road; during his flight he suffers from hunger and thirst and is sick: every item in the catalogue of the unfortunate is paralleled in the book. The irony lies partly in the fact that he rejects or strikes down those who do try to "minister unto" him—Mrs. McEachern, Miss Burden, Gail Hightower. But we are invited to believe that by the time these attempts to help him came he was beyond being able to respond to them except with rejection.

The motif of Christmas's adult life takes its pattern in part from the *Agnus dei* of the service of Holy Communion. In the *Agnus dei* the worshipper calls upon the "lamb of God" first to have mercy and then, in culmination, to "grant us thy peace." "All I wanted was peace,"

Christmas thinks after he has killed Miss Burden; and on another occasion, though the word used here is the close synonym "quiet": "That was all I wanted . . . That was all, for thirty years." In his boyhood he had slain a sheep and dipped his hands in the blood, thus in fantasy and symbol being "washed in the blood of the lamb." When he is killed and his own blood flows he seems to find peace at last.

For a long moment he looked up at them with peaceful and unfathomable and unbearable eyes. Then his face, body, all, seemed to collapse, to fall in upon itself and from out the slashed garments about his hips and loins the pent black blood seemed to rush like a released breath. It seemed to rush out of his pale body like the rush of sparks from a rising rocket; upon that black blast the man seemed to rise soaring into their memories forever and ever.

It is perhaps the last irony of Joe Christmas's life that at his death there is a kind of metaphoric ascension. There is a sense in which he himself has become "the slain sheep, the price paid for immunity," to use a phrase applied earlier his taking Bobbie Allen into the fields. Those who witnessed his death, into whose memories his blood has "ascended," are never to lose their memory

in whatever peaceful valleys, beside whatever placid and reassuring streams of old age, in the mirroring faces of [107] whatever children they will contemplate old disasters and newer hopes. It will be there, musing, quiet, steadfast, not fading and not particularly threatful, but of itself alone serene, of itself alone triumphant.

The career of Joe Christmas constitutes a rebuke to the community, a measure of its sin of racial arrogance and of its corruption of Christianity from a religion of love and life to one of hatred and death, from Jesus to Doc Hines and McEachern. But Christmas is not the only source of the rebuke. The novel opens with Lena, an "unconscious Christian"; it moves, except in the sections on Christmas's childhood, largely through the minds of Byron Bunch and Gail Hightower, Christians of two different kinds; and it closes with Byron and Lena. The story of Christmas is thus framed and illuminated by the stories of several kinds of practicing Christians. McEachern and Hines, it would appear, do not give us the whole picture. Each is true to those aspects of religion under condemnation, but taken alone they would constitute a caricature. The force of the criticism comes from the recognition that they are so typical, their errors of practice or doctrine so widespread.

Meanwhile there is Lena to suggest a Christianity different from that of McEachern or Hines. She is not only a kind of nature or fertility goddess, but also a witness to the efficacy of the three theological virtues, faith, hope, and love. Her trust is in the Lord, as Armstid recognizes when he recalls how "she told Martha last night about how the Lord will see that what is right will get done." She may have been created with a passage from St. Paul in mind; at any rate she suffers long, and is kind, does not envy and is not (like Joe Christmas) too proud to accept help, is never unseemly in her conduct, and (to shift to the Revised Standard Version) "is not irritable or resentful"; she "bears all things, believes all things, hopes all things, endures all things." Considering that she is so saintly an image, it is remarkable that she seems so real to us. Novelists have seldom been successful in portraying saints. No wonder there is what has been called a "pastoral" quality in the Lena episodes. No wonder she moves "with the untroubled unhaste of a change of season." Unlike Christmas she is not in flight. [108]

And Byron Bunch. He is the portrait of the unlettered practicing Christian. He works alone at the mill on Saturday afternoon to avoid any occasion of sin, thus following good Catholic precept. (He finds that even so he cannot avoid temptation.) Only Hightower knows that he "rides thirty miles into the country and spends Sunday leading the choir in a country church—a service which lasts all day long." He immediately offers Christmas a part of his lunch when they first meet (the reply is typical: "I aint hungry. Keep your muck.") and refuses to pass judgment on him when he is told that Brown and Christmas are bootleggers. He holds himself responsible for having listened to the gossip: "And so I reckon I aint no better than nobody else." He thinks of Miss Burden and her reputation and the negative judgment the town makes of her; he makes no such judgment. He is a friend of the ruined outcast minister Hightower, not simply "befriending" him, refusing to share the town's harsh judgment, but recognizing in him a kindred spirit, seeking him out for advice, paying him the compliment of putting burdens upon him that he would ask no one else to bear. He pities and tries to help not only Lena and Hightower but Christmas's grandparents, bringing them to Hightower for advice. He extends his compassion to Christmas himself and might have been effective in his intended aid if Hightower had not refused until too late to accept the responsibility Byron tried to get him to see was his.

Byron Bunch has learned to bear the burden of being human. Generally inarticulate, he yet manages several times to define that burden for Hightower:

I mind how I said to you once that there is a price for being good the same as for being bad; a cost to pay. And it's the good men that cant deny the bill when it comes around.

What Byron knows, he has had to learn in painful experience. We see him repeatedly tempted to deny the bill. No man, he often feels, should have to bear what he has to bear. But in the end he discovers that he can bear even the thought that all his efforts have succeeded only in getting Lena married to Burch. "It seems [109] like a man can just about bear anything. He can even bear what he never done." His burden, finally, is total recognition of the impurity, the injustice, the unresolvable irony of life itself. When he has learned this, he knows not to ask for justice but for mercy and the strength to persevere. Like Lena, Byron is travelling the road recommended by the saints.

And Hightower. Here the picture is more complicated, so complicated that many readers have had difficulty putting the pieces together. Fundamentally, Hightower is a romantic idealist who, confronted with a reality less pure and heroic than his dreams, has retreated to a spot where he hopes life cannot reach him to hurt him again. His master symbol is the galloping horsemen; he cannot steadily face the fact that the horsemen were engaged in raiding a chicken house. When he sits at his window at sunset waiting for the dusk and the image of the galloping horsemen, a part of him knows that he is really waiting only for death,

waiting for that instant when all light has failed out of the sky and it would be night save for that faint light which daygranaried leaf and grass blade reluctant suspire, making still a little light on earth though night itself has come.

"Daygranaried": the natural light imagery here cannot be freed of its religious associations. The light of his religious faith has gone from Hightower and he has nothing to wait for now but the little light reflected, stored up perhaps from the source, but now coming, or seeming to come, from the earth itself, before the final coming of night. When he is about to die he thinks he should try to pray, but he does not try.

"With all air, all heaven, filled with the lost and unheeded crying of all the living who ever lived, wailing still like lost children among the cold and terrible stars."

Yet he finally atones for whatever sin has been his by trying to protect Christmas from his pursuers, at a terrible cost to any pride he has left. Like Joe Christmas, Hightower thinks on one occasion that all he has ever really desired was peace; thinking too that it [110] should rightly be his now, that he has earned it through suffering endured. It is Byron Bunch who teaches him that peace is not to be had by retreat, by taking no chances, that the purity achieved by denying the bill, refusing the risks of his humanity, is more like death than like life. As Hightower explicitly recognizes when he thinks Byron has left town without saying goodbye, Byron has restored him to life, or life to him. And so at the end he acts for once not like the romantic idealist and absolutist he has always been but like Byron, the practicing Christian, the doer of the word who can submit to unreason and persevere in good works. Telling the pursuing men that Christmas was with him on the night of the murder, Hightower takes on himself the opprobrium of the town's worst surmise.

Before his death Hightower has learned that he is not simply a victim, that in some degree at least he has brought his martyrdom on himself. He sees that he has been "wild too in the pulpit, using religion as though it were a dream," getting religion and his romantic idolization of the past all mixed up together, using perhaps, he suspects, even his wife as a means to the end of his self-inflicted martyrdom. If he could pray at the end of his life he would pray not simply for peace but for mercy, as a sinner. He learns late what Byron Bunch has known all along. Before this when he and Byron sit together he looks "like an awkward beast tricked and befooled of the need for flight. . . . Byron alone seems to possess life." Yet at the end if he has neither faith nor hope he has shown himself capable in the supreme test of acting in terms of love, "the greatest of these." Hightower too is finally a redeemed and potentially redemptive character.

Joanna Burden is more complex than Byron Bunch and perhaps more perfectly realized than Hightower. Faulkner's critics have generally passed over her in silence, leaving her unrelated to the central themes of the book. But I think that if we consider the clue offered by her name, we shall find a key to at least the most significant aspect of her symbolic role. To do so seems not to be capricious in considering a book filled with suggestive names: [111] Hightower, who spends most of his life *above* the battle and only at the end of his life comes down into the common life of man; Bunch, whose name suggests something common and solid and unromantic; Grimm; Christmas. Miss Burden, then, may be seen in a preliminary way as one who has taken the opposite road from the one followed by Hightower during his years of isolation. She accepts the burden of working for human betterment and the other, often painful, burdens it entails. Her isolation in a hostile community has been the price *she* has had to pay, in Byron's terms, for working for the cause of Negroes. For her, the white man's burden is her own burden.

But her conscience is not just sensitive, it is sensitive in a special way, the way of her grandfather the abolitionist. Though she has responded to life by commitment instead of flight, she is fundamentally as "idealistic" and "absolutist" in her reactions as Hightower. She accepts Joe Christmas, paradoxically, because he is, or she thinks he is, a Negro, not because he is a human being. The crisis in their relationship comes when she tells him her plan to send him to a Negro college. Her very idealism forces her to *place* him, in black or white. Thus she ends by reinforcing for him the terrible need that has driven him all his life, the need to know what he is. He has become her world, and she cannot accept a mixed, impure, ambiguous world, any more than Joe himself can, or Hightower before Byron teaches him. Like

Melville's Pierre, she finds "the ambiguities" intolerable, just because she is so much an idealist. Her cause is finally more important to her even than Joe, and in her inflexible conscientiousness she drives him to murder her.

She is not, of course, an obvious sinner like Doc Hines and the other "righteous" characters in the story. There is real nobility in her that sets her quite apart from all the "idealists" but Hightower. She pays the price of goodness unflinchingly. But she can function only in a world of black and white; gray leaves her baffled, helpless. There is one burden, then, she cannot bear: precisely Byron Bunch's burden, the perception of essential irony. She is murdered by a man neither white nor black, but in a deeper sense she is destroyed by [112] her abolitionist grandfather, for whom moral issues were perfectly clear and unambiguous.

In these people and their relationships the theme of the novel finds whatever expression it gets. There are no author's intrusions, no pointing fingers to tell us what it means. The meditations of Hightower come closer than anything else in the book to the voice of Faulkner the moralist but Hightower is portrayed as so clearly the victim of his own delusions that we are left to make our own decision as to which of his ideas are sound and which mere symptoms of his spiritual sickness. Byron Bunch is nearly as inarticulate as Lena, and we are given every opportunity to dismiss them both as essentially creatures of tender comedy in a pastoral idyl. The only characters of whom we may say that a definite and single judgment is required are McEachern, Hines, and Grimm; these are the only important characters approached wholly from outside, without any sympathetic identification with them on Faulkner's part.

Yet the novel "says" some things clearly enough. To the region in which it is laid it says that its racial injustice is a sin of the most terrible proportions and consequences (not merely a mistake or an accident—there is no moral relativism here or anywhere else in Faulkner) but also an opportunity for moral action. It says that suffering is the universal lot of mankind: in every man's death, even in that of a Joe Christmas, there is a kind of crucifixion. It says that the test of character is the individual's response to suffering: the hatred of Joe Christmas, the flight from responsibility of Hightower, the humble engagement of Lena and Byron.

The fact that these two open and close the novel seems to me crucial and not to have been given sufficient weight in most interpretations. It is not enough to say that the beginning and end are comic relief from the pure tragedy of the major part of the work. Lena and Byron *are* comic, of course, and the ending is an anticlimax, but it is also an affirmation of the possibilities of life. The voice of the travelling man from Memphis is the voice of sanity which makes no excessive demands on life, the voice of "realism" [113] if you will, but a realism capable of seeing two people of precisely Byron's and Lena's qualities as those who offer hope. That only Byron and Lena, in the end, are capable of carrying on is to be expected. We have been prepared for this kind of affirmation by Dilsey and Cash. Certainly one meaning of the ending is that though knowledge of absolutes is not granted to man, yet what he is given to know is enough, if he has the moral and religious qualities of Byron and Lena. If this is the central meaning of the ending, the final implication of the book is a kind of Christian existentialism which could be explicated in terms of the theology of a Tillich or a Bultmann. Byron and Lena have the courage and the faith to *be* in a world where man does not see God face to face and any localizing of the absolute is a mark of pride.

This much is tolerably clear, but there is a good deal that is not, and even this is likely to seem most plausible if we keep our attention centered on the contrast between Byron and Lena, on the one hand, and Hightower, Christmas, and Joanna Burden, on the other—as of course the structure of the book in the largest sense suggests that we should. There is a theological ambiguity and a moral one, each of which tends in some degree to run counter to what I have described as the implication of the ending. The theological seems not crucial in the context which the story itself has created. Whether ultimate meaning here should be thought of in a humanist or in a Christian sense, in Hightower's way or in Byron's way, it is perfectly clear that the humble commitment of Byron and Lena is presented as the only alternative to suicide or destruction. If God exists, and cares, he demands this of us; if He does not we must live, if we are to live at all, by the old virtues anyway. Humanists may be living only by "day-granaried" light, light stored up from a higher source that now only *seems* to seep up from below; or the light may really come from below, from the earth. In either case, the "old truths of the heart" are valid. The theological ambiguity is not crucial to an interpretation of the main thrust of the novel.

But the moral ambiguity is not so easily disposed of. It concerns, as so often in Faulkner, the problem of freedom and responsibility. [114] We have seen Hightower as one who has demanded purity and, not finding it, has tried to isolate himself from an impure world; in this sense he is a victim of his own delusion and so in another sense not a victim at all but a man who has been mistaken. But most of the time during his years of seclusion he sees himself, and Faulkner seems to see him, as an innocent victim of other people or of life. His parishioners, the townspeople, the church, his wife, God, all seem to him to have failed him; and since we see them from his point of view, it is not entirely clear that he is wrong. Or at least it is not until toward the end. Then he thinks, "After all, there must be some things for which God cannot be accused by man and held responsible. There must be." Presumably there must, but it is not entirely clear to Hightower or to the reader what they are. It is significant, I think, that after Hightower achieves this insight and the reader comes to see him in terms of what it implies, the man himself becomes clear and believable to us at last. His dying meditation is one of the most powerful passages in all of Faulkner.

The same ambiguity is more troublesome in the portrait of Christmas. We see him chiefly as a "bad" man who cannot help being what he is. Living and dead he is a condemnation of an unjust society and a perverted religious conscience. But it is difficult if not impossible for us to picture a man as *simply* a victim. We may withhold judgment, refusing to try to decide what he can be held responsible for in the Last, and true, Judgment, but we must assume that he has some degree of moral responsibility if we are to see him as fully human. Apparently Faulkner must, too. Though the chapters on Christmas's childhood and boyhood, constituting a kind of case history of the growth of a sadomasochist, seems to remove from him all responsibility for what he later becomes, there are passages in which choice is imputed to Christmas. There are others in which, choice being denied but felt by the reader, the effect is sentimental. A couple of examples will serve to illustrate the point sufficiently.

When, after striking McEachern in the dance hall, Christmas runs away, there is a definite imputation of choice: [115]

The youth . . . rode lightly . . . exulting perhaps at the moment as Faustus had, of having put behind now at once and for all the Shalt Not, of being free at last of honor and Law.

But the point of the Faustus myth is that Faustus, with full knowledge and acceptance of responsibility, made a choice. Most of the portrait of Christmas has the effect of suggesting that he was simply a victim, made no choices.

Again, and in contrast to the Faustus passage, the treatment of Christmas's experience with Bobbie Allen culminates in an apparent acceptance by Faulkner of Christmas's own view of the experience, a view which makes this the final betrayal, the last bitter blow of fate. "Why, I committed murder for her. I even stole for her," Christmas thinks. But that is not quite the way it was. As for the stealing, he had been stealing for some time before, and this particular "theft"—he took Mrs. McEachern's money in her presence, knowing well that she would have given it to him gladly—was not so much a theft as a final premeditated blow to the woman who had tried to help him. As for the "murder," whether or not McEachern died from the blow we are not told, but we do know that the boy had been waiting for the opportunity to deliver it for a long time and "exulted" when the opportunity came to "get even." It was not then in any real sense a murder committed "for her." Yet there is no indication in the writing at this point that these rationalizations of the boy's are not to be accepted at face value. The effect of the passage is sentimental.

A final example. As a part of the summary of Christmas's years between the time when he ran away from the McEacherns and the time when he came to Jefferson we are told of the effect on him of his first experience of sexual relations with a white woman.

He was sick after that. He did not know until then that there were white women who would take a man with a black skin. He stayed sick for two years.

I am afraid I shall have to say that this seems to me just plain nonsense. The implication that he was sick for two years not simply [116] "after that" but because of "that" is wrong from several points of view. Would this amazing discovery make a well man sick, and for two years? Anyway, he does not have a "black skin." It is already perfectly clear, and even explicit, that he was very sick indeed psychologically long before this discovery, and is sick long after the two years are up. The passage is melodramatic in its imputation of too great an effect to too little a cause, and it is sentimental in its implication, once again, of innocence betrayed. It tells us more about Faulkner's own mixed racial feelings than it does about Joe Christmas.

No doubt this was how Christmas remembered the incident, but the passage could be effective only if there were some indication that Faulkner himself did not accept Christmas's sick notion of cause and effect. Faulkner's submergence of himself in his characters, which accounts for some of his greatest triumphs, also sometimes accounts for his failures. Here he has become Joe Christmas, sickness and all, as he thinks "back down the street, past all the imperceptible corners of bitter defeats and more bitter victories."

It seems to me, finally, that all the street and corridor imagery, applied chiefly to Christmas but also, less conspicuously, to several of the others, comes to less than it should. Perhaps its chief effect is to imply that for a person with (possibly) mixed blood life is a one-way street with no exit, no escape, leading inevitably to defeat and death. This at least is the effect of the passage in which Christmas finds that the street has turned into a circle, that he is inside it, and that there is still no escape. But this idea is both banal and untrue, or true only in a sense that needs just the kind of qualification a novel could give it. Only one aspect of this too prominent image pattern seems to me interesting, and that one only partially justifies the elaborate and repeated treatment of the pattern. There is some indication that Lena is in a street or a corridor too, as in the passage which begins

Behind her the four weeks, the evocation of *far*, is a peaceful corridor paved with unflagging and tranquil faith and peopled with kind and nameless faces and voices . . . [117]

or in the description of Armstid's wagon as "a shabby bead upon the mild red string of the road." It depends, apparently, how we *take* our corridor, whether it is "peaceful" or bitter, a string of beads, each bead intrinsically valuable, or an avenue of flight. Percy Grimm too has his corridor and to him it means an escape from the necessity of choice: "his life opening before him, uncomplex and inescapable as a barren corridor." With her face lighted by the "unreason" of her faith, Lena finds friendly and helpful people everywhere, while Christmas finds only hatred and frustration.

These technical failings have the cumulative effect of creating an undeniable element of obscurity in a work nevertheless distinguished by its passion and immediacy and the seriousness of its imaginative grasp of reality. The obscurity here is quite different from the intentional ambiguity of *The Sound and the Fury* or *As I Lay Dying*, and different from the ultimately functional obscurity of *Absolom, Absolom!* This obscurity must be seen as an aesthetic weakness. I have suggested that it may be related to the mood of despair that dominates *Sanctuary*. But perhaps we should say only that *Light in August* attempts more than Faulkner could perfectly accomplish. [118]

. . . *Light in August* offers hope, but only by shifting levels, changing perspectives. The central story of Joe Christmas is unrelieved tragedy; the story of Lena and Byron is tender comedy. The hope is real, but inevitably qualified by our feeling that we must smile at Lena and Byron even as we admire them: *we* are more like Hightower or Miss Burden, or even Joe Christmas. I have argued that we must not undervalue Lena and Byron, that certainly we must not dismiss them as bumpkins before we see their moral and religious implications; but I should certainly not want to imply that we can take them in the same way that we take Hightower or Christmas.

Hope may be found in *Light in August* only by giving up the intellectual and emotional struggle for ultimate certainty embodied in Hightower and Christmas and turning to the humble and unselfconscious engagement of Lena and Byron. Because this means, in effect, turning to what is likely to strike us as a lower level of apprehension, the novel is perhaps in its final effect more unrelievedly tragic than *The Sound and the Fury*. If we agree that Dilsey has [119] truly heroic qualities we may say that redemptive hope in *The Sound and the Fury* lies within the tragedy itself. Because we feel Dilsey's nobility, we feel that we move upward to identify with her and to achieve her view of life. But because we smile at Lena and Byron, though by an act of judgment appreciating their virtues, we must in a sense move down to a vision less serious than the tragic to reach the hope which they alone offer in *Light in August*. As we sit with Hightower in the twilight, we are likely to feel that the darkness is more powerful than the light. [120]

Joe Christmas: The Hero in the Modern World

JOHN L. LONGLEY

—Aristotle has not defined pity and terror.—said Stephen Dedalus—I have. Pity is the feeling which arrests the mind in the presence of whatsoever is grave and constant in human sufferings and unites it with the human sufferer. Terror is the feeling which arrests the mind in the presence of whatsoever is grave and constant in human sufferings and unites it with the secret cause.—

It is appropriate that Joyce's Stephen Dedalus should formulate this definition, for, different as he is from Joe Christmas, they are alike in being heroes who are distinctly modern and who must make their way in a cosmos that is violent, chaotic, and absurd. Stephen's plight is only slightly less desperate than Christmas', and Stephen's motto *non serviam* is very close to Christmas' rigid determination not to submit to those forces that compulsively attempt to shape him to their will.

Sutpen and John Sartoris, especially when viewed in their dynastic patterns, are tragic heroes in the grand and completely tragic mold, partly because, of course, they are located in a remote and more "heroic" time, when presumably there existed that scope of action and choice large enough for heroic gestures.

But even assuming Faulkner's possession of a tragic sensibility and granting him the ability to shape it into art, how can the very long jump to Joe Christmas as tragic hero be made? There are perhaps two possible approaches to this question, and perhaps both of them should be used: to what extent is Christmas [192] authentically tragic by traditional criteria, and to what extent can it be shown that he is tragic by some entirely modern, different set of criteria? To oversimplify vastly, the modern protagonist should be one who is typical of the age and not so remote from typical human beings as to make emotional identification difficult for the spectator. In some highly symbolic fashion, the modern hero must typify the major myths and major problems of our century. In a cosmos where all is chaos and all standards have disappeared, he will very likely be destroyed as a result of his failure to define himself correctly in relation to that cosmos. Lastly, he must somehow embody the perpetual human constants which are the property of any age. Bypassing for a moment this very interesting second possibility, let us examine Christmas in the light of traditional, classic tragic criteria. At first glance, this procedure appears unpromising.

Granting his acts of persistence, his arrogance and pride, how can Christmas be called noble? How can he be said to be illustrious in rank and fortune? Above all, how can a human being so conditioned, so utterly predestined to violence and death, ever be called free: free to choose and free to act or not act? It is my belief that this reservation is precisely the point.

Aristotle awarded the palm for classic tragedy to the *Oedipus Tyrannus* of Sophocles. If this is not quite the same thing as saying Oedipus is the most perfect example of the tragic protagonist, perhaps he will do for comparison. Everyone knows his tragic story, at least in outline, for it is one of the ironies of history that he has given his name to the folklore of psychology. In that same folklore, we in the modern world give tacit agreement to the belief that human free will is all but impossible. In the Greek world, once the oracle had spoken, who was ever so hopelessly "pre-destined" as Oedipus?

But, as everybody knows, that is not it at all. Oedipus becomes tragic only because he does strive against the prediction. Resolved to know, he goes to the oracle himself and hears the dire prophecy repeated. His mistake is in believing that by running away he can circumvent the dreadful events. His *hubris* lies in thinking [193] he has escaped by his own strength and cleverness and in boasting that such is the case. But we know what he does not know, that far from escaping his destiny, he has run full tilt to meet it. When we first see him he is *tyrannus*, "first of men," a king who has made himself king by strength and cunning. But there is more dramatic irony: the tyrannos who killed the sphinx and assumed the throne and the queen is really the rightful ruler of Thebes, the true son of Laius. His confidence still unbroken, he is convinced he can save Thebes again as he did before. He pronounces the curse on the unknown polluter of the city, and as the process of ferreting out the guilty one goes on, Oedipus' search becomes one of finding his own identity. As the dark hints begin to accumulate, he boasts of his contempt for prophecy; his father is still alive and his mother is far away. As the flawlessly plotted action unfolds, there comes the crushing peripeteia: all along he had been nearer home than he knew.

We could say that Oedipus' fault lies in trying to beat the rap. But again, everyone knows that his tragedy has to mean more than that; that this expenditure of human striving and achievement and suffering has to stand for something grave and constant in the eternal human condition. It is very true that his is the classical *hubris*, the sin of pride and arrogance and overconfidence in his own ability. But far more to our purpose, we can say it is a failure to achieve self-knowledge, a failure of self-definition. Oedipus is saddled with an incredibly horrible, inevitable future. He has not asked for it and has done nothing to deserve it; it is all "decided" before he is born. But he persists and demands to know the truth. Bernard Knox has noted how in the Greek original there is the constant, cruelly ironic interrunning of *Oedipus, oidi* ("swell," as with pride or arrogance), and *oida,* "I know," a word that is often, too often, in Oedipus' mouth. At the beginning of the play there is too much that he does not know, and at the end there is too much that he does. It is in the interweaving of guilt and innocence, in the willing of his own actions, in the god-like insistence on knowing *who* he is and the crushing ruin that this knowledge brings him, that the tragic glory of Oedipus lies.

Consider another hero. About his birth there is mystery also. [194] He too is spirited away as an infant because dreadful things are whispered about him, and he too is brought up by foster-parents whom he leaves hurriedly for fear he may have killed his foster-father. In a direct way, it can be said that his very begetting caused the death of his real father. He brings terrible shame, agony, and death to his real mother. After a great deal of wandering, he returns to that part of the world which, unknown to him, is the scene of his begetting and birth. Early in life he was give a free choice of two lines of conduct, one of which would have removed all danger from him. He persists in the other because it is necessary to the terms of his own definition of himself. He lives connubially with an older woman, who, as a result of his drive toward self-definition, dies a horrible death. The fearful rumors about him break out afresh. There is an old, mad visionary who claims to have special insight into the truth about him, and as a result, his fellow men are convinced he is a ritual pollution in the community. Pursued by them, he is harried for days and is eventually sacrificed in a particularly horrible ritual murder. He has been saddled with a terrible, inevitable curse. He did not ask for it and does nothing to deserve it; it was all "decided" before he was born. The second hero is, of course, Joe Christmas.

If the fall of Oedipus comes as a direct result of his terribly mistaken idea of who he is and his insistence on finding out, then the death of Joe Christmas is a result of his insistence that he already knows who he is and his persistence in the demand for the right to be himself, to live on the terms of his own self-definition. To state the paradox in another way, the classic tragic protagonist such as Oedipus, Othello, Hamlet, or Macbeth rejoices in an existence that allows him a superb scope of action in which to achieve self-realization, including self-knowledge, even though in this same drive toward self-fulfillment he destroys himself. The modern tragic protagonist, the hero of a Dostoyevsky, a Conrad, a Kafka, a Faulkner, a Hemingway, or a Warren, must use all his intelligence, his strength, his luck, merely to travel the tightrope between Cosmic Chaos on the one hand and

Cosmic Absurdity on the other. He can trust in nothing, hope for nothing, and accept [195] nothing at face value until he has put it to the test. He may have heard of determinism, but he does not believe in it; in the face of those joyous theories of self-exculpation formulated by present-day psychology and sociology that presumably give the individual the right to scream, "It's not my fault! It's not my fault!" his preference is much nearer the dreadful freedom of the existentialist: since existence is prior to essence, the individual is totally free and totally accountable for his own view of things, for with total freedom comes total responsibility.

In the case of Joe Christmas, Faulkner takes pains to make this freedom absolute. Here we must be blunt: previous critical opinion seemed almost never to be aware of that freedom. Partly because, one supposes, the term "conditioning" is now a household word, it was decided that Christmas is the helpless victim of his own conditioning. But surely it is obvious that the wellspring of all his actions is his refusal to surrender to that conditioning.

One of Faulkner's clearest strokes of genius is in leaving the question of whether Christmas has Negro blood unanswered. We, no one, will ever know if he has it or not. If he does have it, the percentage is very small, something that not only adds to the irony but leaves him free to "pass" if he chooses. Although he is, largely through the efforts of Old Doc Hines, putatively a Negro child at the orphanage, he is adopted and brought up as a white child by the McEacherns. ("He don't look no more like a nigger than I do," says a white character.) This is probably the most crucial point in the book. Christmas is free to choose what he will be, and his freedom is infinite. Precisely as Oedipus, he must find out who and what he is. One remembers a scene in the orphanage: Old Doc Hines is recalling how the five-year-old Christmas begins following the Negro yard-boy around:

. . . until at last the nigger said, 'What you watching me for, boy?' and he said, 'How come you are a nigger?' and the nigger said, 'Who told you I am a nigger, you little white trash bastard?' and he says, 'I aint a nigger,' and the nigger says, 'You are worse than that. You dont know what you are. And more than that, you wont never know. You'll live and you'll die, and you wont never know. . . .'

But he must know, as with his determination to keep his own name. And because he is free, he cannot ever passively acquiesce. [196] He cannot let others tell him how or what to be. All his life, people attempt to force him to be what they insist he must be: McEachern's beating him to inculcate worship of the Moloch-Jehovah; Mrs. McEachern's sickening attempts to make him as cringing as herself; Joanna Burden's final insistence that he "become a nigger." His method is active. In the fifteen years of wandering he tries life as a

black man living with Negroes and as a white man attempting to live
with whites. But ultimately he chooses to be neither—he will simply be
himself. Until the very end, the community cannot decide what he is;
their deep distrust grows from his refusal to declare himself one or the
other in a social pattern in which this is the most important distinction
of all. He will insist on his right simply to be; he has defined himself
and has fought hard for the definition. The murder of Joanna Burden
and his own death are the fruits of that insistence.

Granted he has freedom and choice; what about rank and fortune? The modern hero, like Oedipus and Macbeth, makes his own.
Christmas' distinction lies in the strength of his proud, ruthless,
arrogant, cold self-sufficiency, as rigid as that of a Richard or an Ahab
and more adequate to the strain placed upon it than Macbeth's. As
with any modern hero, the simple fact that he is still alive may be as
much good fortune as he can expect. It is far more important to prove
he is typically human.

Part of the difficulty in understanding Christmas again lies in the
form and structure of the novel. The sequence of telling is such that he
is first seen as the utterly sinister alien and is revealed early in the book
as a brutal murderer. It is only as the flashbacks begin to unfold and
we see him as a child and youth that we are made aware of his simple
humanity. He is presented for the most part at a distance, and his
inmost thoughts and feelings are not often enough open to us. However, at rare intervals a momentary flash of insight will give a total
revelation: for instance, we see the denial of love and belonging in the
orphanage and the beatings by McEachern. The effect of these is of
course cumulative, but the moment of revelation comes when Christmas hears his name will be changed:

"He will eat my bread and he will observe my religion," the stranger
said. "Why should he not bear my name?" [197]
The child was not listening. He was not bothered. He did not especially
care, anymore than if the man had said the day was hot when it was not
hot. He didn't even bother to say to himself *My name aint McEachern. My
name is Christmas* There was no need to bother about that yet. There was
plenty of time.

We are shown the idyllic relationship with Bobbie, the stunted
and no-longer-young waitress who is a working prostitute in her spare
time. His slipping away from the McEachern farm at night to be with
her is part of his program of defiance, but it is truly, at least at the
beginning, the adolescent's first tentative, awestruck discovery of the
body of the beloved and all its possibilities. Again, before the dawn of
the day on which he will murder Joanna Burden, when the pressures
that will compel either murder or complete surrender are building past
endurance, he muses on the past:

. . . it seemed to him, sitting on the cot in the dark room, that he was hearing a myriad [of] sounds of no greater volume—voices, murmurs, whispers: of trees, darkness, earth; people: his own voice; other voices evocative of names and times and places—which he had been conscious of all his life without knowing it, which were his life, thinking *God perhaps and me not knowing that too* He could see it like a printed sentence, fullborn and already dead *God loves me too* like the faded and weathered letters on a last year's billboard *God loves me too.*

His humanity, and perhaps even his own completely tragic awareness of his situation, is revealed in that incredible week in which we run with him while he eludes mobs, sheriff, deputies, Lucas, and bloodhounds. All that has gone before in the novel is brilliantly recapitulated as Christmas, still wrapped in the rags and tatters of his self-sufficiency and pride, works himself slowly away from the violence of the attack on the Negro church toward his tragic reconciliation with his fate, his acceptance of the price and the risk of the human condition. The incidents of his life which have "pre-destined" him toward the proud denial of his own humanity are echoed. Aware, as perhaps never before, of the simple joy of merely being alive and breathing, he watches another day begin:

It is just dawn, daylight: that gray and lonely suspension filled with the peaceful and tentative waking of birds. The air, inbreathed, [198] is like spring water. He breathes deep and slow, feeling with each breath himself diffuse in the neutral grayness, becoming one with loneliness and quiet that has never known fury or despair. 'That was all I wanted,' he thinks, in a quiet and slow amazement. 'That was all, for thirty years. That didn't seem to be a whole lot to ask in thirty years.'

"That didn't seem to be a whole lot to ask. . . ." No, it is not—simply the right to live and be one's own self, to expect perhaps a little peace, a little love; but knowing the price. (Who now hears the far-off echo of Thomas Jefferson: "We hold these truths to be self-evident . . ."?) But Christmas' dilemma is the truly tragic one: he is caught not between right and wrong but between right and right. Rejected, feared, hated, he has sought and been proud of that rejection and fear; but pushed too far he has gone too far, and unable to reconcile conflicting responsibility, he has committed a brutal murder.

Now he must go back. But it is impossible to go back, only forward. He must accept responsibility for the freedom of choice he exercised in his actions and pay the price of that freedom. But because he is truly tragic, he will not practice a mere passiveness and wait for the men with the dogs to come up and shoot him. He will actively seek his human reconciliation: his problem is how to begin to get back inside the human community. It is not easy; he has been isolated for too many years. He waits in the dawn for a farmhouse to come alive and the men to leave for the fields. Then he approaches the farm wife, who recognizes him, and quietly, from a respectful distance, he asks: "Can you tell me what day this is? I just want to know what day this is."

Even though the white woman sends him away, the symbolism is clear. He wants to begin again by reaccepting the limitations of one of the most human and communal inventions: time. The next step involves a basic human need and social ritual. Having violently rejected the offer of food on a number of symbolic occasions, he approaches a Negro cabin to ask for a meal.

He was sitting at a table, waiting, thinking of nothing in an emptiness, a silence filled with flight. Then there was food before him, appearing suddenly between long, limber black hands fleeing too in the act of setting down the dishes. It seemed to him that he could hear without hearing them wails of terror and distress quieter than sighs all about [199] him, with the sounds of the siren mounted toward its unbelievable crescendo, passing out of the 'And they were afraid. Of their brother afraid.'

He has made his first gestures, but it is not enough. He stops two Negro children and a Negro man to ask again the day of the week. They fear him as wildly as do the whites and reject him also. So, having shaved himself as carefully as he can with the razor, the murder weapon, he strikes across country to find his way to Mottstown. Given a ride on a wagon by a Negro youth who does not know who he is, he reviews his life:

. . . he is entering it again, the street which ran for thirty years. It had been a paved street, where going should be fast. It had made a circle and he is still inside of it. Though during the last seven days he has had no paved street, yet he has traveled farther than in all the thirty years before. And yet he is still inside the circle. 'And yet I have been farther in these seven days than in all the thirty years,' he thinks. 'But I have never got outside that circle. I have never broken out of the ring of what I have already done and cannot ever undo,' he thinks quietly, sitting on the seat, with planted on the dashboard before him the shoes, the black shoes smelling of Negro: that mark on his ankles the gauge definite and ineradicable of the black tide creeping up his legs, moving from his feet upward as death moves.

The symbol is perfectly chosen. For thirty centuries or so, the black-white, light-dark, Apollonian-Dionysian, rational-irrational opposition has existed in Western civilization. If this were the only meaning of the symbol, its use would be forgivable but hardly brilliant. It should be remembered that Christmas gleefully exchanged his own shoes for these that had been worn by a Negro woman, to throw the bloodhounds off the scent. (At this stage Christmas, like Oedipus, is "full of devices.") But now, completely alone, he is feared and rejected by both black and white. Urged on by the frantic greed of Lucas Burch and the fanatic madness of Old Doc Hines, the white community considers Christmas a Negro, hunts him as a Negro, and will lynch and mutilate him as a Negro. Continuing to wear the shoes, he looks at that mark "moving upward from his feet as death moves." The murder he committed was the direct result of his refusal to choose, black or white. While choice of action remains (which may not be long), he will *choose* his means of reconciliation. Had [200] he chosen sooner, or had he merely gone away, as he was also free to do, Joanna Burden would not be dead, and he himself would not be about to die. As surely as he sees the blackness (his acceptance of Negro status) creep up his body, so surely his body is sinking into the darkness, the extinction, of death. He walks quietly about the streets of Mottstown until he is captured.

At this point only the last of the tragedy remains to be played out. The reader may decide that Christmas has been unable to sustain his resolution, that his breaking away from the officers only to be shot and castrated by Percy Grimm reveals an artistic defect on the part of Faulkner. But Oedipus and Lear have moments toward the end when the old rage and arrogance blaze out. Antigone, St. Joan, Richard—all have moments when human fear of absolute extinction overwhelms human integrity. The moment is there for a conscious artistic purpose: to give us that ultimate awareness of pity and terror by reminding us that the protagonist is not a hollow tragic mask but a living human being, only a little less lucky than ourselves. There is a further meaning: free to the end, Christmas has held on to his life until this proper moment has come to give it, the moment most filled with reconciliation.

As Gavin Stevens says, no one will ever know what Christmas hoped for from Hightower, but it was the conflict in his blood that let him run but would not let him escape, that made him snatch up the pistol but would not let him kill Grimm with it. (It is Stevens who posits the black-white opposition. Faulkner has never said if there is Negro blood or not.) The meaning has taken on almost universal significance. It is the light-dark opposition that is in the blood of all of us; the savage pull between bright rationality and the darkness so feared by the Greeks, that leads to irrationality and death.

Little else in modern literature has the speed and inevitable onward sweep of the chapter in which Percy Grimm pursues Christmas and kills him. Taken merely as evocative realism, the writing is superb: the shots, the shouting; the blind rushes and clotted confusion of the mob; the added detail of the fire siren, a characteristic sound of our time, screaming the rise and fall of its meaningless message; the early resolution of the pursuit into a [201] personal contest between Christmas and Grimm. The rendition of Grimm as a type is as merciless as anything else of the sort ever done. Grimm is as the embodiment of pure force so often is: his rather colorless personality and appearance are in ghastly disproportion to his ability to produce evil and violence. He is Faulkner's equivalent of the classic Nemesis of the Furies—machine-like, unerring, impersonal, mindless. Here the problem of belief is no problem at all.

Still guided perhaps by his irrational hope, Christmas runs into Hightower's house holding the pistol he has snatched up on the way. He could kill Grimm easily, but with nothing to lose by another killing, he does not; this is his final gesture of human reconciliation. Grimm empties the magazine of his automatic into Christmas' body, but this is not all.

When the others reached the kitchen they saw the table flung aside now and Grimm stooping over the body. When they approached to see what he was about, they saw that the man was not dead yet, and when they saw what Grimm was doing one of the men gave a choked cry and stumbled back into the wall and began to vomit. Then Grimm too sprang back, flinging behind him the bloody butcher knife. "Now you'll let white women alone, even in hell," he said. But the man on the floor had not moved. He just lay there, with his eyes open and empty of everything save consciousness, and with something, a shadow, about his mouth. For a long moment he looked up at them with peaceful and unfathomable and unbearable eyes. Then his face, body, all, seemed to collapse, to fall in upon itself, and from out the slashed garments about his hips and loins the pent black blood seemed to rush like a released breath. It seemed to rush out of his pale body like the rush of sparks from a rising rocket; upon that black blast the man seemed to rise soaring into their memories forever and ever. They are not to lose it, in whatever peaceful valleys, beside whatever placid and reassuring streams of old age, in the mirroring faces of whatever children they will contemplate old disasters and newer hopes. It will be there, musing, quiet, steadfast, not fading and not particularly threatful, but of itself alone serene, of itself alone triumphant. Again from the town, deadened a little by the walls, the scream of the siren mounted toward its unbelievable crescendo, passing out of the realm of hearing.

They are not to lose it, nor, I think, are we. In Stephen Dedalus' terms, we feel pity and terror to a degree that is almost unbearable. One does not know why we feel these [202] emotions or even less why the tragic spectacle is so compelling. It may be that it is better that we don't know. Certainly, as Nietzsche claimed, the tragic emotions lurk in the dark, irrational part of the blood, and very likely the rational mind wants no part of them. "Pity is the feeling which arrests the mind in the presence of whatsoever is grave and constant in human sufferings and unites it with the human sufferer." This part at least is no problem. We unite with Joe Christmas because he is the modern Everyman. In a cosmos where the only constants are absurdity and instability, we have the right to expect anything except rationality. Any one of us could become the victim. His suffering far transcends the time and place and means Faulkner has used and comes to stand for everything that is grave and constant in the human condition.

"Terror is the feeling which arrests the mind in the presence of whatsoever is grave and constant in human suffering and unites it with the secret cause." The union with the secret cause is almost as terrible as the suffering itself, because it gives a moment of true insight into ourselves. Part of this insight is perfectly symbolized in *Light in August* when the injured Hightower, in a scene that might have come straight out of Dostoyevsky, is working himself toward complete self-knowledge. As the wheel of his memory turns on and on, he comes to realize that his own cold selfishness, his absorption in the Confederate grandfather, has caused his wife's disgrace and death. As the crowd of faces in his memory struggles to come into focus, one of them becomes the dead face of Christmas, but the focus is not clear; another face is struggling with that face, struggling to become clear and be recognized. Suddenly it emerges: it is the face of Percy Grimm, gunman, mutilator, avenging fury, lyncher extraordinary. Hightower never saw either of them before the lynching, but their terrible failure and terrible guilt are somehow directly related to his own failure to live up to his humanity. Somewhere at the root of the secret cause of things as they are, we are all related; we are all involved. We are all responsible because we are all a part of mankind. So far as the rational mind goes, the union with the secret cause is a moment of awareness, of realizing that grave and constant human suffering is truly constant. Once we achieve [203] this awareness, the acceptance of the tragic human situation, with all its absurdity and irrationality, becomes possible, and with the acceptance come the emotions of peace and tranquility.

Yet the union with the secret cause has another side, which is less commendable. This emotion, which we are not so willing to let swim up to conscious awareness, can be curtly put as "There but for the Grace of God. . . ." The hero has fallen, but we, for the moment at least, are safe. Let society pick its victims as it pleases, so long as the victim is not I. It is in just this area of playing upon our deep, instinctual fears and misgivings that Faulkner has succeeded in achieving a favorable comparison with classic tragedy. It was impossible to put the Furies believably on the stage, but Faulkner found the perfect equivalent in the lynch mob, which one way or another elicits a strong emotion in all of us, or better still, a mixed one. In an age in which the very name of Oedipus has been explained away, tamed and embalmed in the clinic, in which almost no one can truly feel why Macbeth should think the murder of a king so much worse than any murder, and in which no one believes in the absurdity of an ancestral curse, the beholder is simply asked: "Did Joe Christmas inherit a curse?" Or rather, it is not necessary to ask, since we know. Faulkner has used the subconscious fear of mutilation and distrust of miscegenation that lurks in all of us, the love of and response to violence and death, the simultaneous love and hate of the loved one, to arouse these emotions or their equivalents in us. We love the violence and evil because we acquiesce in them. No doubt these emotions are despicable, but no doubt the emotions aroused by the spectacle of what Oedipus did were despicable also. The doctor who tamed the legend of Oedipus and rechristened it a complex only found out very late what the Christian world had known all along: when there are guilt and filth in the human psyche, the only possible remedy is to cast them out.

This chapter has dealt only with the analysis of Joe Christmas as a modern tragic protagonist. It has hardly mentioned the many other excellences of *Light in August,* leaving until a later chapter the cases of Joanna Burden and Hightower, who are also classic [204] examples of the tragedy of isolation, strongly underlining the case of Christmas.

Tradition tells us that the Greeks demanded that each trilogy submitted in the great dramatic contests be accompanied by an outrageous and lewd satyr play, which preferably would burlesque the very elements and events just presented as tragedy. Perhaps some such comic relief is essential. After the human emotions have endured all they can, after the *katharsis,* something has to sustain us until we can touch earth again. Perhaps this is one explanation of the bawdy, almost folksy humor of the Lena-Byron episode in the last chapter of *Light in August,* so often dismissed with bewilderment or anger as an artistic botch. The direct experience of pity and terror is a little like being caught up in a cyclone, or to use another metaphor, like being at the heart of what goes on in a thermonuclear explosion. In contemplating the question, "When will I be blown up?" the author of *Light in August* has always been willing to risk a small side bet on Mankind. This risk and this faith are also a part of the tragic paradox. The Greeks knew, as did the Elizabethans after them, that, in contemporary terms, once the mushroom cloud has blown away and the fallout has ceased to fall there is always the continuing residue of humanity. It, as the author would no doubt say, will endure. [205]

Frozen Movement in
Light in August

DARREL ABEL

FAULKNER's *Light in August* DOES NOT (EXCEPT WITHIN THE ARBITRARY perspective of any given character in the novel) delineate a single complete action with a beginning, a middle, and an end. For Faulkner's reality, like Bergson's, is a "becomingness"—not static, but dynamic; not formed, but fluid. To Faulkner, "The present does not exist, it becomes. . . ."[1] According to Bergson, "Reality is mobility. There do not exist *things* made, but only things in the making, not *states* that remain fixed, but only states in process of change."[2]

A writer's insight into this moving reality, his escape from the static and particular into the vital and general, is intuitive. It is the poetic faculty alluded to in "Tintern Abbey," by which "the heavy and the weary weight / Of all this unintelligible world is lightened" and "We see into the life of things." Bergson defines intuition as *"knowledge which establishes itself in the moving reality and adopts the life itself of things"* (p. 227). He contrasts "intelligence," as an effort to know reality by hypostatizing and analyzing it, with "intuition":

To think intuitively is to think in duration. Intelligence starts ordinarily from the immobile, and reconstructs movement as best it can with immobilities in juxtaposition. Intuition starts from movement, posits it, or rather perceives it as reality itself, and sees in immobility only an abstract moment, a snapshot taken by our mind, of a mobility. Intelligence ordinarily concerns itself with things, meaning by that, with the static, and makes of change an accident which is supposedly superadded. For intuition the essential is change: as for the thing, as intelligence understands it, it is a cutting which has been made out of the becoming and set up by our minds as a substitute for the whole. (p. 39)

Bergson calls artists men who "are born detached," and who have "a [32] much more direct vision of reality" than other men (pp. 162–163).

If Faulkner has, as I think, a similar conception of reality in flux, and a similar theory of the imaginative writer's gift and function, his technique must master a paradox: in order to fix reality in a literary construct, it must freeze movement. "Faulkner appears to arrest the motion at the very heart of things; moments erupt and freeze, then fade, recede and diminish, still motionless."[3] In Bergsonian terms, the artist's "intelligence" must make "cuttings" out of the "becoming" which his "intuition" perceives: "Our mind, which seeks solid bases of operation, . . . has as its principal function, in the ordinary course of life, to imagine *states* and *things*. . . . It substitutes for the discon-

---

[1] Jean-Paul Sartre, "Time in Faulkner: *The Sound and the Fury*," trans. Martine Darmon, in Frederick J. Hoffman and Olga W. Vickery, *William Faulkner: Two Decades of Criticism* (East Lansing, Michigan: Michigan State College Press, 1954), p. 183. Reprinted from *Situations*, 1, "Le Bruit et la fureur" (Paris: Gallimard, 1947), pp. 70–81.

[2] Quoted by permission of the publishers, The Philosophical Library, from Henri Bergson, *The Creative Mind*, trans. Mabelle L. Andison (New York: The Philosophical Library, 1946), p. 222. All subsequent quotations cited by page numbers enclosed in parentheses in the text refer to this edition.

[3] Sartre, "Time in Faulkner," p. 182.

tinuous the continuous, for mobility stability. . . . This substitution is necessary to common sense, to language, to practical life" (p. 222).

The resource of the intuitive artist in conveying his intuitions to practical men, who must have reality represented to them in "states" and "things," is symbolism. Intuition "will have to use ideas as a conveyance. It will prefer, however, to have recourse to the most concrete ideas, but those which still retain an outer fringe of images. Comparisons and metaphors will here suggest what cannot be expressed" (p. 48). "No image will replace the intuition of duration [i.e., of "becomingness," of "mobility"], but many different images . . . will be able, through the convergence of their action, to direct the consciousness to the precise point where there is a certain intuition to seize on" (p. 195). Although symbolization is the artist's best expedient for communicating his intuitive knowledge of the mobile and continuing reality, it is still only a suggestive makeshift; it conveys no absolute insights, only relative conceptions: "*Relative is symbolic knowledge through pre-existing concepts, which goes from the fixed to the moving*" (p. 227). "Relative" knowledge "depends on the viewpoint chosen and the symbols employed," but "absolute" knowledge (i.e., "intuition of duration") "is taken from no viewpoint and rests on no symbol" (p. 187). Symbolism is merely a means by which "we lean our communication up against a knowledge that our interlocutors already possess" (p. 81).

In *Light in August* Faulkner attempts to contrive through symbols an immobile representation of mobility, and at the same time to suggest how "relative" and arbitrary any distinct and arranged version of mobile reality must be. He endeavors to represent a fluid reality in the [33] static terms "necessary to common sense, to language, to practical life"; and at the same time to disclose that the static images through which he makes the fluid reality visible are merely arrested and discontinuous blinks—what Bergson calls "snapshots" or "cuttings made out of the becoming."

Such a symbolic shuttering of reality controls the narration from the opening pages, which offer an image, immediately augmented into a symbol,[4] of the mule-drawn country wagons in which Lena Grove made her enchanted, ineluctable progress from Alabama into Mississippi; "backrolling now behind her a long monotonous succession of peaceful and undeviating changes from day to dark and dark to day again, through which she advances in identical and monotonous and deliberate wagons as though through a succession of creak-wheeled

---

[4] I use the terms "image," "symbol," and "figure" in this paper in the different senses which I think they usually carry: "image"—a distinct, unified sense-impression of an object; "symbol"—an image which is the nucleus and sign of a congeries of not readily explicable meanings and sensations; "figure"—pattern or design, possibly a configuration of images in time or space; also, any kind of trope.

and limp-eared avatars, like something moving forever and without progress across an urn."[5]

In this figure the countryside across which Lena travels is, like the "silent form" of Keats's urn,[6] a designated image or visible metaphor of eternity. The stories of Lena Grove and Joe Christmas constitute the "legend" (or "brede" or "frieze") seen against this immutable image of eternity. A legend is both an inscription and an old story, especially an "old story" in the colloquial sense of something happening over and over again from time immemorial. Against the background of country-side which is Faulkner's equivalent of the "silent form" of Keats's urn, the comic and pathetic leaf-fring'd[7] legends of [34] Lena Grove and Joe Christmas are seen to be, although interesting as individual his-tories, even more significant as expressions, moments, postures, phases of a human reality into which all personal realities fade. The stillness of urn and countryside represent, not immobility itself, but "deserts of vast eternity"—so vast that in such perspective all particulars and moments are lost.

Faulkner's somewhat peculiar use of the word "avatar," in charac-terizing the progressive appearances or apparent progress of both Lena Grove and Joe Christmas through space and time, makes their stories legends of arrested human striving like the "brede / Of marble men and maidens" on the urn. Lena "advances as though through a succession of avatars"; Joe, "as in numberless avatars" (Chaps. I, X). The main signification in Faulkner's use of the term "avatar" is of course simply "embodiment."[8] The avatar-figure, which converts per-

---

[5] Quoted by permission of the publishers, Random House, from William Faulkner, *Light in August* (New York: Modern Library, 1950), Chap. 1. All sub-sequent quotations cited by chapter numbers enclosed in parentheses in the text refer to this book.

[6] For more explicit allusions by Faulkner to Keats's "Ode to a Grecian Urn" which show how persistently Keats's urn-symbol has haunted Faulkner's imagina-tion, see Faulkner's article "Verse Old and Nascent: A Pilgrimage," *Double-Dealer,* VII (1925), 130; and "The Bear," *Go Down Moses* (New York: Modern Library, 1955), p. 297. Norman Holmes Pearson has commented on Keats's urn-symbol as employed in *Light in August* in "Lena Grove," *Shenandoah,* III (1951), 3–7.

[7] Professor Pearson ("Lena Grove," p. 6) remarks that Lena's family name (Grove) alludes to the "leaf-fring'd"; probably, despite the change of vowel, Burch's name also has this reference. That *Light in August* is "a kind of pastoral" has been noted by Cleanth Brooks in "Notes on Faulkner's 'Light in August,'" *Harvard Advocate,* cxxxv (1951), 27.

[8] Thus, for example, Faulkner calls the old mulatto Lucas Beauchamp in *In-truder in the Dust* an "avatar" ("Lucas in ten thousand Sambo-avatars") of the Negro in a position of moral superiority to the white man who has injured him (*Intruder in the Dust* [New York: New American Library, "Signet Books"], Chap. IX). In the "Appendix" to *The Sound and the Fury* which he wrote for *The Portable Faulkner,* ed. Malcolm Cowley (New York: Viking Press, 1946), Faulkner speaks of old Brigadier General Jason Lycurgus Compson II as "now completing the third of his three avatars—the one as son of a brilliant and gallant statesman, the second as battle-leader of brave and gallant men, the third as a sort of privi-leged pseudo–Daniel Boone–Robinson Crusoe." In the same "Appendix" Faulkner

sonal histories into a mere succession of envisagements of a continuous and moving process of human "becoming," determines the conception of the other characters in the novel too. In Faulkner's sense of "avatar," Hightower's whole inert existence is a kind of prolonged or aborted avatar, in consequence of his belief "that I skipped a generation. . . . I had already died one night twenty years before I saw light" (Chap. xx). Even Byron Bunch philosophically questions his own determinateness as a self, his own identity: "*You just say that you are Byron Bunch. . . . You are just the one that calls yourself Byron Bunch today, now, this minute*" (Chap. xviii). Faulkner apparently uses the avatar-figure to indicate that a person's sense of distinct and stable identity is simply a hypostatization of the streaming subjective life in which he [35] transiently exists and which his private consciousness defines for him as *his* life.

A less conspicuous device of Faulkner's for indicating that the "fixed" is only an arbitrary arrest of the "moving" is his frequent mention of the omnipresent muted hum of natural life,[9] furnishing a vague, monotonous, repetitious, generalized accompaniment to foreground action. Thus Joe Christmas, voicing his finally definite intention to murder Joanna Burden, heard around him "a myriad sounds, . . . voices, murmurs, whispers: of trees, darkness, earth, people: his own voice; other voices evocative of names and times and places . . ." (Chap. v). As he entered the house later, to commit the deed, "The dark was filled with voices, myriad, out of all time that he had known, as though all the past was a flat pattern. And going on: tomorrow night, all the tomorrows, to be a part of the flat pattern, going on" (Chap. xii). After Christmas' capture, as Hightower hears from Mrs. Hines the story of his early life, "through the open window there comes now only the peaceful and myriad sounds of the summer night" (Chap. xvi). And later, as Hightower is alone in his house, struggling to suppress his humane impulse to sympathize with and help "poor mankind": "Beyond the open window the sound of insects has not ceased, has not faltered" (Chap. xvi). These generalized, remote, anonymous voices of changing, enduring reality constitute an audible image of the continuous and moving, just as urn and countryside are its visible image.

---

tells of Jefferson's mousy librarian spending "her life trying to keep *Forever Amber* in its orderly overlapping avatars . . . out of the hands of highschool juniors and seniors": the "avatars" of *Forever Amber*, that is, are the whole succession of forbidden sexy novels which titillate feverish adolescent fancy. "Avatar," in these various instances, seems to signify a periodic succession of embodiments of an essentially identical reality—or, as in "ten thousand Sambo-avatars," perhaps multiple simultaneous embodiments.

[9] Faulkner's "myriad voices, out of all time" correspond to what Bergson calls "the uninterrupted humming of life's depths" (pp. 176–177). Faulkner externalizes and objectifies the concept by finding an "objective correlative": the summertime chorus of insect-sounds.

If, then, *Light in August* eschews classical form—lacks a single complete action with a beginning, a middle, and an end—it does so because there is no alpha or omega in Faulkner's alphabet of reality. His novel ends, but his story does not: it is merely a harsh and prolonged suspiration swelling out of and subsiding into the "myriad voices, out of all time." Faulkner's story is about convergent or connected human destinies, which have as their nexus the burning of the Burden house, an event which any individual character views as a fixed and understood reality, but which is in fact a symbol capable of as many significances as the various individuals who view it are enabled to read into it from their own experience, their own ideas. To the [36] stranger who brings Lena to Jefferson, it is merely "a house burning" (Chap. i). But as a crucial moment in each of the human histories which converge in it, it is variously interpreted. To each, it brings "light in August" in a different way, provides a glaring but transient interval of illumination and realization.

"There is at least one reality which we all seize from within, by intuition and not by simple analysis. It is our own person in its flowing through time, the self which endures" (p. 191). "If, instead of claiming to analyze duration . . . , one first installs oneself in it by an effort of intuition, one has the feeling of a certain well-defined *tension,* whose very definiteness seems like a choice between an infinity of possible durations" (p. 218). The central perception offered to readers of *Light in August* is expressed in Bergson's sentence, "The higher the consciousness, the stronger is this tension of its own duration in relation to that of things" (p. 105). Such a "tension" requires a consciousness of at least two "possible durations": the intuition of our own duration, "which we all seize from within"; and the intuition of some possible duration more comprehensive than our own. Duration consists of "the addition to the present feeling, of the memory of past moments" (p. 211). "The distinction between our present and past is . . . , if not arbitrary, at least relative to the extent of the field which our attention to life can embrace" (p. 179). Thus, intuitions grasp "durations" which vary infinitely in comprehensiveness. They may include awareness of immediate and instant reality, or of our whole lives since birth, or of generations of our family, or of the continuing life of the human species, or of the vast transcendent flux in which the *élan vital* endlessly reshapes reality in novel and more complex forms.

Of the major characters in *Light in August,* the one with least awareness of "this tension of its own duration in relation to that of things" is Lena Grove, for her intuition of her own duration is a very contracted one, and she has no intuition of any other duration. Her "attention to life" embraces only what immediately confronts her; there is little addition to her present feeling "of memory of past events." She cares nothing for her own past or for her family, and never thinks of them; she is fully content with the moment which she occupies, and with the bliss of being in it. As the book opens, she reflects, *"Although I have not been quite a month on the road I am already in Mississippi";* [37] and as it ends, she says, "Here we aint been coming from Alabama but two months, and now it's already Tennessee" (Chaps. I, XXI). The brief span of her attention to the past is clearly marked in such reflections: the only past she ever speaks of is a very recent one, and she speaks of it only as the antecedent of the present in which she is almost wholly engrossed. Her consciousness has "an inward-lighted quality of tranquil and calm unreason" (Chap. I). "The duration of things" is not measured for her by the tides of God or the clocks and calendars of man, but solely by the elemental urges and responses of her nature to her immediate surroundings. She knows no reality beyond her subjective moment. She represents ordinary naive mankind, inviolably innocent because it cannot enter the realm of ideas. To Hightower she stands for *"the good stock peopling in tranquil obedience to it the good earth"* (Chap. XVII). She is too unsophisticated to comprehend good and evil. Faulkner assigns her the first and last speeches of the novel because, just as hers is the least conscious and sophisticated, so is it the most elemental and enduring, aspect of humanity. She is one of Sandburg's "people who live on," a primitive character like Hardy's "man harrowing clods."

If *Light in August* at all anticipates Faulkner's later statement, in his Nobel Prize acceptance speech, that "man will not merely endure; he will prevail," it does so by identifying the "crucified" Joe Christmas with Lena's child, and by exhibiting her calm and confident onward travel at the end of the story. The hate, mistrust, and evil will which impel mankind to crucify some of its members are counterbalanced by the love, trust, and good will tendered to Lena and her child. Lena prevails, not by her understanding, but by her complacent trust in others, a trust amounting almost to obstinacy and stupidity. Although her story is a comedy of rustic innocence, a comic pastoral, Faulkner dignifies instead of disparaging her.

In contrast, Joe Christmas' story is tragic, or at least pathetic. Although Lena is hardly more than an expression of the will to live of the species, Joe is a person struggling to establish his selfhood, and aware of overwhelming influences extending into his life from a long reach of time and a broad range of human relationships. He saw his own history as a struggle to gain status in white society, or, failing that, to revert to primitivism. A long passage near the end of Chapter V serves as figure for his life. It relates how, on the night before he murdered Joanna Burden, he wandered into the Negro section of [38] Jefferson, Freedman Town, "like a phantom, a spirit, strayed out of its own world and lost. . . . It was as though he and all other man-shaped life about him had been returned to the lightless hot wet primogenitive Female." He ran in frantic revulsion "out of the black hollow," but became calm when he reached a white neighborhood with "clustered lights: low bright birds in stillwinged and tremulous suspension." He said of the white life around him, "That's all I wanted. . . . That dont seem a whole lot to ask." As he walked on, he saw behind him "the far bright rampart of the town . . . and the black pit from which he had fled . . . black, impenetrable, in its garland of Augusttremulous lights. It might have been the original quarry, abyss itself" (Chap. v).

In retrospect Christmas saw his career as a vain striving to emerge from the black, primitive, earthy, female, passionate "allmother of obscurity and darkness" (Chap. x) into light, civilization, manliness, volition, identity. In the course of this vain striving, his hatred of the "lightless hot wet primogenitive Female" grew into a complex obsession. His first indelible impressions, at the orphanage, were of females, sex, guilt, and the rejection of Negroes as inflictions divinely and irrevocably decreed. At the McEacherns', throughout his boyhood, these impressions were all confirmed and deepened. His first experience of sex made it for him thereafter simply an overmastering lust: "something liquid, deathcolored and foul" (Chap. viii). After his young innocence and affection had been outraged by the malformed whore Bobbie Allen (an episode grotesquely caricaturing love's young dream), he tried to coerce by injury and hate the world into which he could not find a way by generosity and love. Even at the age of five in the orphanage he had learned to believe that "*I am different from the others*" (Chap. vi), and he never was able to surmount the difference.

After his decisive rejection by the white world, he tried to return to primitive black life. In Detroit

he lived with Negroes, shunning white people. . . . He now lived as man and wife with a woman who resembled an ebony carving. At night he would lie in bed beside her, . . . trying to breathe into himself the dark odor, the dark and inscrutable thinking and being of Negroes, with each suspiration trying to expel from himself the white blood and the white thinking and being. And all the while his nostrils at the odor which he was trying to make his own would whiten and tauten, his whole being writhe and strain with physical outrage and spiritual denial. (Chap. x)

Christmas failed to recover "the dark and inscrutable thinking and being of Negroes," not because they refused to accept him, but [39] because his upbringing had conditioned him against it. He had not gained a place in the white world, but he had been unfitted for a place in the black world. His was the tragedy of "black blood" in a "pale body" (Chap. xix), an antagonism of two possibilities so equal in strength that each negated the other. Thus Gavin Stevens summed up his tragedy:

It was not alone all those thirty years [of his personl existence] . . . , but all those successions of thirty years before that which had put that stain either on his white blood or his black blood, whichever you will, and which killed him. . . . His blood would not be quiet. . . . It would not be either one or the other. (Chap. xix)

Thus Faulkner shows that the conviction of his outcast fate which dogged "Christmas, the son of Joe" (Chap. xvi) grew in his mind like a fatality. When he anticipated murdering Joanna Burden, he did not acknowledge that he willed to do it, but that he was fated to do it: "*Something is going to happen to me*" (Chap. v). When he murdered her, he "believed with calm paradox that he was the volitionless servant of the fatality[10] in which he believed that he did not believe" (Chap. xii). He transvaluated murder into something like a creative act, however, since it was for him a symbolic annihilation of the world which had denied his claims to selfhood and status. Joanna Burden was his appropriate victim, for she combined in one person the three elements of coercion which Joe had experienced: femaleness, Calvinism, and obsession with color-difference.[11]

Since Christmas could not find a secure life anywhere, his only alternative was to die: to accept and hasten the doom that he thought was determined for him. After the murder, as he looked at his feet in the black Negro shoes that he had put on to throw the pursuing bloodhounds off the scent, it "seemed to him that he could see himself being hunted by white men at last into the black abyss, which had been waiting, trying, for thirty years to drown him and into which now and at last he had actually entered, bearing upon his ankles the definite and ineradicable gauge of its upward moving" (Chap. xiv). [40]

Just as Lena represents the comedy of ordinary life, so does Joe represent the tragedy of extraordinary life. Hated, corrupted, and persecuted from the hour of his birth, he was not only accused of being evil by those who "crucified" him for righteousness' sake (Hines in the name of God, Grimm in the name of patriotism and society); he *was* evil, for he had been imbued with all the sin and corruption of humanity; he was a scapegoat burdened with the accumulated evils of his generation. But even his persecutors were not responsible for the tragedy. Although Hines and Grimm were persecutors rather than victims, although Lucas Burch was Judas rather than Christ, all alike were servants of the general and traditional obsessions which assigned their roles in the tragedy. Byron Bunch's opinion about the town of

---

[10] Most of the principal characters in the novel (Grimm, McEachern, Joanna Burden, and even Gail Hightower) act as if their wills were determined by some overruling necessity. For an excellent brief discussion of the theme of fatality in Faulkner, see Rabi, "Faulkner and the Exiled Generation," in *William Faulkner: Two Decades of Criticism,* especially pp. 132–134.

[11] For discussion of the conjoined Negro-sex motifs in *Light in August* see Phyllis Hirshleifer, "As Whirlwinds in the South: An Analysis of *Light in August,*" *Perspective,* vii (1949), 237–238.

Jefferson's long harassment of Hightower applies equally well to Christmas' "crucifixion": "The entire affair had been a lot of people performing a play and . . . now and at last they had all played out the parts that had been allotted to them" (Chap. III).

"Installed in universal mobility, . . . consciousness contracts in a quasi-instantaneous vision an immensely long history which unfolds outside it. The higher the consciousness, the stronger is this tension of its own duration in relation to that of things" (p. 105). Gail Hightower is the most significant character in *Light in August* because only he attained the higher consciousness which "contracts in a quasi-instantaneous vision an immensely long history which unfolds outside it." Hightower suffered even more than Joe Christmas, for he who experiences most suffers most. Hightower tried to maintain that he had "bought immunity" (Chap. XIII) from involvement in the affairs of living men, but his long-suppressed humanity impelled him "to come back into life" (Chap. XIII) to assist at a birth and try to prevent a death. His identification with the human beings whose fates, when he was forced to sympathize with them, illustrated both the hopeful and tragic possibilities of the life he had evaded made him comprehend the general fate of mankind, which is to serve the compulsive ideas which are its inheritance. Hightower's own story is an exaggerated rendering of the truth that all men are directed by ancestral ghosts and do not fully possess their own realities. He had chosen to withdraw into his ancestral ghost, rather than to let the human past summed up in him enter the present; but his story, like Joanna Burden's and [41] Joe Christmas', shows the persistence through generations of a pattern of transmitted ideas and tendencies which effectually make each inheritor their instrument, because they are not externally dictated to him but are constitutive of his own character.

Because Hightower had so long lived a "dead life in the actual world," "dissociated from mechanical time" (Chap. XVI), had not enacted a vital role in the present, he was able, like God in a high tower in a medieval mystery play, to see that present with detachment. He had breadth of understanding and depth of compassion, and rose to contemplation of those principles of human action, those conditions of human life, which are so recurrent in time that they seem ulterior to time, and "tease us out of thought / As doth eternity." If, in a naturalistic cosmos, Joe Christmas is Jesus Christ, Gail Hightower is God Himself. Lena Grove, a pagan generatrix, is mankind aware of its existence only through participation in the burgeoning life of nature; Joe Christmas lives and dies in a world of ideas of good and evil; but Gail Hightower, by his intuition of "universal mobility," philosophically transcends both the natural and moral worlds.

The concluding revery of Hightower (to whom light in August

comes more effulgently than to any other character, although all the witnesses of Christmas' death, like the witnesses of the crucifixion of Jesus, have a half-comprehended enlightenment) shows him in an instant when "consciousness contracts in a quasi-instantaneous vision an immensely long history which unfolds outside itself." In his agony of comprehension, of realization, Hightower sits "in the lambent suspension of August into which night is about fully to come," and all the faces of the recent past rise before him, but "not shaped with suffering, not shaped with anything: not horror, pain, not even re-proach. They are peaceful, as though they have escaped into an apotheosis" (Chap. xx). The figure which structures his revery is a rapidly revolving wheel of thought,[12] or consciousness, which slows and [42] stops to focus the static images and characters which per-ception distinguishes in the continuous, moving reality. But the wheel in rapid revolution is a halo full of faces that "all look alike, composite of all the faces that he has ever seen" (Chap. xx).

In this apocalyptic instant in Hightower's vision the faces of Christmas and Grimm, in mortal life obsessed and murderous oppo-nents, "fade and blend." "Then it seems to [Hightower] that some ultimate dammed flood within him breaks and rushes away. He seems to watch it, feeling himself losing contact with earth, lighter and lighter, emptying, floating. . . . He [thinks,] 'With all air, all heaven, filled with the lost and unheeded crying of all the living who ever lived, wailing still like lost children among the cold and terrible stars. . . .'" (Chap. xx). Thus, for an instant, Hightower escapes from the static and discontinuous appearances which constitute reality to ordi-nary perception: leaves the temporal world of frieze and legend and enters the eternity of the urn-world itself. When, by philosophic intui-tion, man is able to "arise from a frozen vision of the real . . . to perceive all things *sub specie durationis*," "all things acquire depth,— more than depth, something like a fourth dimension. . . . What was immobile and frozen in our perception is warmed and set in motion.

---

[12] Faulkner, in representing what Bergson calls "intuition of duration," gen-erally uses cyclic figures. Movement across an urn is of course cyclic movement. Joe Christmas feels that for thirty years he has been running "inside a circle" (Chap. xiv). Lena thinks of her movement along a country road as being "like already measured thread being rewound onto a spool" (Chap. i). This simile is also used by Bergson to suggest the sense of "our own person in its flowing through time" (p. 191): "It is, if you like, like the unrolling of a spool. . . . But it is just as much a continual winding, like that of thread into a ball" (pp. 192–193). Richard Chase has discussed the contrasting significances of what he calls "linear discreteness and curve" in "The Stone and the Crucifixion: Faulkner's *Light in August*," *Kenyon Review*, x (1948), 539–551 (reprinted in *William Faulkner: Two Decades of Criticism*). I think that his argument, although per-ceptive and valuable, miscarries somewhat because he thinks in terms of the form of Faulkner's cyclic images, instead of noting that they are essentially images of duration.

Everything comes to life around us. . . . A great impulse carries beings and things along. We feel ourselves uplifted, carried away, borne along by it" (p. 186). In the Dionysian dance of life there comes a serene moment of Apollonian vision.

The climactic symbol of *Light in August,* the lambent wheel which Hightower sees in his highest moment of vision as an image of eternity, is an archetypal symbol whose richness can be best apprehended in comparison with literary parallels. The most obvious is Dante's recurrent conjunction of images of light and a rapidly revolving wheel in the *Paradiso* (e.g., Cantos, i, xii, xxviii), especially the elaborate image of the circle of fire, or rapidly whirling wheel haloed with light, which Dante views in the ninth heaven (Canto xxviii). Dante quotes in connection with this image a passage from Aristotle's *Metaphysics* on the *primum mobile,* the "unmoved mover" which is the center and source of this dazzle of cyclic movement. Similarly, Plato's *Timaeus* designates the stars in their courses as "a moving image of [43] eternity"—a passage which may be the source of the famous opening stanza of Henry Vaughan's poem "The World":

> I saw Eternity the other night
> Like a great ring of pure and endless light,
>   All calm, as it was bright,
> And round beneath it, Time, in hours, days, years,
>   Driven by the spheres
> Like a vast shadow moved, in which the world
>   And all her train were hurl'd.

I think it likely that such reminiscences, whether conscious or not, have contributed to Faulkner's symbol of the haloed wheel of Hightower's vision. If Hightower, like Dante, is regarded as one who, while still in mortal life, is afforded a vision of eternity in all its phases, his experience exhibits something of hell, of purgatory, and of heaven. His inferno consists of his witnessing and participating in the complicated tragedy of human evil and mortality which is consummated in the "crucifixion" of Joe Christmas. His purgatory is the initial stage of his revery after Christmas' death, when finally, in "a consternation which is about to be actual horror," he admits his guilt as an "instrument of [his wife's] despair and shame," while "sweat begins to pour from him, springing out like blood" (Chap. xx). He sees, beyond his own guilt, the determinism which fixed this complicity in evil upon him: "If I am the instrument of her despair and death, then I am in turn the instrument of someone outside myself" (Chap. xx). Purged by his abandonment of delusion, his admission of truth, he enters his paradise, his moment of perception of an eternal truth which leaves his stale and corrupt "body empty and lighter than a forgotten leaf and even more trivial than flotsam lying spent and still . . . ; so that it can be now Now"[13] (Chap. xx).

But, although *Light in August* contains a *Divina commedia,* a *Comédie humaine* encompasses it: Lena, the almost primitive embodiment of the human species' persistent effort to seek attachments and find durable satisfactions in local, temporal, and personal terms, is presented to us first and last. Her primacy in the story does not mean, I think, that Faulkner rejects Hightower's vision of reality for her view of it, but rather that he regards Lena's reality as the almost universally and constantly available one, and Hightower's as a difficult, fleeting, and rarely attainable one. [44]

The Calvinistic Burden of
Light in August

ILSE DUSOIR LIND

PURITANISM AS A DOMINANT THEME OF *Light in August* WAS FIRST OBserved two decades ago. Although subsequent studies have noted that religion and repression are recurrent themes linking the stories of Hightower, Lena Grove, and Joe Christmas, they have failed to show specifically how these two motifs in the various narratives are interrelated. The textual explications which have appeared in recent years have been useful for their alignment of patterns of imagery, but only to a limited degree because of their inadequate orientation to the structure and design of the novel. Many "figures in the carpet" have been traced, but no one has solved the mystery of the novel's coherence. More than one critic has pronounced the work structurally imperfect.

Repeatedly, however, we discover that Faulkner's seeming defects are failures of our own perception, which is not prepared for the new uses to which he applies his resources. *Light in August* presents three interwoven stories, as we readily enough observe, but what we have not seen is the basis of their inner coördination. They are, to begin with, three quite different types of narrative: a tragedy (Christmas' story); a problem novel (the ordeal of Hightower); and a comedy

---

[13] Faulkner's "now" is a verbal device for signaling the moment of Hightower's passage from a temporal now to the Eternal Now. Compare "yesterday today and tomorrow are Is: Indivisible: One" (*Intruder in the Dust*, Chap. IX).

(the Lena Grove–Byron Bunch romance). Each is distinct and is elaborated with extraordinary textual richness on its own conceptual principle, yet all form a harmonious synthesis. The story of Christmas occupies the largest area of interest, but the remaining narratives are in no sense sub-plots. Each story has its own mood, tempo, plot, and theme. The vision of *Light in August*, as in *The Sound and the Fury* (where the structural units are blocks of consciousness, rather than narratives), resides in its total effect, and rests upon our comprehension and response to each unit as an entity, each unit in thematic [307]   relation to each other, and all the units seen as a series of outlooks or attitudes transcending each other progressively toward an artistic resolution. The effect, in brief, is contrapuntal. The writer who had achieved consummate control in the management of multi-level poetic narration in *The Sound and the Fury* and *As I Lay Dying* undertook a greater challenge in *Light in August*. Where in the earlier novels he had used a series of limited points of view, he now chose a triple narrative scheme, exploiting the new possibilities inherent in the use of independent narratives. The result is a greater range and depth of treatment at the same time that the reader's interest in plot action—which had been relatively subordinate in the earlier masterpieces—is constantly recharged. The success of his strategy in heightening the immediate appeals of the work without lessening its intellectual and emotional complexity is proved by the fact that *Light in August* is one of Faulkner's most popularly enjoyed novels, even while—from a critical point of view—it remains essentially obscure.

The Christmas story, or tragedy, is the subject of this study. For purposes of analysis, it is here isolated from the body of the text for consideration as a thematic and structural entity. Its relation to the remaining narratives may be schematically indicated as follows: the Christmas tragedy, a tale of personal and social violence, poses the problem which the remaining narratives must resolve. Its communicated sense of moral injustice and appalling endlessness are forthrightly confronted in the story of Hightower. Hightower's commitment to life—his involvement in Lena's delivery—halts the "wheel" of tragic recurrence. Lena's infant, as the symbolic representation of the future, enters a world which has been liberated by Hightower's ordeal and sacrifice. The final outlook of the novel represents the triumph of the comic over the tragic vision.

In approaching the Christmas narrative it is perhaps best to state at the outset that the story of Christmas is developed by Faulkner along two lines, and that the confusion of these two has been the chief stumbling block in critical interpretation. [308] As the tragic hero—or, better, victim—Christmas is traced from birth to death. Formative influences are given in great detail, so that we understand the necessity of his violence. After his murder of Joanna Burden, his negation and outrage are shown mounting to a point where he hurls defiances to

God from the pulpit of a church he has invaded, then subsiding to a recognition of all men as brothers (simultaneous with the wish for death, for he has ceased to want food), and finally to his voluntary surrender and ugly mutilation by Percy Grimm. As a psychological study, it is the best in literature of an alienated personality who is not articulate or intellectual. Our interest in him as an individual sustains our suspense as to his ultimate fate throughout the novel and tempts us, understandably enough, to assume that his personal experience, like that of Billy Budd—another fictional protagonist symbolized as a Christ figure—is the key to the meaning of the novel.

But many problems arise as a consequence. If the book is considered as primarily Christmas' story, then the adult years—as some critics have protested—are slighted by the allocation of no more than a few pages for the events of Christmas' life occurring between adolescence and the age of thirty-three. Equally problematic is the bearing of the Christ symbolism, which, if its purpose is merely to identify Christmas with Christ, is laid on with an extremely heavy hand. The Christ symbolism is strongly reinforced at the end of the novel, for example, in the scene of Christmas' capture (the assembled multitude, the five wounds, Percy Grimm as Roman soldier, the age of Christmas), but the attempt to apply this terminal emphasis to Christmas as a person leads only to bafflement. Spiritually enervated, he is inadequate to represent the renewal implied in the myth, and the pathos of his plight, increased by association with the Crucifixion cannot be the final effect we are meant to ponder; it is refuted by the story of Lena, which concludes later. Actually, each of the narratives contains a Christ figure, and this is why the symbolism is excessive in emphasis and direction when seen in relation to Christmas [309] alone. The story of Christmas as an individual is compelling in the extreme, but it is not on this level that the narrative of Christmas is integrated with the remaining narratives in a meaningful composite.

Analyzing the Christmas narrative as an entity, what becomes evident is that the central motif is not Christmas' growth of consciousness or his encounter with "justice," but the conflict between Christmas and Joanna Burden. This conflict comes to its crashing climax (the murder) only a little past the middle of the novel as a whole, in the twelfth chapter (of twenty-one).

Miss Burden has received almost no critical attention as a significant symbol in the novel, probably because her personality and background, unlike those of Christmas, are conveyed tersely (in her sharply highlighted monologue on her family history) and with almost clinical objectivity (in Faulkner's account of her erotic conduct with Christmas). The result is that she appears monstrous, whereas Joe, whose disturbed personality we understand because of the detail and skill lavished on his early years, seems poignantly human. Yet that Faulkner intends to equate Joanna and Joe as victims of analogous cultural neuroses is suggested in his designation of them as name-twins (Joe and Joanna) and in his care to supply each with a genealogy covering three generations. Joanna's past, coming as it does just at the point in the novel where we are tempted to skip pages to learn what in Joe's illicit relationship with Joanna incited him to kill her and flee, is easily overlooked as a thematic crux. But attention to it is essential if we are to discover why Joanna bears the obviously allegorical surname of Burden and why her forebears carry given names as rich in historical connotation as Calvin and Nathaniel.

An astonishing symmetry emerges when the biographical and psychological data contained in the accounts of Joanna and Joe are assembled. The forces which shaped Christmas are identical with those which shaped Joanna. Only on one issue—the status of the Negro—are the forebears of Christmas [310] and Joanna opposed. The encounter and mutual destruction of Joe and Joanna, each the product of identical but conflicting impulses in the culture which produced them, represent, therefore, a profound irony of history. On the highest level of significance, Christmas and Joanna Burden are historical symbols, dramatic personifications of cultural forces. To understand the cunning with which Faulkner has personified in two neurotic personalities forces at work in the culture of the South, it is necessary to trace the psychological problems of Joe Christmas and Joanna Burden in the process of formation, to recognize the relevance of all that is specifically given us about their personal and social past.

Christmas' problem of self-identity is created, first of all, by his grandfather, "Doc" Hines, who shapes Joe's early years according to a fantastic vision. The general impression left upon the reader by Hines is that he is a raving lunatic; certainly, the sanity of a man who abducts his own grandson, both of whose parents he has in effect killed, and who watches over the infant with a hatred more doting than the intensest love, is at best dubious. He revels in the dietitian's torment when she is found by little Joe in "lechery and fornication" with wild exultation. No less frenzied is his incitation of the mob, almost thirty years later, to "Kill the bastard."

The motives underlying Hines's conduct, tinged as they are with madness, are not easily discerned, but the importance of Hines's mission in the life of Christmas requires that we sift the data concerning him with extreme care.

At the time of Christmas' birth, Hines was in his forties. What his occupation had been in the years preceding is idly speculated upon by the citizens of Mottstown after he settles there. Of the various theories put forward, some derisively, that most generally held (and that which best accords with all that is elsewhere given about him) is that he had once been a minister. At this stage of his life he bears little resemblance to the frothing dotard who is to demand Christmas' violent death. He is [311]

. . . a hard man, in his prime, a man who should have been living a hard and active life, and whom time, circumstance, something, had betrayed, sweeping the hale body and thinking of a man of fortyfive into a backwater suitable for a man of sixty or sixtyfive.

The people of Mottstown recognize that some intense private conviction has taken him out of a realm in which he once exercised authority:

. . . he talked a little about himself, with a self confidence not alone of the independent man, but with a further quality, as though at one time in his life he had been better than independent, and that not long ago. . . . It was . . . the confidence of a man who has had the controlling of lesser men and who had voluntarily and for some reason which he believed that no other man would question or comprehend, changed his life.

His religious affiliation is not disclosed, but we may infer from his repeated allusions to God's "foreordained Will," "His Purpose and His Vengeance," that its leanings were Calvinistic. It is also clear that assumptions about the inferiority of the Negro in the eye of God figured in his faith. Historically, such a combination fits well enough the branch of Presbyterianism which, during the religious controversy preceding the Civil War, evolved the theories of Divine sanction for slavery. This branch was no longer officially recognized in the 1890's (when Hines would have been in his forties), yet it was near enough to have caught up a man living in a cultural "slack backwater." The theological reasoning by which Hines brought himself, during the years he lived in Mottstown, to enter remote Negro churches and preach "humility before all skins lighter than theirs" and "the superiority of the white race . . ." had been forged by Southern churchmen some fifty years earlier. The citizenry of Mottstown, who tolerated Hines and his wife without much concern for their activities because the couple was old and ineffectual, had only a vague notion of their mission, believing them just "crazy on the subject of Negroes," or "Maybe . . . Yankees." The couple subsisted [312] almost wholly on food brought by Negroes in a confused return of gratitude for the white man's "selfdedication to the saving of Negro souls" on a demeaning Biblical argument. The Hineses persisted, Faulkner suggests, as cultural anachronisms "like two homeless and belated beasts from beyond the glacial period."

Adherence to a doctrine of white supremacy maintained on religious grounds is sufficient to account for the shattering of Hines's past when, by a fate he could not avert (though he tried desperately enough to procure an abortionist for his daughter), a presumed part-Negro child is born of his own blood. Such an event, impossible in his eyes as a true expression of God's will as set forth in the Bible, he can only construe as an extraordinary providence, representing God's will in reverse, divine "vengeance." Snatching the child up from its dead mother's body and seeing that it will live, Hines pronounces the significance of its birth in the eyes of the Lord and declares his own future role in relation to it: "It's the Lord God's abomination, and I am the instrument of His will." The "abomination" had, in Hines's construction of God's inscrutable purpose, no human spiritual identity. It was "dead to God." Hines's life henceforth is given over to waiting for the evil which is to come from evil.

Depositing the child on the doorstep of a white orphanage (thereby to enhance its opportunity to bring about evil), he finds his omen-seeking act rewarded when on Christmas Eve the dietitian and her physician lover, desecrating the sacred anniversary with eggnog and lovemaking, discover the "abomination" wrapped in its blanket and name it carelessly in honor of the day, or—as Hines sees it—"in sacrilege" of God's Son. He now takes a janitor's job at the orphanage, and from his station in the yard watches the "abomination" until the intensity of his gaze is felt by both the boy and his playmates, setting Christmas apart and evoking the pejorative, "nigger." Hines notes with assurance that God is actively ". . . polluting the earth with the working of that word on him," just as he [313] is convinced that the dietitian's dilemma, upon discovering that Joe may have been witness to her act of surreptitious carnality, is a further confirmation of evil by evil. He is as profoundly obsessed by the sinfulness of sexuality in all its aspects (he had pronounced the onset of his daughter's menses "the womansign of God's abomination"), as by the spiritual inferiority of blacks to whites.

By the time young Christmas has completed his stay at the orphanage, Hines's hatred, the dietitian's deviousness, and the children's epithets have already crystallized for him into a puzzled awareness of his peculiar alienation. Of Hines he asks, when rejection by the other children has forced him to lonely reflection: "Is God a nigger too?" To which the bigot replies, with wild irrelevance: "He is the Lord God of wrathful hosts, His will be done. . . ." Looking next to the Negro working in the yard to establish some identification, Christmas asks: "How come you are a nigger?" To which the colored worker replies, resenting the term of address innocently employed: "Who told you I am a nigger, you white trash bastard? . . . You are worse than that. You don't know what you are . . . And more than that, you wont never know. . . . God ain't no nigger." The effect of these words upon the five-year-old orphan is shuddering to contemplate.

These exchanges soon faded from conscious recollection, but they did not fade from consciousness ("Memory believes before knowing remembers"). During his boyhood and adolescence with the McEacherns, the question of Christmas' origins was never raised beyond McEachern's futile attempt to pry assurances from the stubbornly "liberal" matron. The course which Faulkner has sketched out as crucial in Christmas' psychological development continues, however, to be one in which religion is the most pervasive influence.

McEachern lacks Hines's belligerence of temperament; he is a self-mastered, predictable man. But he is equally a dogmatist of the sect which places God on a "wrathful and retributive Throne," and conceives life on earth to be a penance of [314] toil for man's original sins, the whole book of which he holds Joe accountable for at one point: "sloth, ingratitude, irreverence . . . blasphemy . . . lying . . . and lechery." His sect is Presbyterian. What is more, he is Scotch, and Scotch Presbyterianism in the South was known for its extreme literalism of Calvinistic doctrine. An enormous Bible and an opened Presbyterian catechism lie on the lamp-table in his parlor. He is a faithful communicant; even though other churches are nearby, he drives a whole hour to attend the Presbyterian church, five miles away. He sets himself expiations, and in his prayers at table he not only gives thanks for his food but asks forgiveness for the need to eat it. In the unforgettable scene in which Joe faints from hunger because McEachern has not yielded on the memorizing of the catechism, the inhuman coldness of the man is what chiefly shocks us. We remember only on second thought the object involved—the book of elemental instructions in the principles of his faith—which authorizes McEachern's persistence in his own mind.

At worst, McEachern is not perversely cruel; this is why the boy comes to feel a certain security with his foster father. McEachern's actions always conform to his principles, but these principles, as he understands and applies them, are merciless. They make no provision for human frailty; they outlaw the affections. The Calvinistic conception of an austere Providence and of divinely delegated order in secular government—in this case government of the family—sets forth for him his rôle as a father, just as it had determined the rôle into which he had cast himself as a husband. Mrs. McEachern's subordination had been long ago accomplished. "Timid," "hunched," with a "beaten face," she looked "fifteen years older than the rugged and vigorous husband . . . as if she were the medium and . . . the husband the control." McEachern's sovereignty over her is moral, impersonal, and absolute: "Kneel down, Woman," he orders, when he discovers her attempted collaboration in Joe's lie about his suit, "Ask grace and pardon of God, not of me."

His duties as a parent he accepts in the spirit of a stewardship [315] emanating from God and entailing above all the responsibility of moral-theological discipline. To the matron at the orphanage he had declared of Joe: ". . . he will eat my bread and observe my religion." To Joe, on the ride home, he had said: "You will find food and shelter and the care of Christian people. For I will have you learn that the two abominations are sloth and idle thinking, the two virtues are work and the fear of God."

McEachern replaces Joe's "heathenish" name with his own, takes him regularly to church, assigns him a round of chores, and when Joe reaches adolescence gives him a calf for his first private possession. Outwardly, this regimen has much to commend it. Unfortunately, since every element of this program derives in McEachern from a sense of duty which refuses to communicate itself through affection, it is rejected by the boy emotionally even while he submits physically, with impassive demeanor. The name Christmas he restores at his first opportunity (while talking to the waitress during their first private conversation); the church-going affects him so adversely that association with any of the girls who attend he rules out of the question *a priori*. ("To do so would be . . . a retraction of his religious hatred.") He stealthily sells the calf, realizing, no doubt—as McEachern tells him soon enough—that his status as possessor is ambiguous, his title to the calf being meant as just another lesson: "To teach you . . . responsibility of the owner to that which he owns under God's suffrance."

Sexual phobia was commonly enough an accompaniment of Calvinistic rigor. McEachern possesses it no less than does Hines. His clairvoyant knowledge of the place where Christmas has taken Bobbie to dance is the seeming "intuition" which is bred of repressed speculation; he has long been fighting Christmas' "temptations" vicariously. His enraged outburst in the dance hall (he had never met the girl; and the dance itself was in the schoolhouse, attended mostly by simple country boys): "Away Jezebel, away harlot!" is completely unwarranted. [316]

McEachern's ultra-puritanical attitude drives Christmas to express through sexual activity his impulses of defiance and escape, and his longing for some undefinable cessation of his tensions which he calls "peace." Northward and westward, through white communities and black, Christmas journeys on a road which never ends, telling the facts of his Negro origins to the white prostitutes with whom he consorts, trying to absorb their meaning from the black woman whom he takes for a while as wife. Acceptance is not what he seeks, in actuality; had it been, he would have found it, for he is not always turned away. Lacking self-acceptance, he cannot tolerate acceptance by others, even when it is tentatively offered. Over and over he enacts a pattern of defiance and flight, carrying with him his "Calvinistic burden," the heritage of those who have reared him, bearing the psychic weight of multiple rejections—rejection before God, rejection as Negro, rejection as human being. Rigid, solitary, cold, with a latent compulsion toward a joyless violence, he finds "peace" nowhere. At thirty-three, the momentum of his flight propels him into relationship with Joanna, into whose kitchen he breaks to steal food.

Joanna Burden is the granddaughter of Calvin Burden, an anti-slavery agitator from New England, who in the 1880's had been shot by Colonel Sartoris "over a question of Negro voting." She is the daughter of Nathaniel Burden, who had settled in Jefferson during the Reconstruction after having received a commission from the government to come South "to help with the freed Negroes." A spinster, now living alone on the outskirts of Jefferson, she is, like Hines and his wife, disregarded by the townsfolk, who dismiss her as a Yankee, "crazy on the subject of Negroes." She devotes herself primarily to the cause of Negro education. Her voluminous mail consists of correspondence with ". . . the presidents and faculties and trustees . . . and . . . young girl students and even alumnae, of a dozen Negro schools and colleges throughout the South." These schools she also visits, and—in complete disregard of what she knows to be the attitudes of Jefferson—receives alone [317] the Negroes who come to her house seeking educational advice. She gives her personal business affairs, "including her will, with instructions for the disposal of her body after death," into the hands of a Negro lawyer who is a trustee of one of the schools she assists. Negroes come through the woods to her house, bringing dishes of food in expression of their gratitude.

So single-minded a dedication to an inherently good cause deserves admiration; yet, in the terms of the novel Joanna's mission brings about Christmas' "crucifixion," as well as her own violent death. The meaning of this meliorative impulse must therefore be established unmistakably. For its delineation Faulkner uses both the account which Joanna gives Christmas of her forebears and the psychological analysis of Joanna which is implicit in her conduct during the love affair.

The religious orientation of the Burden "mission," suggested in the given name of Joanna's grandfather, is without question its most determining aspect. Calvin Burden, whose early years were spend in New Hampshire, professed Unitarianism, which we associate chiefly with New England and which is the direct historical descendant of Calvinism. Calvin Burden left New Hampshire in the 1820's or 1830's, at a time when New England Unitarianism was a modification of Calvinism only to the extent that it differed on the doctrine of the Trinity and that it placed greater emphasis upon practical Christianity, but its core (the Five Articles, including total depravity) remained essentially the same. Calvin's own father, Nathaniel Burrington,[1] the minister who named his son in honor of the great Protestant reformer, was, of course, a Calvinist. In his home, we may presume, he applied the principles of the older faith with unyielding strictness; young Calvin rebelled at the age of twelve by running away and becoming converted to Catholicism.

In California Calvin spent a year in a Catholic monastery; ten years later, dissatisfied with the stand of the Catholic [318] church on

---

[1] Calvin, nearly illiterate, changed the family name from Burrington to Burden to simplify the spelling.

slavery (he was living in Missouri during the years of agitation over
the repeal of the Missouri Compromise), he turned anti-Catholic,
formally renouncing his allegiance. When his first son was born he felt
the need to revive his original faith. There being no Unitarian meeting-
house in St. Louis, he created a private version of his inherited religion
out of a Spanish Bible he had brought from the mission and from his
memory of the sermons he had heard in his boyhood and in the West,

. . . producing services which interspersed the fine sonorous flowing of
mysticism in a foreign tongue with harsh, extemporized dissertations composed half of the bleak and bloodless logic which he remembered from his
father on interminable New England Sundays, and half of immediate hellfire
and tangible brimstone of which any country Methodist circuit rider would
have been proud.

This perversion of his native faith he inflicted upon his children in
family services in the parlor on Sunday mornings, driving home mainly
two ideas, one theological, in direct descent from the Calvinistic
conception of a god of wrath, and the other social, reflecting the same
furious righteousness: "I'll learn you to hate two things . . . hell and
slaveholders."

Having killed a man in an argument over slavery in St. Louis, he
moved westward to Kansas, where he lost an arm in the bloody civil
strife in the 1850's as a member of a troop of partisan guerillas. He was
much involved in the political aspects of the slavery issue as well,
hating the Democrats, but the basis of his anti-slavery conviction was
essentially religious. On the day of his son's wedding, having had too
much whiskey, he interrupted the ceremony with a speech:

He got off on Lincoln and slavery and dared any man there to deny that
Lincoln and the Negro and Moses and the children of Israel were the same
and that the Red Sea was just the blood that had to be spilled in order that
the black race might cross into the Promised Land.

His son Nathaniel inherited Calvin Burden's anti-Catholic [319]
as well as anti-slavery prejudices, waiting twelve years to legalize his
marriage to his Spanish common-law wife rather than allow a priest to
perform the ceremony and make his twelve-year-old illegitimate son
(also named Calvin) a "heathen." After the war a Washington commission sent him and Calvin Burden to the South to work on behalf of
the freed Negroes. An election day argument with an ex-slaveholder,
Colonel Sartoris, resulted in the killing of both his father and his son.
Whatever fanaticism may have been latent in the man (Joanna
remembers very little about her father as a person) was brought out
by this event, which left him bereft and embittered. He had thoughts
of leaving the South, but the death of his wife deferred the move. He
stayed on, and at fifty married again (this time a woman sent to him

from New Hampshire), and sired Joanna. The broodings of grief and outrage took him often to the secret burial ground of his slain kin, whose deaths he construed as God's will and the curse of Adam expressing themselves in the Southern race problem. This grim philosophy he expounded to Joanna, then four years old:

Your grandfather and brother are laying there, murdered not by one white man but by the curse which God put on a whole race before your grandfather or your brother or me or you were even thought of. A race doomed and cursed to be forever and ever a part of the white race's doom and curse for its sins. Remember that. His doom and his curse. Forever and ever. Mine. Your mother's. Yours, even though you are a child. The curse of every white child that ever was born or ever will be born. None can escape it. . . . Not even you. Least of all, you.

This extreme puritanism, which to the burden of original Biblical transgression added, for the white man, the burden of supporting the Biblical curse God had put on the sons of Ham, was Joanna Burden's religious heritage. Born late in the lives of parents already set in ideas and outlook, she was unduly exposed to these concepts, unduly "shaped" psychologically. Forty years later she recalls for Christmas, in her touching attempt [320] to establish communication with him on terms meaningful to her, the impact made by the great descending weight of this compounded moral responsibility upon her childish soul:

. . . I seemed to see them [Negroes] for the first time not as a people, but as a thing, a shadow in which I lived, we lived, all white people, all other people. I thought of all the children coming forever and ever into the world, white, with the black shadow already falling upon them before they drew breath. And I seemed to see the black shadow in the shape of a cross. And I seemed to see the white babies were struggling, even before they drew breath, to escape from the shadow that was not only upon them but beneath them too, flung out like their arms were flung out, as if they were nailed to the cross. I saw all the babies that would ever be in the world, the ones not yet even born—a long line of them with their arms spread, on the black crosses.

This ghastly vision prefigures her own crucifixion on the black cross of her elected mission, for surely it cannot be doubted that Joanna, any less than Joe, is crucified. Her ugly slaying is no less replete with meanings than Christmas' twenty-year record of theft, assaults, and killings.

But to complete the tracing of a pattern: Joanna's own fanaticism in her mature life is rabid. Prayer is the issue which brings about her murder. In the mounting guilt and remorse of the last phase of her relations with Christmas, she begins to talk to Joe of "hell" and "expiation" and damnation "forever and ever," and to pray privately. Once

Joe submits to staying with her during her ritual of penance, watching her "talk to God as if He were a man in the room with two other men," hearing her naming the obscenities which they had engaged in, for which she believed them both to be damned. After Joe's definite and unshakable refusal to become a Negro lawyer, she insists that he pray with her before proceeding to what is, for her, the only resolution of their torment, joint suicide. When he still remains adamant, she backs the request with a pistol. Her words, reflecting a will which has become absolute under [321] the delusion of having surrendered itself to the Almighty, might be McEachern's: "I don't ask it. It's not I who ask it. Kneel with me."

Two of the occasionally observable concomitants of the more judgmental Protestant sects are suppression of the "soft" emotions and the self-licensing to physical violence in the name of righteousness (often for the outlet of other emotions which have been suppressed). On Christmas' side, the quiescent urge to do something rash has its source and parallel in Hines's murder of Christmas' father, his furious fist-fights, and in McEachern's whippings and onslaught upon the waitress. On Joanna Burden's side the continuity of aggressiveness is even more militant and dangerous. The black pistol with which Joanna threatens Joe had been carried by her grandfather and had been used many times lethally: Joanna's father also had "killed a Mexican who claimed he stole his horse," not to mention the dead or wounded left behind in such enterprises as "helping some Rangers that were cleaning up some kind of mess where some folks had a deputy treed in a dance hall."

Defiance and revolt, as the consequence of a too judicial early training, is no less a pattern in the Burden family than in the life of Joe Christmas. In the former it is given in the bare outlines of family history, in the latter in psychological closeup. Calvin Burden ran away from home at twelve, his son Nathaniel at fourteen. When Nathaniel meets his father again for the first time some sixteen years later, bringing with him his bride, the old man stands ready with the strap to "learn" him not to run away. In Joanna, the affair with Christmas itself symbolizes psychological revenge. Experiencing a hysterical pregnancy in the later stages of the affair, Joanna muses on its value as defiance: "A full measure. Even to a bastard Negro child. I would like to see father's and Calvin's faces."

Sexual repression in modern literature has been associated with New England puritanism so frequently that the meaning of Joanna's sexual conduct with Christmas in the novel hardly requires comment; it is integrally related as a study of the [322] effects of intense and prolonged repression. On the first occasion that Christmas possesses her, "the . . . untearful and unselfpitying and almost manlike yielding of that surrender" leaves him incredulous: "It was as if he struggled with another man for an object of no value to either." The thwarting of femininity in Joanna, shown also in her plain attire and her imperviousness to fear of living without protection against molestation, has been so complete that she is not aroused even when she gives herself. In Christmas' second attempt she has willed assent beforehand, but she manifests no feeling. Infuriated, Christmas possesses her brutally, with the result that she bars the door to him for over a half-year.

In the second phase, her frigidity manifests itself obversely as nymphomania. There has, of course, been no female surrender, and never is. During the months that Joanna had kept herself aloof, the tensions of long-accumulated desire and guilt, heightened by those of the climacteric, break in a fury of lust. Christmas now finds himself an actor in her drama of wild self-damnation, living "not in sin but in filth." The inventions of her polluted mind now so far exceed his primitive education in depravity that he is stunned. Grasping at its meaning beyond simple carnality, he is perhaps aware, Faulkner suggests, "of the abnegation in it . . . ," aware that her "abject fury" is "the New England glacier exposed suddenly to the fire of the New England biblical hell." When remorse begins for Joanna, Christmas observes the wrestling of two personalities within one body with more aloofness, having already acquired detachment by being unfaithful to her on his trips to Memphis. He sees now with greater distinctness the "two sisters" grappling within one psyche: "The cold, contained woman of the first phase, impervious and impregnable . . ." and the one who "in furious denial of that impregnability strove to drown in that black abyss of its own creating that physical purity which had been preserved too long now even to be lost." The "cold, contained" self-directed Joanna of the writing desk and the cotton housedresses is truly the daughter of the widower who [323] at fifty had ordered from New Hampshire a "good New England woman," and "efficient housekeeper," to be sent him for wife and who had married the stranger on the day of her arrival. She is no less the descendant of her grandfather, that strong-willed Puritan, who had declared on the day of his marriage that he "reckoned he'd better settle down"—referring only to his religious wild oats—and who promptly did so, without further spiritual vacillation.

Joanna, at the height of her orgiastic frenzy, cries out in mad exultation "Negro! Negro!," crowning her triumph in evil by compounding miscegenation with lust. The added value which miscegenation has to her as symbolic evil and defiance suggests a descent from Doc Hines, rather than from a family of Abolitionists. In truth, however, the Burden mission is characterized throughout by a curious ambivalence on the subject of the Negro. Calvin Burden, who often risked—and ultimately lost—his life in the fight to achieve equal rights for Negroes as citizens, greeted with "bewildered outrage" the dark-skinned Spanish wife his son had brought from Mexico. She was the image of his own wife, Evangeline, except for her darker complexion. "Damn, lowbuilt black folks," he maundered, "low because of the weight of the wrath of God, black because of the sin of human bondage staining their blood and flesh. But we done freed them now, both black and white alike. They'll bleach out now. . . ."

Nathaniel, also receiving his mission from the Bible, explains more precisely the "Burden" interpretation of the white man's relation to the black man's curse: "The curse of the black race is God's curse. But the curse of the white race is the black man who will be forever God's chosen own because He once cursed him." Having lived in the South longer than his father, however, Nathaniel is less sure that the Negro will eventually "bleach out"; that is, achieve fundamental equality. Joanna must struggle to "raise the shadow"; but, he warns her, "You can never lift it to your level. I see that now, which I did not see until I came down here." [324]

In Joanna, the sense of Joe's "difference" supplants all awareness of him as a person, reducing itself to three formulas governing three patterns of conduct, all different and contradictory: herself in relation to a Negro in the sexual act; herself in relation to him as the white mistress of a Southern household; and herself in relation to him as an agent for his regeneration. The erotic significance to her of his mixed blood has already been indicated. As a tenant of the deserted cabin (a cabin originally built to house the slaves attached to the plantation whose charred ruins lie in the meadow nearby) and as the frequenter of her house, he is a "nigger," in the social sense that this word is used in common Southern parlance. Although she sets food for him in the kitchen, she never stays while he eats or sits while talking to him (with one exception); she never invites him into the house proper or gives him leave to enter any room but the bedroom, with the result that he feels, as he must—with his own acute awareness of Southern pro-priety—a perpetual invader.

As the object of her mission he is nothing human at all; he is the Negro race seen "not as a people, but as a thing." The question that she puts to him when, her lust spent, she resumes her enterprise of racial benevolence with new frenzy ("Do you realize you are wasting your life?"), reverberates with irony backward over the whole narrative of Joe's life. The dramatic impact of these words, addressed to the being whom Faulkner has created for us as Joe Christmas, should be sufficient in itself to guarantee Faulkner's immortality; they belong inscribed over the desk of every compulsive do-gooder. Her subse-quent projects for the reconstruction of his future all center with deadly accuracy upon the wound of Christmas' unresolved identity. Compared to this, the sheriff's strapping of the Negro who refuses to tell what he knows about Miss Burden's affairs when the manhunt for her slayer is on, is the gentlest humanity. The sheriff comprehends that the Negro's stubborn silence is self-protective uncoöperativeness which has become cultural habit; he acts swiftly and decisively to [325] protect him from an immediate danger of mob violence which the latter has undercalculated. The contrast is intended; it is one of the many minor implications of the Burden "mission."

Turning to the Christmas-Burden narrative as a whole to survey its dominant themes, we observe that the most prominent on the psychological level is the devastation wrought by morally willed coldness. The fanaticism depicted is, of course, extreme, so that the consequences in alienation and repression are psychopathological, but the overdrawing sharpens the outlines of a pattern recognizable and recurrent in Western culture as perhaps the greatest single source of personal anguish. Because a disturbed personality of necessity imposes its disturbance upon the world, most often fatefully through its own progeny, no surcease of pain can be optimistically forecast. On this level, the Christmas-Burden narrative is a psychological horror story of unprecedented magnitude.

In its broader social application, the theme of alienation and repression is seen in a variety of ways: in relation to criminal violence in modern culture (the murder itself); to sectional violence (the activities of the Hineses and the Burdens, the Civil War, the continuation of the racial conflict in Southern society); and to international violence (World War I, which Percy Grimm was too young to take part in, so that he expresses his drives in the capture of Christmas instead). The vastness of Faulkner's conception here is suggested in the irony that Christmas, martyred by the austerity of a faith rooted in the Old Testament, becomes a symbol of the suffering endured by Christ in the New. The Judeo-Christian religious tradition, therefore, is seen as embodying in its very origins the will to extreme self-suppression and the need to crucify. Christmas, in his agony, revitalizes for us the symbolic meaning of Christ's death. He does not, of course, share Christ's role as a moral teacher. It is Faulkner as artist, creating Christmas as a person stirring our hearts to pity and love, who transfers the essence of the myth. The Christmas-Burden narrative arouses our tender awareness of human existence as "perpetual crucifixion." [326]

On the historical level, the Christmas-Burden narrative pursues a somewhat different line of inquiry. Faulkner is a Southerner whose acute moral consciousness has stimulated him to grapple more deeply with the problems of his historical past than any other American novelist, and his exploration is singularly searching and exact. The setting of the novel is the contemporary South (1925 or 1926), and the question which Joe's murder of Joanna poses is this: In what light is the violence of the modern South, especially on the Negro issue, to be viewed? The entire novel, naturally, has bearing upon this problem; insofar as the Christmas-Burden conflict alone is concerned, it is clear that Faulkner means to indicate that the extreme Calvinism and white supremacy of Hines are native to the South, but that equally rooted in contemporary Southern culture are influences stemming from New England Calvinism. These influences express themselves as impulses for Negro equality and education but are impaired by an excessive valuation of principle over awareness of the Negro as a human being. Joanna and Joe Christmas are symbols of abstract historical forces which meet and clash on Southern ground. In a certain sense, the representation of Joanna as Northern attributes the causes of Southern disturbance to outsiders—to the North—but the old sectional dispute is bypassed by the balancing of Hines and Joanna as perverted reformers; by the representation of Joanna as isolated from community (both North and South); by the greater share of guilt to be borne by the South through the enthusiasm (no longer religious) of the young white supremacist, Percy Grimm; and by the Southern people themselves, of whom Hightower observes:

Pleasure, ecstasy, they cannot seem to bear: their escape from it is in violence, in drinking and fighting and praying; catastrophe, too, the violence identical and apparently inescapable. *And so why should not their religion drive them to crucifixion of themselves and one another?*[2] [327]

And yet, Hightower's equation of Southern religion with Southern violence is not quite Faulkner's. It is Hightower's own attempt to assume a guilt from which the awareness of history as tragedy must eventually free him. He makes this formulation early in his narrative; later he will progress to a better understanding of the Southern religious problem than this. Faulkner himself, as the artist in command, transcends the crisis of Hightower in the story of Lena and Byron. It is well to remember that neither Byron nor Lena, in whom the hope of the future is vested, is disassociated from religion. Byron used to "spend all day singing in country churches" and Lena's pilgrimage is governed by the faith that "the Lord will see to [it]" that a family will "all be together when a chap comes."

In the Christmas-Burden narrative, which poses the religious and cultural problem to be solved, only the older theological and racial attitudes which linger in the modern South are studied. These attitudes, in their earlier aggressive forms, are not general in the South (neither Doc Hines nor Joanna Burden, in thirty years, becomes part of the Southern communities in which they are tolerated), but their inevitable persistence is a spark igniting the tinder among the populace. As Robert Penn Warren, in the interviews comprising the recent volume, *Segregation,* has a young Southerner state, thereby unwittingly summing up the extent to which the South is a prisoner of its own history: "Race prejudice . . . ain't our hate; it's the hate hung on us by the old folks dead and gone." In *Light in August* Faulkner

---

[2] Faulkner's italics.

probes the relation of this hate to the entire history of Southern religion. The old Calvinism he condemns, but to the complexity of the Southern religious problem in the novel as a whole he does full justice. No contradiction exists between his recognition of the importance of religion in the South, as seen in *Light in August,* and his appeal to his countrymen in a recent article on segregation:

> There are all the voices in fact, except one. That one voice which would adumbrate all into silence, being the superior of all since [328] it is the living articulation and sovereignty of God and the hope and aspiration of man. The Church, which is the strongest unified force in our Southern life since all Southerners are not white and are not democrats, but all Southerners are religious and serve the same God. . . . Where is that voice now? [329]

The Stillness of *Light in August*

ALFRED KAZIN

Light in August BEGINS UNFORGETTABLY WITH A PREGNANT WOMAN FROM Alabama sitting beside a road in Mississippi, her feet in a ditch, her shoes in her hand, watching a wagon that is mounting the hill toward her with a noise that carries for a half mile "across the hot still pine-winey silence of the August afternoon." She has been on the road for a month, riding in a long succession of farmwagons or walking the hot dusty roads with her shoes in her hand, trying to get to Jefferson. There, she firmly expects, she will find her lover working in a planing mill and ready to marry her, and there—that is the big city—she will put her shoes on at last.

This opening chapter, so dry and loving in its pastoral [257] humor, centering on the picture of Lena and her precious burden being carried in one wagon or another, by one farmer after another, to her hoped-for destination in a husband, ends sharply on the outskirts of Jefferson, from which she can see smoke going up from a burning house. It is the house of Joanna Burden, who has just been murdered by Joe Christmas. The images that have crowded us—the dust and heat of the unending road; the young woman continually amazed at how far a body can go; the serenity of her face, "calm as a stone, but not hard"; the "sharp and brittle crack and clatter" of identical and anonymous wagons "weathered and ungreased wood and metal"; the mules plodding in a steady and unflagging hypnosis; the drowsy heat of the afternoon; Lena's faded blue dress, her palm leaf fan, her small bundle in which she carries thirty-five cents in nickels and dimes, and the shoes that she takes off and carries in her hand as soon as she feels the dust of the road beneath her feet—all these, we soon discover, provide us with that foundation in the local and the provincial, the earth and the road which man must travel on it, against which are set images of fire and murder, of aimless wandering and of flight, embodied in the figure who soon enters the book and dominates it in his remorseless gray anonymity. Joe Christmas does not even have a name of his own, only a mocking label stuck on him at the orphanage where he was deposited one Christmas Eve. "Joe Christmas" is worse than any real name could be, for it indicates not only that he has no background, no roots, no name of his own, but that he is regarded as a *tabula rasa,* a white sheet of paper on which anyone can write out an identity for him and make him believe it.

It is the contrast of Lena Grove and Joe Christmas, of [258] the country girl and the American wanderer, who is a stranger even to himself, the ultimate personification of modern loneliness, that frames the book—literally so, since Lena Grove begins and ends it, while Joe Christmas' agony and crucifixion are enacted as within a circle round which he runs in an effort to catch up with himself. When he finds that he cannot run out of this circle and stands still at last in order to die, the book comes back to Lena Grove and ends on her ritualistic procession up the road with her baby and Byron Bunch—Faulkner's version of the Holy Family. By the time we have finished *Light in August,* we have come to feel that the real greatness of Faulkner in this book (and indeed of his extraordinary compassion) lies in the amazing depth which he brings to this contrast of which American writers—particularly in the South—are so fond: between the natural and the urban, between Lena Grove's simplicity and the world in which Joe Christmas walks all city pavements with the same isolation and indifference, eats at the coldly smooth wooden counter, and is murdered. Faulkner even leads up to a strange and tortured fantasy of Joe Christmas as Lena Grove's still unnamed son. There is virtually an annunciation to Lena, in the moving last phase of the book when Lena, delivered of her child just as Joe Christmas is running for his life, hears Mrs. Hines, Christmas's grandmother, calling the baby "Joey"—he who is a "nigger" murderer, and whom Lena has never seen. The reader comes to this with a shock, only because of Faulkner's reckless, desperate eagerness to wrest all the possible implications from his material, to think it out interminably, since there is no end to all one's possible meditations round and round the human cycle. One of the conflicts of which the book is made—between life and [259] anti-life, between the spirit of birth and the murderous abstractions and obsessions which drive most of the characters—is in Faulkner himself, in his attempt to will his painful material into a kind of harmony that it does not really possess.

But in any event, it is Lena who opens the book, Lena's world,

Lena's patience, that set the ideal behind the book—that world of the permanent and the natural which Joe Christmas seeks all his life without knowing that he does, and seeking it, runs full tilt into the ground. "Light in August" is itself a country saying: light as a mare or cow is light after delivery. And it is this world of Lena Grove from Doane's Mill—the tiny hamlet too small for any post-office list, though Lena, living in the backwoods, had not seen it until her parents died— with the sound of the wagon wheel taking her away from it, that becomes in the book not merely a world that Faulkner celebrates but a mythic source of strength. As indeed it is. For it is this intense sense of the earth, this superb registering of country sights and sounds as the stillness is broken by the creaking and lumbering wagon coming up the hill, that is the secret of Southern writing. In his attachment to the irretrievable, in his obstinate feeling for the earth, the good Southern writer makes so much writing in America seem as shallow as if it had been composed by a young instructor in English sitting in his study surrounded by manuals on the great novels. Albert Camus, talking appreciatively about Southern novelists, once remarked to a friend of mine that what he liked about their books was "the dust and the heat." And to the man from North Africa, with his memories of the blazing world described in *Noces*, that world into which Paris can never enter, Faulkner's sense of local color must be especially [260] moving. But after all, it is this sense of place that is the great thing about American writing. It is the "mossy scabs of the worm fence, heap'd stones, elder, mullein and pokeweed" in *Song of Myself;* the landscape that in *Walden* seems always to be reflected in water; the strong native sense of the here and now that is the basis of Emerson's esthetic; the edge of the world seen from Hemingway's Michigan woods; "reading the river" in *Life on the Mississippi* and *Huckleberry Finn;* the "snow, the real snow" seen only beyond Chicago that Scott Fitzgerald described so rapturously in his memories of Midwesterners in Eastern colleges going home for Christmas. And if we ask what is so remarkable about that sense of place which is, after all, essential to imaginative writing, the answer is that we Americans are in fact just the opposite of the homogeneous mass we are always trying to be, and that what distinguishes American writing is exactly the fact that we are strangers to each other and that each writer describes his own world to strangers living in the same land with himself.

Now of all parts of the United States the South is certainly the strangest to the others; it is, in fact—or used to be—a separate nation. And almost all the good Southern writers have this sense of local color to an extreme, for to the degree that the South is what it is because of its rural background, its "backwardness," its isolation, its comparatively homogeneous white population—to that degree does the American's need to value and venerate his own region or place as the only escape from American bigness, American smoothness, American abstractness, American slogans, the juggernaut of American progress, find (at least it used to find) its deepest expression in the South. Even poverty, which in America certainly is a disgrace, becomes [261] in Southern writing a sign of the natural man (Huckleberry Finn) or the earth-mother (Lena Grove). And, as so often happens in Southern writing—for sensitive Southerners are likely to feel that they are lost in the modern industrial world and, in mourning their traditional homeland, to see the immediate world around them as damned—Faulkner's pictures of the impersonal modern world, the opposite of Lena's sacred grove, are lurid. As Lena is all fertility, so the others are all barrenness. Destruction, fire, obsession, inhumanity, anonymity, the "friction-smooth" wooden counter at which Joe Christmas eats, the hard cold eyes of Bobbie the prostitute and Mame the madam and Max the pimp—these against the images of locality, the farmers in their faded and patched but clean overalls, and of time, the wagon along the road and the "heelgnawed porch" of the country store around which farmers sit. As soon as we get to Jefferson, we catch the typical dialectic of life and anti-life, the contrast of birth and destruction on which the book is built, in the fact that the slow patient rhythms of Lena, the wagon, the road, are immediately followed by the whine of the saw in the planing mill, the reiteration of *smooth*. The world is narrowing down to the contest between the good Christian laborer, Byron Bunch, the very essence of the common ordinary good man, and those who, like Lena's seducer, have either taken on a name which is not their own, "Brown," a name too conventional even to be *his* name, or who, like Joe Christmas, have no name to begin with.

This contrast is familiar enough in Southern opinion, and one can find the same horror of miscegenation, of uprooting, of the city man's anonymity, in any expression of Southern agrarianism. But Faulkner does not stop at the abstraction of the alien: he carries it on, he carries it out [262] to astonishing lengths. And it is this intensity of conception that makes the portrait of Joe Christmas so compelling rather than believable, that makes him a source of wonder, of horror, yet above all of pity, rather than of pleasure in the creation of a real human being. For Joe Christmas remains, as he is born, an abstraction; from the moment he appears, "there was something definitely rootless about him, as though no town nor city was his, no street, no walls, no square of earth his home." He comes to work in the only clothes he has, a serge suit and a white shirt; and Bryon Bunch, watching him, knows that Joe Christmas "carried his knowledge with him always as though it were a banner, with a quality ruthless, lonely, and almost proud." So from the moment Joe Christmas appears, he is seen as what others say about him, he is only a thought in other people's minds. More than this, he is looked at always from a distance, as if he were not quite human, which in many ways he is not.

We see Joe Christmas from a distance, and this distance is the

actual space between him and his fellows. It is also the distance
between the name "Joe Christmas," which is clownish, and the actual
suffering of someone who has to live up to the non-humanity of his
name, to the obsession (founded on hearsay, not on actual evidence)
that his father had "some" Negro blood in him. Joe Christmas, then, is
really "man" trying to discover the particular kind of man he is. He is
an abstraction created by the racist mania of his grandfather, a former
preacher whose tormented life is spent insisting that Negroes are
guilty in the eyes of God and must serve white men. When his
daughter ran away with a "Mexican" circus hand, Doc Hines not only
killed the man, and after his daughter died in childbirth on Christmas
Eve, left the baby on the steps of an orphanage, but [263] later took a
job as a janitor in the orphanage in order to make sure that his "nigger"
grandson would never be allowed to contaminate anyone. This obsession about race goes hand in hand with a Calvinist obsession of the
elect and of the hopeless sinfulness of others, an obsession which is
found both in Joe Christmas' rigidly doctrinaire foster-father, Calvin
McEachern, and in his future mistress, Joanna Burden, a descendant
of New Hampshire Puritans who remains in the South though she is
the sworn enemy of its ways. All these obsessions about purity and
guilt are, Faulkner indicates, the remnants of an inhuman religion that
has added bigotry and arrogance to the curse of slavery. They are the
symbols of a church that has lost its spiritual function and that has
been deserted by the Reverend Gail Hightower, who spends his days
in endless reveries of the South's irretrievable glory. The obsessions are
all summed up in the fate of Joe Christmas, who is trying to become
someone, a human being, to find the integrity that is so ripely present
in Lena Grove. Lena does not have to try; her symbol is the wheel on
the road. Joe Christmas' is flight: flight on the same road, but flight
toward himself, which he cannot reach, and away from hatred of
himself, which he cannot escape. Only his pursuers catch up with him,
to murder and to castrate him.

Joe Christmas is an abstraction seeking to become a human being.
In the race-mad South, many a Negro—and Mexican, and Jew—is
turned into an abstraction. But this man is *born* an abstraction and is
seeking to become a person. He is an orphan, brought up in a found-
ling home, who in earliest childhood is watched by his own grandfather as if he were a caged beast. He is then bribed by the dietitian,
whom he has heard making love with the intern, as [264] if he knew
enough to betray her. He is adopted by a farmer who re-names him,
lectures him, starves him, beats him for not learning the catechism. He
is robbed and beaten by the pimp of the prostitute with whom he has
fallen in love. He is constantly treated by his Negrophile mistress,
Joanna Burden, as if his own personality were of no account and is
beseeched in her sexual transports as "Negro." And finally, after being
starved, betrayed, flogged, beaten, pursued by bloodhounds, he is

castrated. The essential picture behind Joe Christmas is his grand-father's carrying him to the orphanage and then from it in a savage parody of loving care. Joe Christmas is nothing but the man things are done to, the man who has no free will of his own, who is constantly seeking a moment of rest ("When have I ever eaten in peace?") and who looks for an identity by deliberately provoking responses that will let him be *someone,* if only as a white man among Negroes, or as someone calling himself a Negro in an effort to shock the white prostitute he has just slept with. His passivity, his ability to lend himself to situations and to people who will "carry" him for a while, is immense and pitiful.

Joe Christmas is the most solitary character in American fiction, the most extreme phase conceivable of American loneliness. He is never seen full face, but always as a silhouette, a dark shadow haunting others, a shadow upon the road he constantly runs—a foreshadowing of his crucifixion, which, so terrible and concentrated is his suffering, already haunts the lives of others like a black shadow. For, almost *because* he does not look it, he becomes the "Negro," or the thought of, the obsession with, Negroes in the minds of those who, looking at Joe Christmas, can think of nothing else. And Joanna Burden, whose abolitionist grandfather [265] was murdered in the South, whose whole life has been an obstinate carrying on, deep inside Mississippi, of her family's coldly abstract espousal of Negroes, shows us how much of an abstraction Joe Christmas is when she makes love crying to him "Negro! Negro!" Whether the "Negro" represents the white man's guilt or the white man's fear, he is always a thought in the white's mind, and—in the South—an obsession. So Joanna Burden, who befriends him, and Doc Hines, who hates him, come to see in him the cause of guilt that is finally the image of guilt. "I thought," Joanna says to her lover,

of all the children coming forever and ever into the world, white, with the black shadow already falling upon them before they drew breath. And I seemed to see the black shadow in the shape of a cross. And it seemed like the white babies were struggling, even before they drew breath, to escape from the shadow that was not only upon them but beneath them, too, flung out like their arms were flung out, as if they were nailed to the cross.

And she quotes her father:

"In order to rise, you must raise the shadow with you. But you can never lift it to your level. I see that now, which I did not see until I came down here. But escape it you cannot. The curse of the black race is God's curse. But the curse of the white race is the black man who will be forever God's chosen own because He once cursed Him."

The grounds of this obsession, then, can be a compassion for the Negro that is as profound as hatred, and equally removed from brotherhood. This compassion seems to me the essence of Faulkner's approach to Joe Christmas, and the triumph of the book is Faulkner's ability to keep his [266] leading character a shadow, and yet to make us feel all his suffering. Compare Joe Christmas with the types of the Northerner, the city man, the "stranger" in Southern writing, to say nothing of the Negro, and you realize that where so many neo-orthodox Southern literary critics are hysterically fearful of the "stranger," Faulkner, by a tremendous and moving act of imagination, has found in Joe Christmas the incarnation of "man"—that is, of modern man, reduced entirely to his unsupported and inexplicable human feelings. There are no gods in Faulkner's world; there are only men—some entirely subject to circumstances, some protesting against them, and some even moved to change them. The hero of *A Fable* is of the last; Joe Christmas is of the first. He is human to us because of the experiences he undergoes, but his passivity is so great that he is finally a body castrated, a mere corpse on a dissection table—or someone whose body has been turned into the host, material for a ritual, so that his last agony will earn him the respect he never earned while he was alive. He is not, like the Christ of *A Fable*, a man who gives new meaning to life; like Benjy in *The Sound and the Fury*, he is an incarnation of human suffering, unable to speak—except in the tremendous action near the end of the book when he stops running from his pursuers and waits for them, and attains in this first moment of selfhood, the martyrdom that ends it.

We see Joe Christmas always from a distance. This distance from ourselves to him seems to me the key to the book, for it explains why Joe exists for us principally as a man who is described, not seen. He is so far away that we cannot see him; he is reported to us. And this distance is filled with the stillness of a continuous meditation. [267] *Light in August* tells a story of violence, but the book itself is curiously soundless, for it is full of people thinking to themselves about events past. As soon as Lena Grove arrives in Jefferson, at the end of the first chapter, the story of Joe Christmas comes to us through flashbacks, through talk by the other men at the planing mill, through a whole chapter of summary biography, Chapter VI, through rumors and gossip of the townspeople, and at the very end, when Joe Christmas' whole story is put together for us, by Gavin Stevens' telling a stranger about the grandparents. Almost everything we learn about Joe Christmas comes to us in the form of hearsay, accusation, the tortured memories of others; even his death is told as an incident in the life of his murderer, Percy Grimm. All these reports about the stranger sufficiently suggest his alienation. But in themselves they also create that stillness, that depth of meditation into which all the characters are plunged.

This meditation begins in Joe Christmas himself, who in his distance from other men is constantly trying to think himself back to life, and who, without knowing exactly how his ordeal began—and certainly not why—finds himself like a caged animal going over and over the same ground. We hear him talking to himself, and we follow his slow and puzzled efforts to understand the effect of his actions upon others. We see him as a child in the orphanage, eating the toothpaste, frightening the dietitian out of her wits because he is staring straight at her trying to understand what she is accusing him of. We watch him walking the path between his cabin and Joanna Burden's house for his meals, thinking out everything he finds between the four walls of her kitchen. Finally we watch him running, and thinking deliriously in his flight, until, in that magnificent and piercing [268] scene near the end of his flight, he falls asleep as he runs. The pressure of thought, the torture of thought, is overwhelming—and useless—since Joe Christmas does not know who he is and so cannot locate the first cause of his misery. But still he thinks, he broods, he watches, he waits. And it is this brooding silence in him, fixed in attention over he knows not what, that explains why he is so often described in the book as looking like a man in prayer—even like a "monk." There is a strange and disturbing stillness about him that eases him, more swiftly than most men, into the stillness of non-being.

The stillness of the book has, of course, an immense reverberation within it. Describing Doc Hines, Faulkner notes about him "a quality of outworn violence like a scent, an odor," and the actual violence of Joe Christmas is always felt about him even when he sits rigidly still at counters like a man in prayer. When Joe's past history is run off in the rapid newsreel style of Dos Pasos, one feels not only his personal insignificance, but the just leashed violence of American life of which Joe is, in his way, completely the creature:

He stepped from the dark porch, into the moonlight, and with his bloody head and his empty stomach hot, savage, and courageous with whiskey, he entered the street which was to run for fifteen years.

The whiskey died away in time and was renewed and died again, but the street ran on. From that night the thousand streets ran as one street, with imperceptible corners and changes of scene, broken by intervals of begged and stolen rides, on trains and trucks, and on country wagons with he at twenty and twenty-five and thirty sitting on the seat with his still, hard face and the clothes [269] (even when soiled and worn) of a city man and the driver of the wagon not knowing who or what the passenger was and not daring to ask.

Yet it is a stillness of thought that generally pervades the book, in the form of enormous meditations by which Faulkner tries to lift his material into place. The stillness is interrupted by shooting, burning, beating, the barking of bloodhounds and Percy Grimm's mutilation of Joe Christmas, which interrupts the pervading stillness like the sound which nails must make when they are driven into wood through human flesh. Yet, just behind this obvious figure of the Roman soldier torturing Christ, there is a pastoral world. As Irving Howe has noted, the arrangement of the book "resembles an early Renaissance painting—in the foreground a bleeding martyr, far to the rear a scene of bucolic peacefulness, with women quietly working in the fields." Despite its violence, *Light in August* is one of the few American novels that remind one of the humanized and tranquil landscape in European novels. Its stillness is rooted in the peaceful and timeless world which Lena Grove personifies and in which she has her being. It is the stillness of the personal darkness inside which Joe Christmas lives. But his stillness is also the sickly, after-dark silence of the Reverend Gail Hightower sitting in his study, with his stale clothes and stale thoughts, going over and over the tragedy of his life, his grandfather's "glorious" death, his wife's desertion and suicide—and finally and typically summing it all up into a stale round of human illusion and defeat. Faulkner wishes us to understand that Hightower finally cuts the gordian knot of his thoughts when he delivers Lena's baby and is struck down by Percy Grimm as he stands between him and Joe Christmas. But Hightower, whether brooding out [270] upon the street, or sitting behind the green lamp in his parlor when he receives Byron Bunch, his only visitor, enlarges the stillness, increases its weight, by personifying what is immediately present in the book, and throughout Faulkner's novels—the Southern effort to explain, to justify, and through some consummation in violent physical action even to lighten, the burden of this obsession with the past.

Hightower, by general consent, is one of the failures of the book: he is too vague, too drooping, too formless, in a word too much the creature of defeat and of obsession, to compel our interest or our belief. But this is so partly because Hightower is both a surrogate figure for Faulkner's meditations and a kind of scapegoat on whom Faulkner can discharge his exasperation with Southern nostalgia and the endless searching in the labyrinths of the past for the explanation of the Southern defeat and of the hold it keeps on the descendants of the Confederate aristocracy. Hightower is a failure because Faulkner both uses and parodies him. Because of the absurdly literal symbolism of his name, his constant watchful position behind the green lamp, his useless reveries, he is never on the same scale with the other characters, who are equally obsessed by the past, but who function on the plane of some positive action. Hightower not only lives by his thoughts; he has no life but his thoughts. We miss in him the life-like element of violence (the only possible end to characters so entirely formed of reverie) that we find in Joanna Burden's degeneration, in Joe Christmas' hatred, in Percy Grimm's fanaticism, in Doc Hines's mania. Hightower, acting in various sections of the book as a foreground observer, brings to them not merely a stillness but a deadness which intervenes between us and the other characters. This shapeless, ghostly body of [271] thought has its symbolic place in the mind of Hightower. For just as his life is over, and he has no function but to brood, so Faulkner has signified in Hightower that wholly retrospective, watchful concern, not with the past but with their bondage to the past, that seems to be the essence of what Faulkner's characters are always thinking about.

Joe Christmas, Joanna Burden, Gail Hightower—each of these is the prisoner of his own history, and is trying to come to terms with this servitude in his own mind. None of them can ever lift themselves out of the labyrinth by taking thought. But in this effort to think man's life out of the circumstances that enclose it, Faulkner sees the condition of man. Man is engulfed in events that are always too much for him. Hightower, listening to Byron Bunch make plans for Lena's confinement, thinks: "It is because so much happens. Too much happens. That's it. Man performs, engenders, so much more than he can or should have to bear. That's how he finds out that he can bear anything. That's it. That's what is so terrible. That he can bear anything, anything." Endurance, as we know, is the key-word in Faulkner's system of values. At least this was so up to *A Fable*. There, as Faulkner himself has told us, the highest value is represented not by the young Jewish pilot officer who says, "This is terrible. I refuse to accept it, even if I must refuse life to do so"; not by the old French quartermaster general who says, "This is terrible, but we can weep and bear it," but by the English battalion runner who says, "This is terrible, I'm going to do something about it." *Light in August* does not arrive at this step. Man never thinks of changing the world; it is all he can do to get a grip on it, to understand some part of what has happened to him and to endure all of it. Any release that occurs is a [272] purely individual one, as when Hightower finally frees himself, in the one profoundly unselfish act of his life, by delivering Lena's baby. In the freshness of the early morning, after Lena has given birth, Hightower feels that he is in touch with the earth again—the symbol throughout the book of rightness, authenticity, peace. But the earth is not his life, as it is Lena Grove's. Man's highest aim in this book is to meet his destiny without everlasting self-concern. Yet this profoundly tragic cast to *Light in August*, so much like a Hardy novel in the implacable pattern that unrolls against a country background and the inarticulate stillness of its leading characters, is matched by Faulkner's ironic awareness that man, in his endless brooding over events, can never stop, that the event is nothing compared with the speculation that follows and in a sense replaces it. One of the most revealing phrases in Faulkner's rhetoric is: "not that"—it is not peace, not an end, that his people ever want. The violence may be "outworn," but it is the human passion. He describes his chorus, the townspeople, scurrying around Joanna Burden's house after her murder, looking "for someone to crucify":

But there wasn't anybody. She had lived such a quiet life, attended so to her own affairs, that she bequeathed to the town in which she had been born and lived and died a foreigner, an outlander, a kind of heritage of astonishment and outrage, for which, even though she had supplied them at last with an emotional barbecue, a Roman holiday almost, they would never forgive her and let her be dead in peace and quiet. Not that. Peace is not that often. So they moiled and clotted, believing that the flames, the blood, the body that had died three years ago and had now just begun to live [273] again, cried out for vengeance, not believing that the rapt infury of the flames and the immobility of the body were both affirmations of an attained bourne beyond the hurt and harm of man. Not that.

We can never let the event go, for that would mean an end to the human history that is lived in retrospection. Just as Faulkner's language is full of words, like "avatar" and "outrage," which are really private symbols left over from his unceasing meditation, and just as his style is formed from the fierce inner pressure of problems which give no solution, so the actual texture of *Light in August* suggests, in the tension and repetition of certain verbal motifs, that man can never quite say what the event originally meant, or what he is to think of it now. Language never quite comes up to the meaning of events. To adapt Faulkner's phrase, it is not that, or that. The townspeople exist in *Light in August,* as in so many Faulkner novels, to ask questions whose very function is to deny the possibility of an answer. Faulkner's grim, sarcastic asides show that he views language as in some basic sense unavailing. The astounding repetition of certain key phrases and verbal rhythms in his work signifies his return back and back on the question.

Call the event history, call it the Fall: man is forever engaged in meditating, not the past itself, for that would bring knowledge, but man's guilt, for that may bring freedom. Guilt, not history, is the nightmare from which all of Faulkner's deepest characters are trying to escape. The guilt arises from man's endless complicity in his own history, as when the innocent, gravely staring child that Joe Christmas was, ate toothpaste and listened to the dietitian making love. Hightower is guilty because his sickly, foolish [274] nostalgia for his grandfather's one day of glory made him unavailable to his own wife, who committed suicide; Joanna Burden feels so guilty that she has remained an alien in the Southern town in which she was born, accepting her isolation as the price of her identification both with her Abolitionist forebears, who were shot down in the South, and with the Negroes, on whom a curse must have been laid. Even Doc Hines and Percy Grimm murder in order to "clean" life of the stain that Negroes have put on it, for as the Negroes were cursed by God, so they have cursed life, and the maniac "saviors" of Southern racial purity have to save their hallowed country from contagion. But just as no one of them can really distinguish the hate they feel for others from self-accusation, so no one can say with whom guilt began, where the ultimate human crime was committed. The paths which lead back to the human past are endless through the human brain, and sitting at his study window after he has gained new self-respect by delivering Lena's baby and by standing up to Percy Grimm, the dying Hightower still ruminates, goes over and over the past, as "the final copper light of afternoon fades" and "the world hangs in a green suspension in color and texture like through colored glass." The everlasting reverie begins again, but now the wheel of life that brought Lena Grove to Jefferson begins to slow down, runs into sand, "the axle, the vehicle, the power which propels it not yet aware." These memories are endless and the style in which they are described is over-colored in a way that shows how static action often becomes in Faulkner's work, how much it serves as the raw material for reflection, which is why he can lavish so many Joycean compound words on objects which do not seem to move of their own accord, but to be rallying points in Faulkner's tortured concern with guilt.[275]

Guilt is endless; in the labyrinths of the mind, there is turning, but no deliverance. Like T. S. Eliot, Faulkner is a favorite today because he takes his stand on human guilt; this is the side of ourselves that we can recognize, and, curiously, stand by; for in this alone, as we feel, is the possibility of our freedom. When men feel so wretchedly small before their own past, they must be guilty. So runs the legend. This is the argument behind Faulkner's novels: of the God who made Yokna-patawpha County. In the beginning, life was free and good and natural; but something inexplicable, a curse, was put on it. Perhaps the curse is nothing more than man's effort to get the better of events that are "too much for us"; the evil lies in arrogance. Doc Hines hears God addressing him personally, ordering him to act for Him. Calvin Mc-Eachern, Joe Christmas' adopted father, starves and beats him because he cannot memorize portions of the catechism on order. "He asked that the child's stubborn heart be softened and that the sin of disobedience be forgiven him also, through the advocacy of the man whom he had flouted and disobeyed, requesting that the Almighty be as magnani-mous as himself, and by and through and because of conscious grace." Even Joanna Burden tries to play God to her Negro charges. *Light in August* is one of the sharpest criticisms of Calvinism ever written, but unlike so many Southern writers on Puritanism, Faulkner knows that the same religion is found in Doc Hines and Joanna Burden. The guilt that is the mainstay of their faith is embodied in the assumption of excessive authority by fathers, law-givers, teachers, ministers. Everyone wants to play God to the orphan Joe Christmas. In Faulk-ner's eyes, life is an ironic and tragic affair that is beyond human rule and mis-rule; but Calvinists [276] like Doc Hines and Calvin Mc-Eachern, the children of Calvinists like Joanna Burden, even murder-ing simon-pure "patriots" like Percy Grimm, take life in their hands, they dominate and they murder. Joe Christmas is their favorite pupil; he is the man "things are done to." His final ignominy comes when his mistress, Joanna Burden, regarding him in her new phase as a Negro charge to be "brought up," tells him that she wants him to go to school so that he can become a lawyer. And it is at this point that he breaks. It is this point that has always been the signature of the everlasting victim. Other men are the law-givers; the law is passed out to him, through him, inflicted on him. And so finally he murders and dies, a pure victim, shot, castrated, treated like a thing. It is the final ignominy. But in the very unattainability of his suffering, in its inexpressibility, is the key to his healing power over others. For where life exists so much in the relation of master to man, of the elect to the sinner, the only possible consummation man can ever reach, for Joe Christmas as for Uncle Tom, is in the final consistency of his suffering, in a fate so extreme that it becomes a single human word which men can read. This is what Faulkner means in that exalted passage after Joe Christmas' immolation:

. . . when they saw what Grimm was doing one of the men gave a choked cry and stumbled back into the wall and began to vomit. Then Grimm too sprang back, flinging behind him the bloody butcher knife. "Now you'll let white women alone, even in hell," he said. But the man on the floor had not moved. He just lay there, with his eyes open and empty of everything save consciousness, and with something, a shadow, about his mouth. For a long moment he looked up at [277] them with peaceful and unfathomable and unbearable eyes. Then his face, body, all, seemed to collapse, to fall in upon itself, and from out the slashed garments about his hips and loins the pent black blood seemed to rush like a released breath. It seemed to rush out of his pale body like the rush of sparks from a rising rocket; upon that black blast the man seemed to rise soaring into their memories forever and ever. They are not to lose it, in whatever peaceful valleys, beside whatever placid and reassuring streams of old age, in the mirroring faces of whatever children they will contemplate old disasters and newer hopes. It will be there, musing, quiet, steadfast, not fading and not particularly threatful, but of itself alone serene, of itself alone triumphant.

Joe Christmas has attained the stillness that will finally allow us to see him. Of sufferings alone is he made, and in this sense, and in this sense alone, is he a figure whose condition is so total that he reminds us of Christ in the sense of Christ's integrality. That tortured and would-be Christian philosopher, Simone Weil, understood this when she found that *malheur*, affliction, could become so much in itself that she felt riven to the universe by bonds of pain. The arch-victim may not be a "martyr," as students of totalitarianism have noticed; but there is a kind of suffering in our time which is so extreme that it becomes an integral *fact* of the human condition. Father Zossima bowed down to Dmitri Karamazov because of all the affliction he would undergo. So marvellous is Faulkner's compassion, he can visualize in the man who was nothing but a victim, the shadow thrown from the Cross of Christ, who was nothing, as it were, but Himself. Men are men because events are always "too much" for them; Joe Christmas became one [278] with his life in that extreme moment when even he had no longer to search out the past. The figure on the Cross is the most tremendous interventive symbol in history; the castrated man on the floor has only one free power in his life—to stop running at last and to face his murderer. Faulkner intends no parody; he is moved by the likeness of totality to totality. But neither is he a Christian. There is no redemption; there is not even in A Fable—but there man has the courage to redeem circumstances by denying their fatality. In Light in August, the past is not merely exigent; it is malicious, the spirit of pure bad luck, a god-like force that confronts man at every turn with everything he has been, and so seems to mock and to oppose him. This spirit is called "The Player": Lena's seducer, "Brown," still running away from her at the last, sends a Negro boy to the sheriff for the reward money he has earned in informing on Joe Christmas, but knows despairingly that he will never see the money.

"He wont do it. He cant do it. I know he cant find him, cant get it, bring it back." He called no names, thought no names. It seemed to him now that they were all just shapes like chessmen—the negro, the sheriff, the money, all—unpredictable and without reason moved here and there by an Opponent who could read his moves before he made them and who created spontaneous rules which he and not the Opponent, must follow.

This is the Opponent that Joe Christmas decides finally not to elude again, the "Player" who moves Percy Grimm unerringly from position to position:

He was beside the ditch now. He stopped, motionless in midstride. Above the blunt, cold rake [279] of the automatic his face had that serene, unearthly luminousness of angels in church windows. He was moving again almost before he had stopped, with that lean, swift, blind obedience to whatever Player moved him on the Board. He ran to the ditch.

All things are fated; man is in any place because the Player moved him there. Our past sets up the positions into which we fall. This is why Joe Christmas' grandmother, Mrs. Hines, utters the most significant lines in the book when, at the end, she pitifully cries:

"I am not saying that he never did what they say he did. Ought not to suffer for it like he made them that loved and lost suffer. But if folks could maybe just let him for one day. Like it hadn't happened yet. Like the world never had anything against him yet. Then it could be like he had just went on a trip and grew man grown and come back. If it could be like that for just one day."

And it is in these terms that we come to understand why Joe Christmas, in running away from a past that he cannot escape, seems constantly to be looking back as he runs. Not only is no one free of his past; he even has, at the most critical moments, the sense of not moving at all, but of being silently lifted from position to position. It is because of this curious effect of immobility in Faulkner's characters as they run (as if they were held up in the air by wires) that Faulkner can lavish such idle poetic largesse upon them: can see in a Percy Grimm that "serene, unearthly luminousness of angels in church windows," and at various points throughout the book emphasized Joe Christmas' rigid likeness to a man in prayer. Even the countrymen in overalls move at one point "with almost the air of monks in a [280] cloister." The reason is that all these characters are lost in contemplation as they are moved here and there by the Player. There is no free action for anyone; everyone is carried, as Lena Grove was carried to Jefferson in a whole succession of farmwagons, by the fate that was and so shall be.

Faulkner's world is grim—a world in which the past exerts an irresistible force, but against which there is no supernatural sanction, no redeeming belief. He believes in original sin, but not in divine love, and he is endlessly bemused by the human effort to read fate or to avoid it. The highest reach of his belief is the effort to become "a saint without God" (Albert Camus), but this is a point not yet tried for in *Light in August*. Correspondingly, there is great power in his work, but little color, and *Light in August*, for all its brilliance, somehow wears the lack-lustre look of the year in which it was published, 1932. It is a grim book, and the countryside described in it already has the pinched, rotted look that one sees in so many depression novels about the South. The greatest fault of the book is its over-schematic, intellectualized past. Although Faulkner himself has lived more like Joe Christmas than like the Sartorises, he is socially far from the world of Joe Christmas and Lena Grove, and there are tell-tale signs in the novel that it is written *down*—for Faulkner, too much from his head down, and about people whom he tends to generalize and to overpraise, as if he saw them only as symbols rather than as entirely complex beings. And it is a simple fact that the opening of *Light in August* is so beautiful that nothing after quite comes up to it.

On the other hand, it is one of Faulkner's greatest [281] books, and although it does not have the blazing directness of *The Sound and the Fury* (a book written more directly out of Faulkner's own experience), it has much of the creative audacity which is Faulkner's highest ideal in art. With this book, published in 1932, Faulkner completed a period of extraordinary fertility. He was only thirty-five; since 1929, he had published, in rapid order, *Sartoris, The Sound and the Fury, As I Lay Dying, Sanctuary,* and *Light in August*. It was a period of tremendous creative power. When he was recently in Japan, Faulkner said of this period:

I think there's a period in a writer's life when he, well, simply for lack of any other word, is fertile and he just produces. Later on, his blood slows, his bones get a little more brittle, his muscles get a little stiff, he gets perhaps other interests, but I think there's one time in his life when he writes at the top of his talent plus his speed, too. Later the speed slows; the talent doesn't necessarily have to fade at the same time. But there's a time in his life, one matchless time, when they are matched completely. The speed, and the power and the talent, they're all there and then he is . . . 'hot.'

Light in August comes out of that "one matchless time." The only possible objection one can have to the book is the number of implications which Faulkner tries to bring out of his material—for just as the characters' own lives are "set" for them to mull over, so Faulkner constantly mulls over them, wringing a poetry that has grandeur but also an intensity of contemplation that is sometimes more furious in expression than meaningful in content. If we see Faulkner's narrative method as essentially recollective, in the form of individual meditation over past [282] events, we can recognize the advantage he has over most "naturalistic" writers and we understand why Faulkner refers to himself as a "poet." For what makes the portrait of Joe Christmas so astonishing is the energy of imagination lavished upon it, the consistency of texture that derives from the poet's sense that he has not only to *show,* in the modern realistic sense, but to *say*—that is, to tell a story which follows from his contemplation of the world, and which preserves in the nobility of its style and in the serene independence of its technique, the human victory over circumstances.

It is this that makes us hear Faulkner's own voice throughout the book, that allows him to pull off the tremendous feat of making us believe in a character who in many ways is not a human being at all—but struggling to become one. And this, after all, is the great problem of the novelist today. Joe Christmas is an incarnation not only of the "race problem" in America, but of the condition of man. More and more, not merely the American novel, but all serious contemporary novels, are concerned with men who are not real enough to themselves to be seriously in conflict with other men. Their conflicts, as we say, are "internal"; for they are seeking to become *someone.* Joe Christmas lives a life that is not only solitary but detached. He lives in society physically, but actually he is concerned only with the process of self-discovery, or of self-naming, even of self-legalization. This is a fate which, as we know, can be as arduous and deadly as that of the classic heroes. But in Joe Christmas' case, there is no conflict from positions of strength, no engagement between man and man—only the search of the "stranger," *l'étranger,* to become man. [283]

The Unity of Faulkner's
Light in August

C. HUGH HOLMAN

THE NATURE OF THE UNITY IN WILLIAM FAULKNER'S *Light in August*, in fact, even the existence of such unity, has been seriously disputed by his critics. The debate has ranged from Malcolm Cowley's insistence that the work combines "two or more themes having little relation to each other" to Richard Chase's elaborate theory of "images of the curve" opposed to "images of linear discreteness."[1] Those critics who see a unity in the novel find its organizing principle in theme or philosophical statement—"a successful metaphysical conceit," a concern with Southern religion, the tragedy of human isolation, man's lonely search for community—but they fail to find a common ground for the unity they perceive because they neglect properly to evaluate the objective device which Faulkner employs in the novel as an expression of theme.[2] That device is the pervasive paralleling of character

---

[1] Introd., *The Portable Faulkner*, ed. Cowley (New York, 1946), p. 18; "The Stone and the Crucifixion: Faulkner's *Light in August*," *William Faulkner: Two Decades of Criticism*, ed. Frederick J. Hoffman and Olga W. Vickery (Michigan State Coll., 1951), pp. 205–217. Between these 2 extremes a great variety of attitudes have been held. Irving Howe, although he praises the novel, feels that it "suffers from a certain structural incoherence" resulting from its use of "a triad of actions" (*William Faulkner: A Critical Study*, New York, 1952, pp. 153, 149). Conrad Aiken feels that it fails because Faulkner's excessive concern with formal technique is not here "matched with the characters and the theme" ("William Faulkner: The Novel as Form," *Faulkner: Two Decades of Criticism*, p. 145). George M. O'Donnell also feels that the novel is a failure "because of the disproportionate emphasis upon Christmas—who ought to be the antagonist but who becomes, like Milton's Satan, the real protagonist in the novel" ("Faulkner's Mythology," ibid., p. 57).
[2] Harry M. Campbell and Ruel E. Foster find unity in the book through an interplay of its incidents in terms of their contribution to "a successful metaphysical conceit" (*William Faulkner: A Critical Appraisal*, Norman, Okla., 1951, pp. 68 ff.). William V. O'Connor believes that it achieves unity through its pervasive concern with Southern Protestant mores ("Protestantism in Yoknapatawpha County," *Southern Renascence: The Literature of the Modern South*, ed. Louis D. Rubin, Jr. and Robert D. Jacobs, Baltimore, 1953, pp. 153–169. This essay is reprinted in an abridged and modified form as Ch. vi of O'Connor, *The Tangled Fire of William Faulkner*, Minneapolis, 1954, pp. 72–87). Jacobs sees the book as centered in the tragedy of human isolation ("Faulkner's Tragedy of Isolation," *Southern Renascence*, pp. 170–191). Carl Benson finds its theme in man's tragic

traits, actions, and larger structural shapes to the story of Christ. Viewed in terms of this device the novel becomes the story of the life and death of a man peculiarly like Christ in many particulars, an account of what Ilse D. Lind has called "the path to Gethsemane which is reserved for the Joe Christmases of this world."[3] However, that account is in itself perverse, "a monstrous and grotesque irony,"[4] unless the other strands of action in the book—the Hightower story and the Lena Grove story—are seen as being contrasting portions of a thematic statement also made suggestively by analogies to the Christ story. This essay is an attempt to demonstrate that such, indeed, is the basic nature of the novel and that it has a unity which is a function of its uses of the Christ story.

The parallels between Christ and Joe Christmas, the leading character in the novel, have not gone unnoticed. However, although many critics have commented in passing on their presence, they have usually been dismissed as casual or irresponsible.[5] But the publication

---

search for community ("Thematic Design in *Light in August*," *South Atlantic Quart.*, LIII [1954], 540–555). In an interesting but largely ignored examination of the novel just 3 years after its publication, James W. Linn and H. W. Taylor advanced the provocative idea that *Light in August* is a "counterpoint of stories," and said, "Through this . . . device . . . the novelist can, without any distortion of the individual elements of the material, still express his inner vision, his most personal intuitions, not in so many sentences, but in a design, which, like the structure of music, represents nothing but is a sort of meaning in itself" (*A Foreword to Fiction*, New York, 1935, p. 157).

[3] "The Design and Meaning of *Absalom! Absalom!*" *PMLA*, LXX (Dec. 1955), 904.

[4] O'Connor, *Southern Renascence*, p. 169.

[5] For example, Richard H. Rovere says, "Although it seems indisputable to me that some sort of connection [between Christ and Joe Christmas] was in Faulkner's mind at one point or another, I cannot believe that there is much profit . . . in exploring the matter very deeply or in using it to interpret the novel" (Introd., *Light in August*, Modern Library ed., New York, 1950, p. xiii). Richard Chase says, "Faulkner seems not to sense exactly how the Christ theme should be handled, sometimes making it too overt and sometimes not overt enough. His attempts to enlarge Joe's character by adducing a willed mythology remind one of Melville's similar attempts in *Pierre*" (*Faulkner: Two Decades of Criticism*, p. 212). Carl Benson says, "I am not certain as to just how far we may push the Christ-Christmas parallel (which has often been recognized as a troublesome problem in the book)" (*South Atlantic Quart.*, p. 552). Irene C. Edmonds states: "One feels that he had a very definite connection in his mind between Christmas and Christ. The vagueness with which he establishes the connection suggests that the magnitude of his theme was too great for the limits of his imaginative powers to assimilate. . . . One feels that Faulkner, a Southerner, when confronted by the enormity of his attempt to liken a man with Negro blood in his veins to Christ, could not find the moral courage to make the analogy inescapably clear. So it remained a suggestion, trailing away into the obfuscation of It-Could-or-Could-Not Have-Been" ("Faulkner and the Black Shadow," *Southern Renascence*, p. 196). Beekman W. Cottrell's article, "Christian Symbolism in 'Light in August'," *Modern Fiction Studies*, II (Winter 1956–1957), 207–213, which takes seriously Faulkner's

of *A Fable*, [155] with its very obvious and self-conscious use of Christian parallels in highly complex patterns, forces us to accept Faulkner's concern with the Christ story as profoundly serious, and recent criticism has also shown us that such a concern is not a late occurrence in his work.[6] Furthermore, in a recent interview, Faulkner has talked very directly about the use of Christian materials in *A Fable* and the function that he feels that such material has in a novel. He said:

In *A Fable* the Christian allegory was the right allegory to use.

Whatever its [Christianity's] symbol—cross or crescent or whatever— that symbol is man's reminder of his duty inside the human race. Its various allegories are the charts against which he measures himself and learns to know what he is. . . . It shows him how to discover himself, evolve for himself a moral code and standard within his capacities and aspirations. . . . Writers have always drawn, and always will, on the allegories of moral consciousness, for the reason that the allegories are matchless.[7]

Apparently Faulkner intends to use parallels to Christ as devices to invest modern stories with timeless meanings; and Christian allegory, when it appears in his work, may justifiably be viewed as a means of stating theme. Dayton Kohler correctly says, "Faulkner's treatment of Hebraic-Christian myth is like Joyce's use of the Homeric story in *Ulysses* and Mann's adaptation of Faustian legend in *Doctor Faustus*."[8] It is a pervasive and enriching aspect of the total book, and we ex-

---

use of Christian materials in the novel, appeared after the present study had been accepted for publication. However, Cottrell's approach, although illuminating and provocative, is so different from mine that in only one respect, indicated in n. 24, would it have altered my case appreciably. Three other studies have appeared since this essay was written, but they would not have modified seriously the reading given here: John L. Longley, Jr., "Joe Christmas: The Hero in the Modern World," *Virginia Quart. Rev.*, xxxiii (1957), 233–249; Ilse D. Lind, "The Calvinistic Burden of *Light in August*," *New England Quart.*, xxx (1957), 307–329; and Alfred Kazin, "The Stillness of 'Light in August'," *Partisan Rev.*, xxiv (1957), 519–538.

[6] Ward L. Miner, in *The World of William Faulkner* (Durham, N.C., 1952), pp. 139–141; Robert M. Adams, in "Poetry in the Novel: Or Faulkner Esemplastic," *Virginia Quart. Rev.*, xxix (1953), 419–434; and Carvel Collins, in a review of *A Fable* in *New York Times Bk. Rev.*, 1 Aug. 1954, p. 1, have called attention to Faulkner's use of the Holy Week in *The Sound and the Fury* (1929). George K. Smart has shown that the very early newspaper sketches assembled in *Mirrors of Chartres Street* used materials from the Christ story ("Faulkner's Use of Religious Terms," a paper read before the Southeastern Amer. Stud. Assoc., Daytona Beach, Fla., 26 Nov. 1955).

[7] "The Art of Fiction XII: William Faulkner," *Paris Rev.*, iv (Spring 1956), 42.

[8] "*A Fable*: The Novel as Myth," *College English*, xvi (1955), 475. Significantly Faulkner has called Joyce and Mann the 2 great European men of his time and has said, "You should approach Joyce's *Ulysses* as the illiterate Baptist preacher approaches the Old Testament: with faith," *Paris Rev.*, p. 46.

pect to see it bodied forth, not only in fragments and parts, but in the complete design.

Light in August consists of three major and largely separate story strands, what Irving Howe has called "a triad of actions." These strands are the story of Joe Christmas, his murder of Joanna Burden, and his death, together with long retrospective sections that trace his life in considerable detail from his birth to the night of Joanna's death; the story of Gail Hightower, his reintroduction into life through Lena Grove and Joe Christmas, and his death, together with retrospective and narrative sections on his marriage and his ministry; and the story of Byron Bunch and Lena Grove, of her search for the father of her illegitimate child, and of its birth. These strands are tied loosely together by the accident of time, some interchange of dramatis personae, and by the almost mechanical device of having characters in one strand narrate events in another. Lucas Burch, the father of Lena Grove's bastard child, is Joe Christmas' helper and would-be betrayer. Byron Bunch, Lena's loving slave, is a friend of Hightower, narrates much of the Joe Christmas story to Hightower and is himself the retrospective narrator for a good deal of Hightower's early story. Joe Christmas' grandmother attempts, with Bunch's assistance, to persuade Hightower to save her grandson, and Joe turns to Hightower in the last moments of his life. Hightower assists at the birth of Lena's child, and Joe's grandmother confuses Lena with her daughter Milly and Lena's child with Joe as a baby. However, these links are not sufficient to tie the triad of actions into "a single action that is complete and whole."

A certain mechanical unity is imposed upon the novel through Faulkner's establishing the action of the story in the ten days between Joe Christmas' killing Joanna Burden and his being [156] killed by Percy Grimm. However, the significance of these present actions is to be found in the past, and the bulk of the novel actually consists of retrospective accounts of that antecedent action. Faulkner attempts to preserve a sense of present action as opposed to antecedent action by the device of telling in the present tense all events that are imagined to be occurring in a forward motion during these ten days, and in the past tense all retrospective and antecedent events.

Also there are three distinct bodies of material in the book: formal Protestant religion, sex, and the Negro in Southern society. Each of the story strands deals predominantly with one of these matters but contains the other two in some degree. The story of Joe Christmas is centered on the problem of the Negro in Southern society; the Gail Hightower story is centered in the Protestant church; and the sex element is the controlling factor in the story of Lena Grove, her search for the father of her child, and Byron Bunch's love for her. The interplays of these materials among these separate story strands help to knit the parts of the novel into a whole, but these bodies of material and the stories constructed from them find their most meaningful thematic expression as contrasting analogues of the Christ story.

The most obvious of the Christ analogues is in the story of Joe Christmas. Faulkner establishes numerous parallels between Joe Christmas and Christ, some of which are direct and emphatic and some of which are nebulous, fleeting, almost wayward. Strange dislocations in time occur; events in Christ's life have multiple analogies and are sometimes distributed over long periods of time. The parallels often seem perverse and almost mocking, yet they all seem to invite us to look at Joe Christmas as a person *somehow like Christ in certain aspects.* Around his birth and his death events are closely parallel to those in Christ's life; in the middle period of his life the analogies grow shadowy and uncertain.

Joe is the son of an unmarried mother, and the identity of his father is hidden from him and from the world. He is found on Christmas day on the steps of an orphans' home, and he is named Joseph Christmas, giving him the initials JC. His grandfather says that God "chose His own Son's sacred anniversary to set [His will] aworking on" (p. 363).[9] When he is five, his grandfather spirits him away by night to Little Rock to save him from the orphanage authorities who have discovered that he has Negro blood. After he is returned, he is adopted by the Simon McEacherns, and upon his first entering their home Mrs. McEachern ceremoniously washes his feet. The stern Calvinism of Simon McEachern represents the accepted religious order of Joe's world, an equivalent of the Pharisaic order of Christ's, and Joe achieves what he later senses to be manhood and maturity when at the age of eight he sets himself against the formal codification of that order by refusing to learn the Presbyterian catechism. He rejects three temptations: Mrs. McEachern's food and the feminine pity which it represents; the Negro girl whom he refuses when he is fourteen; and McEachern's attempt by means of a heifer to purchase Joe's allegiance to his orthodox conventions. He also rejects food three times, as Robert D. Jacobs has pointed out.[10] Once, when he is taken into Mottstown at the age of eighteen by his foster father, Joe goes to a restaurant where he meets Bobbie Allen and begins to learn about the larger world of which he is a part, the restaurant being a kind of carnal temple and Bobbie and its owners being priests of that world.

His middle years are cloaked in obscurity, but at the age of thirty he comes to Jefferson, and there he is first introduced to us as a man with a name that is "somehow an augur of what he will do" (p. 29).

---

[9] *Light in August* (New York, 1932). All page references are to this edition of the novel. The Modern Readers Series edition, published by New Directions, apparently duplicates the 1932 edition by photoreproduction.

[10] *Southern Renascence,* pp. 175–176.

He is rootless, homeless, "no street, no walls, no square of earth his home" (p. 27). For three years he works in Jefferson. At first he works in the sawmill with Brown who is later to betray him, and Faulkner refers to them as "master" and "disciple" (pp. 40–41). He becomes the lover of a nymphomaniac, Joanna Burden, who, after reveling for a while in depravity, when sex is no longer interesting to her, tries to convert him to the Pharisaic religious order.

Then one Friday night he kills her, striking in self-defense against her use of a pistol to force him to subscribe through prayer to her religion. He flees, and he is betrayed, although ineffectually, by his "disciple" Brown for $1000. On the Tuesday of his week of flight, the day of Holy Week on which Christ cleansed the temple, he enters a Negro church and, using a table leg, drives out the worshippers. On Thursday night, the night of the Last Supper, he finds himself in [157] the cabin of what he calls a "brother" and a meal mysteriously appears before him. Jacobs observes that "this Christ has no disciple except himself and always must eat alone."[11] Faulkner says, "It was as though now and at last he had an actual and urgent need to strike off the accomplished days toward some purpose, some definite day or act" (p. 317). The next morning he frantically questions to learn the day of the week, and, finding it to be Friday, sets his face steadfastly toward Mottstown. Although up to this time he has been walking, he now enters the village riding with a Negro in a wagon drawn by mules. First he gets a shave and a haircut; then a man named Halliday recognizes him and asks, "Aint your name Christmas?" Faulkner reports, "He never denied it. He never did anything" (p. 331). Halliday hits him twice in the face, so that his forehead bleeds. His grandfather, who, being a stern Calvinist, speaks for the Pharisees, tries to incite the crowd to violence, shouting, "Kill him. Kill him" (p. 327). The mob, however, leaves him to the "law." He is moved from Mottstown to Jefferson, another legal jurisdiction, and the Mottstown sheriff yields his responsibility happily. In Jefferson he is guarded by volunteer National Guardsmen, who spend their time gambling. He escapes from the sheriff in the town square, runs to a Negro cabin where he steals a pistol, and then runs to the home of the ex-minister Hightower, where he is shot by the leader of the Guardsmen, a self-important soldier. As he is dying, the Guardsman takes a knife and mutilates him, so that "from out the slashed garments about his hips and loins the pent black blood seemed to rush like a released breath" (p. 440). And Joe Christmas, at thirty-three, as Gail Hightower had earlier prophesied that he would, becomes "the doomed man . . . in whose crucifixion [the churches] will raise a cross" (p. 348).

These parallels have been dismissed as insignificant, I believe, because critics have looked for a theological Saviour, whose death

---

[11] Ibid., p. 176.

becomes an effective expiation for man's guilt, and viewed in these terms Joe Christmas is a cruel and irreverent travesty on Christ. However, Faulkner has defined the function of allegory to be a chart against which man can measure himself and learn "to know what he is." And Christian allegory uses Christ as "a matchless example of suffering and sacrifice and the promise of hope" (*Paris Rev.*, p. 42). The Christ to whom Faulkner parallels Joe Christmas is not the Messiah of St. Paul's epistles but the suffering servant of Isaiah, who is described thus:

he hath no form nor comeliness; and when we shall see him, there is no beauty that we should desire him.

He is despised and rejected of men; a man of sorrows, and acquainted with grief: and we hid as it were our faces from him; he was despised, and we esteemed him not. . . .

He was oppressed, and he was afflicted, yet he opened not his mouth: he is brought as a lamb to the slaughter, and as a sheep before her shearers is dumb, so he openeth not his mouth.

He was taken from prison and from judgment: and who shall declare his generation: for he was cut off out of the land of the living: for the transgression of my people was he stricken. (Isaiah liii.2–3, 7–8)

The central fact in this story of the suffering servant Joe Christmas is his belief that he bears an imperceptibly faint strain of Negro blood, an ineradicable touch of evil in the eyes of the society of which he is a part and in his own eyes as well. This Negro blood exists for him as a condition of innate and predetermined darkness, a touch of inexorable original sin, a burden he bears neither through his own volition nor because of his own acts. In the lost central years of his life his sense of this innate damnation leads him to shock his many women with confessions of his Negro blood (p. 211). At last he finds a woman who is not shocked.

She said, "What about it? . . . Say, what do you think this dump is, any- how? The Ritz hotel?" Then she quit talking. She was watching his face and she began to move backward slowly before him, staring at him, her face draining, her mouth open to scream. Then she did scream. It took two police- men to subdue him. At first they thought that the woman was dead.

He was sick after that. He did not know until then that there were white women who would take a man with a black skin. He stayed sick for two years. (p. 212)

It is from this aspect of himself that Joe runs in such fatal and pre- cipitant flight down "the street which was to run for fifteen years" (pp. 210, 213).

Hightower equates this Negro blood in Joe to "poor mankind" (p. 93); and Joe, running from the Negro quarter of the town, sees it as the "black pit," and thinks, "It just lay there, black, impenetrable. . . .

It might have been the original quarry, abyss itself" (p. 108). It is this black blood that stands between Joe and a natural life. It is his own knowledge of it that stands between him and his becoming "one with [158] loneliness and quiet that has never known fury or despair" (p. 313). And it is this black blood which, in Joanna Burden's impassioned view of the "doom and curse" of the Negro, casts a "black shadow in the shape of a cross" (p. 239).

Gavin Stevens believes that Joe Christmas' actions, after he escapes in the town square, were the results of a series of conflicts between his black blood, which is a form of evil, and his white blood, which represents his humane and good impulses. This conflict reaches its climax when the black blood leads him to strike the minister to whom he had run for help, but, Stevens says:

And then the black blood failed him again, as it must have in crises all his life. He did not kill the minister. He merely struck him with the pistol and ran on and crouched behind that table and defied the black blood for the last time, as he had been defying it for thirty years. He crouched behind that overturned table and let them shoot him to death, with that loaded and unfired pistol in his hand. (p. 425)[12]

After Percy Grimm shoots Joe down, he mutilates him, and then, with the crowd watching, "the pent black blood" rushes from him. Faulkner says:

It seemed to rush out of his pale body like the rush of sparks from a rising rocket; upon that black blast the man seemed to rise soaring into their memories forever and ever. They are not to lose it, in whatever peaceful valleys, beside whatever placid and reassuring streams of old age, in the mirroring faces of whatever children they will contemplate old disasters and newer hopes. It will be there, musing, quiet, steadfast, not fading and not particularly threatful, but of itself alone serene, of itself alone triumphant. (p. 440)

This is Joe Christmas' crucifixion and his ascension, and this outrushing and ascending stream of black blood becomes his only successful act of communion with his fellowmen. Through it, a symbol of his Negro qualities shed for sexual reasons in the house of a man of religion, Joe Christmas becomes one of "the charts against which [man] measures himself and learns to know what he is . . . a matchless example of suffering and sacrifice . . ." (*Paris Rev.*, p. 42).

Joe's life is also shaped by sexual distortions, perversions, and

---

12 Irene C. Edmonds' objection that Faulkner is here indulging in the fallacious "tragic mulatto" theme (*Southern Renascence*, pp. 196–197) seems justified. However, it seems also true that Faulkner's use of "black blood" has here transcended the level of racial qualities, whether true or false, and has been universalized to all mankind.

irregularities. His mother was unmarried; his grandfather's righteous anger at her impurity and at what he believes to be the Negro blood in Joe's father makes him kill Joe's father and refuse his mother the medical assistance which would have prevented her death at his birth. Thus this anger sends Joe into the world an orphan. His accidental witnessing of the illicit relations between an orphanage dietician and an interne results in the dietician's learning of his Negro blood and in his being adopted by the McEacherns. At fourteen, when Joe's turn comes in a group assignation with a Negro girl, he is repelled by the "womanshenegro" and it is against "She" that he struggles and fights, until "There was no She at all" (pp. 146–147). Significantly this early sexual experience is allied in Joe's mind with the Negro.

The menstrual period becomes for him a symbol of darkness and evil. Learning about it from boys' conversation, "he shot a sheep. . . . Then he knelt, his hands in the yet warm blood of the dying beast, trembling. . . . He did not forget what the boy had told him. He just accepted it. He found that he could live with it, side by side with it" (p. 174). This blood sacrifice he is to duplicate himself in his death. But three years after killing the sheep, when he confronts the idea again in connection with Bobbie Allen, it fills him with horror. "In the notseeing and the hardknowing as though in a cave he seemed to see a diminishing row of suavely shaped urns in moonlight, blanched. And not one was perfect. Each one was cracked and from each crack there issued something liquid, deathcolored, and foul" (pp. 177–178). This image of the urn is to appear crucially in each of the major story strands.

Woman thus becomes for Joe a symbol and source of darkness and sin, the dark temptress who is viewed with revulsion alternating with attraction. Joseph Campbell expresses such a duality in attitudes toward women in terms that might have been designed to define Joe's feeling when in his study of religion and mythology he says:

Generally we refuse to admit within ourselves or within our friends, the full-ness of that pushing, self-protective, malodorous, carnivorous, lecherous fever which is the very nature of the organic cell. . . .

But when it suddenly dawns upon us, or is forced to our attention, that everything we think or do is necessarily tainted with the odor of the flesh, then, not uncommonly, there is experienced a moment of revulsion: life, the acts of life, the organs of life, woman in particular as the great symbol of life, become intolerable.[13] [159]

Simon McEachern's harsh and grimly puritan ideal of chastity drives Joe to the prostitute Bobbie Allen, appropriately named for the

---

[13] Joseph Campbell, *The Hero with a Thousand Faces* (New York, 1956), pp. 121–122. It is this aspect of Faulkner's work that seems to bother Edith Hamilton most in her "Faulkner: Sorcerer or Slave?" *Sat. Rev.*, xxxv (12 July 1952), 8–10, 39–41.

hard-hearted heroine of the Southern folk version of the Scotch ballad "Barbara Allen."[14] And this cheap and cruel woman is Joe's closest approach to love and acceptance, and she at last turns upon him, screaming against his Negro blood.

This pattern of unhappy if not unnatural sex reaches its climax for Joe Christmas with the puritanical nymphomaniac Joanna Burden. In a sense, the ministry that Joe performs during his three years in Jefferson is to call to life in this cold, barren woman the primitive sex urge; as he expresses it, "At least I have made a woman of her at last" (p. 223). But what he awakens in her is not a natural urge, but an unnatural and perverted one, for she was too old to bear children, too old to serve the purposes of nature. Faulkner says, "Christmas watched her pass through every avatar of a woman in love. . . . He was aware of . . . the imperious and fierce urgency that concealed an actual despair at frustrate and irrevocable years. . . . It was as though he had fallen into a sewer" (pp. 242, 244). Having perverted his "ministry," she finally denies it and attempts to force him into her sterile religious patterns. It is then that he kills her in an act of self-defense, for she had tried to shoot him; and in an act of spiritual self-preservation, for he could live only by refusing to pray with her; but in an act of suicide, for he could not himself long survive her killing.

It is in the Joanna Burden episode that the sex material of the Joe Christmas story reaches its fullest statement. It is in her episode, too, that the union of this material with the idea of Joe's Negro blood is most clearly stated, for Joanna is the daughter of a Northern father in a Southern town. From her childhood she had been taught that the Negroes were "A race doomed and cursed to be forever and ever a part of the white race's doom and curse for its sins" (p. 239) and that "in order to rise, you must raise the shadow with you . . . the curse of the white race is the black man who will be forever God's chosen own because He once cursed Him!" (p. 240). She first befriends Joe because he is a Negro. And when the flames of her sexual desires die out she wishes to send him to law school and to have him administer her numerous charities for Negro people, but this involves an acceptance of his Negro status, and such acceptance is intolerable to Joe.

Joanna serves adequately to link these two matters, sex and the Negro, to religion, for she is a conventionally devout person, and when she attempts to shoot Joe, thus forcing him to kill her, it is because he refuses to join her in her return to religion through prayer.

The formal Protestant religion, an aspect of which Joanna represents, has been haunting Joe from before his birth. His grandfather Eupheus Hines is a half-mad religious zealot with a special and spiteful hatred of women, of what he calls "abomination and bitchery."

---

[14] See headnote and text, "Barbey Ellen," in Willard Thorp, A *Southern Reader* (New York, 1955), pp. 618–620, for this ballad in its Southern version.

He believes that God speaks directly to him, telling him how to execute His vengeance on earth. In the narrow, vindictive, cruel God to whom Eupheus listens may be seen the primitive Protestant Old Testament Jehovah of anger and jealousy. The Negro has been singled out for the special wrath of this God, and Hines goes about as a quasi minister to Negro congregations preaching to them of God's disfavor. He becomes a kind of perverted and evil divine father for Joe, and he pursues passionately his desire to destroy his grandson. Although his religion is unorganized and brutally primitive, he seems to speak on the lowest level of the religious order and attitudes of Joe's world.

Simon McEachern, Christmas' foster father, into whose hands he is committed when he passes from the orphanage and Hines's control, is a Presbyterian elder. He attempts to instill through grim authority the cheerless pattern of Calvinistic conduct and belief. His only weapon is the flail, and to him love is a deplorable weakness. The crucial occurrence in Joe's relationship with him comes when McEachern attempts unsuccessfully to force Joe to learn the Presbyterian catechism. Finally Joe strikes McEachern down in murderous rage when his foster father comes between him and the closest thing he has known to love, Bobbie Allen.

When Joe is running away after killing Joanna, he re-enacts Christ's cleansing of the temple by interrupting a Negro church service and driving out the worshippers with a table leg. His grandmother, anxious to give him a respite from the punishment he is to suffer, turns to the disgraced Presbyterian minister Hightower and asks him to give Christmas an alibi for the time of Joanna's murder. She tells Joe to go to the [160] minister. When he escapes in the town square, he turns first to a Negro cabin and then to Hightower, but he strikes the minister down, as he has struck down the others who have symbolized church to him.

Significantly, organized religion is represented by the Presbyterian Church rather than the Baptist or the Methodist, both of which are numerically superior to the Presbyterian in Faulkner's country.[15] Yet Faulkner is remarkably ignorant of the government and instruction of that church. He gives it an episcopal government quite contrary to the government by elders from which it gains its name (pp. 456–457).[16] He seems naïvely ignorant of how the catechism is learned, for he has Joe Christmas standing silent with the book in his hands, as though the catechism were a litany to be recited rather than a group of answers to be repeated to questions (pp. 137–146). However, the Presbyterian Church is the doctrinal church of the Protestant sects, the church of

---

[15] *The 1936 Census of Religious Bodies*, Bureau of the Census (Washington, 1941), I, 234–237, shows for Mississippi 150,000 communicants in the Southern Baptist Church, 322,362 in the Negro Baptist Church, 107,245 in the Methodist Church, and only 18,445 in the Presbyterian Church.

[16] See ibid., II, 1382, 1402–1403.

unrelenting Calvinism.[17] As such, it represents the Pharisaic order and is an example of what man does in codifying into cold ritual and inhumane form the warm and living heart of religion.

It is against the dead order of his world as it is defined by this formal religion that much of Joe's rebellion is directed. He defines himself by rebellion against McEachern's catechism and grim and inhumane morality, against Joanna Burden's attempt to force him into her religious patterns, against a symbol of the organized church when he strikes out in flailing anger against the Negro congregation, and against the ex-minister Hightower when he strikes him down. He is pursued and harried by the organized church of his day in a way suggestive of that in which Christ was pursued and harried by the Pharisees.

Joe Christmas is like Christ, so many of whose characteristics his creator has given him, in that he bears our common guilt, symbolized by his Negro blood, that he is denied by the world, and that he is ultimately offered as a blood sacrifice because of the "original sin" he bears. But he is not Christ; he is a rebelling and suffering creature, embittered, angry, and almost totally lacking in love. In his ineffectual death is no salvation. His is a futile and meaningless expiation of his "guilt."

The religious subject matter is pervasive in *Light in August*. The sounds of church bells and of choirs echo throughout the novel, and it is shaped in part by the Protestantism of the South; but the Gail Hightower story strand is the one most completely, although by no means exclusively, drawn from this subject matter.

Hightower is the grandson of a Confederate soldier killed in a raid in Jefferson during the Civil War. He is the son of a pacifist, an abolitionist, a "phantom . . . who had been a minister without a church and a soldier without an enemy, and who in defeat had combined the two and become a doctor, a surgeon" (p. 449). Hightower goes to the seminary seeking an asylum from the world and a means of rejoining his grandfather's ghost at Jefferson.

He believed with a calm joy that if ever there was shelter, it would be the Church; that if ever truth could walk naked and without shame and fear, it would be in the seminary. When he believed that he had heard the call it seemed to him that he could see his future, his life, intact and on all sides complete and inviolable, like a classic and serene vase, where the spirit could be born anew sheltered from the harsh gale of living and die so, peacefully, with only the far sound of the circumvented wind . . . (p. 453)

This "classic and serene vase . . . intact and inviolable" is in contrast to the urn with cracked sides and deathcolored fluid which Joe

---

[17] Ibid., II, 1402–1403, and esp. p. 1444.

Christmas imagined he saw when the revolting animal facts of reproduction were forced upon him.

While in seminary, Hightower marries a girl who is desperately
seeking escape from her life as the daughter of one of the seminary
teachers. He marries her because he quite correctly believes that she
has sufficient influence with the authorities in the church to get for him
a call to Jefferson. But once he reaches Jefferson he proves ineffectual
in every sense. His sermons are half-mad rhapsodies on the last cavalry
charge of his grandfather. The members of his church protest that he is
using "religion as though it were a dream" (p. 56). His church and his
wife, along with everything in the present, seem to him to be meaningless, held in suspension, while reality is "the wild bugles and the
clashing sabres and the dying thunder of hooves" (p. 467). . . . [161]

His frustrated wife is driven into a pattern of promiscuity which
culminates in her suicide and in his being shut out in disgrace from his
church. But he lives on in Jefferson a flaccid, fat, breathing corpse.
Although the possibilities of an effective ministry for him have long
since passed, he remains a symbol of the church and its truth to the
simple religious man, Byron Bunch.

He is called back to an actual ministry to man by Bunch when
that man sends him to help Lena in childbirth and he has to deliver
the baby. He is asked by Bunch and by Joe's grandmother to reassume
his ministry by championing Joe's cause and giving him an alibi. As
Byron introduces the request, he apologizes and yet insists, "But you
are a man of God. You cant dodge that." Hightower protests, "I am not
a man of God," and he argues that the town and the church had
chosen that he should not be; but Byron answers, "You were given
your choice before I was born, and you took it. . . . That was your
choice. And I reckon them that are good must suffer for it the same as
them that are bad" (pp. 344–345). At the last moment, Hightower
attempts to do what Byron and Mrs. Hines have asked and to save Joe
by telling the lie, but the attempt is vain, for when Joe, escaping, turns
to him, it is with raised pistol to strike him down. Yet Hightower has
been given by these actions a sufficiently clear vision of the way in
which he has betrayed his ministry for him to understand himself in
the moments before he dies. Christmas is for him, indeed, the chart
"against which he measures himself and learns to know what he is."

In the senses that Hightower accepts a "call" to the ministry not as
a field of service but as a sanctuary from the "harsh gale of living"; that
he is absorbed in the past rather than the present—a past appropriately, for a Southern minister, built on a false view of Confederate
heroism (the cavalry charge is a hen-house raid)—that his aloofness
prevents his ministering to suffering mankind; that he has a sharp
sense of the ethical values in the human situation (he can properly
instruct Byron, for example) but lacks the human sympathy that
would make him act on his knowledge—in these senses, he exemplified

qualities which Faulkner sees in religion. In Hightower's dying vision of truth:

He sees himself a shadowy figure among shadows . . . believing that he would find in that part of the Church which most blunders, dream-recovering, among the blind passions and the lifted hands and voices of men, that which he had failed to find in the Church's cloistered apotheosis upon earth . . . [He sees] that that which is destroying the Church is not the outward groping of those within it nor the inward groping of those without, but the professionals who control it and who have removed the bells from its steeples . . . He seems to see the churches of the world like a rampart, like one of these barricades of the middleages planted with dead and sharpened stakes, against truth and against that peace in which to sin and be forgiven which is the life of man. (p. 461)

Hightower is here seeing himself and his failure as microcosmic patterns of the failure of the religious spirit in his world. His is not the harsh failure of understanding or vision which the institutional church can sometimes represent and which is shown in this novel in McEachern and Eupheus Hines; for Hightower had known the meaning of the church and of its call to service: "He had believed in the church, too, in all that it ramified and evoked" (p. 453). But this vision has been smothered by his retreat from a positive engagement in life. One evening, listening to the organ music from the Sunday evening prayer meeting, he broods:

The organ strains come rich and resonant through the summer night, blended, sonorous, with that quality of abjectness and sublimation, as if the freed voices themselves were assuming the shapes and attitudes of crucifixions, ecstatic, solemn, and profound in gathering volume. Yet even then the music has still a quality stern and implacable, deliberate and without passion so much as immolation, pleading, asking, for not love, not life, forbidding it to others, demanding in sonorous tones as though death were the boon, like all Protestant music. . . . Listening, he seems to hear within it the apotheosis of his own history, his own land, his own environed blood . . . (p. 347)

Malcolm Cowley has noted Faulkner's tendency to turn Freudian method backward, producing "sexual nightmares" that are in reality symbols on another level,[18] and in the story of Gail Hightower that method is well illustrated. As in a sense the "ministry" of Joe Christmas in Jefferson may be viewed as sexual, so in a more pronounced sense the ministry of Hightower is pictured through sexual parallels: the story of his marriage is in miniature the story of his religious failure.

Hightower is impotent. Faulkner says of him, "[It was] as though the seed which his [162] grandfather has transmitted to him had been

---

18 *Portable Faulkner*, p. 15.

on the horse too that night and had been killed too" (p. 59), and he instinctively is drawn to Tennyson's poetry, which, Faulkner says, is "like listening in a cathedral to a eunuch chanting in a language which he does not even need to not understand" (p. 301). He marries, not for the love of his wife, but to use her to secure the pastorate at past-haunted Jefferson, and she is driven to destruction by his impotence and neglect. He fails equally the church which he neglects her to serve, and in his dying moments he realizes that these two failures are in truth the same one. He says:

I served it [the church] by using it to forward my own desire. I came here where faces full of bafflement and hunger and eagerness waited for me, waiting to believe; I did not see them. Where hands were raised for what they believed that I would bring them; I did not see them. I brought with me one trust, perhaps the first trust of man, which I had accepted of my own will before God [i.e., his duty to his wife]; I considered that promise and trust of so little worth that I did not know that I had even accepted it. And if that was all I did for her, what could I have expected? what could I have expected save disgrace and despair and the face of God turned away in very shame? Perhaps in the moment when I revealed to her not only the depth of my hunger but the fact that never and never would she have any part in the assuaging of it; perhaps at that moment I became her seducer and her murderer, author and instrument of her shame and death. (pp. 451–452)

One of man's basic duties is to the natural order of things, a duty to the race and its propagation. On the one occasion when Hightower works in harmony with that natural order and not against it, on the occasion of his assisting at the birth of Lena's son, he experiences a sudden rejuvenation, a sense of strength and rightness, and he puts away his Tennyson for the redder meat of Shakespeare's *Henry IV* (pp. 382–383). And in his vision of truth he sees man's duty to propagate the race as his "first trust," a duty so elemental that a failure here is a total failure (p. 462).

The stories of Christmas and Hightower are counterparts of the same story, but with reversed roles for the characters. The parallels of Gail Hightower to Joanna Burden are marked. Both are the entangled victims of the heroic past, even to the point of both being the descendants of abolitionists. Both are practically sterile; both destroy those in intimate physical relation to them; both follow religions inadequate to meet their actual problems; both represent distortions and perversions of the natural order as it is represented by normal sexual life and reproduction.

Joe Christmas in his self-destructive relation to Joanna Burden has a parallel role to that of Hightower's doomed wife. Both represent comparatively normal basic urges; both are in quite emphatic ways the victims of the impotence of those to whom they are attached; both are offered religious solace, Mrs. Hightower by the women of the church and Joe by Joanna's attempt to convert him; both reject such solace and elect death.

Thus the stories of Joe Christmas and Joanna Burden and of Gail Hightower and his wife become contrasting personal and institutional aspects of the religious aspirations and frustrations of man, as symbolized by deviations from the sexual norm. Ward Miner is only partly correct when he says, "In *Light in August* the force which destroys Christmas, Hightower, and Miss Burden is institutional Christianity."[19] For Joanna Burden is a destroyer rather than a victim, and she destroys through the same atrophy of natural feeling that has ruined the church as institution. Furthermore, Hightower is a symbol of the atrophy of the religious spirit, a figure indicating how and why the churches fail, rather than a victim of such failure. He is withdrawn from life, remote, indifferent; Faulkner speaks of "his dead life in the actual world" (p. 346).

These stories are finally merged, in a plot sense, near their conclusions by Joe's turning to Hightower, and they then stand as contrasting and complementary portions of the novel—contrasting in that the roles of the actors are reversed and complementary in that both are stories of "suffering and sacrifice" and of the failure of man to find and execute what Faulkner calls "his duty inside the human race" (*Paris Rev.*, p. 42).

The stories of Lena Grove and Byron Bunch form more than a pastoral idyll within which the violence of the other stories plays itself out. They establish a norm for the other actions, a definition of the natural order against which the perversions and distortions of the other stories are to be set. Here it is sex which is the principal subject matter.

Lena Grove in her calm and tranquil way is seeking Lucas Burch, the father of her child whose birth is imminent. Traveling alone in the confident belief that he is waiting for her, she [163] arrives in Jefferson on Saturday morning, the first day of Joe Christmas' flight. At the sawmill to which she has been directed she meets a good, devout, earnest man, Byron Bunch, whose name is a Southern colloquialism for "crowd" or "masses." He immediately recognizes that Burch is "Brown," Joe Christmas' partner and now would-be betrayer, and he decides to shield her from a knowledge of the murder and of who Burch is. Bunch seems to possess on a primitive and unthinking level that aptitude for religious sentiment which Hightower betrays. He and Hightower can talk together, and Hightower has been his religious mentor. He shares with Hightower, too, a desire to retreat from the evils of the world. He

---

19 *World of William Faulkner*, p. 143.

is working on Saturday in order to escape temptation; when Lena
comes, he says, "Out there where I thought the chance to harm ere a
man or woman or child could not have found me. And she hadn't
hardly got there before I had to go and blab the whole thing [that
Burch was in Jefferson]" (p. 284). But Bunch falls hopelessly and
completely in love with Lena, and thus he involves himself increasingly in the problems from which he had been fleeing and attempts to
involve Hightower too. He sees that Hightower is present to assist at
the birth of the baby, sees that the sheriff sends Burch to the cabin to
be confronted by Lena and their son, and learns, since he loves Lena,
that the fact of that son certifies the other and antecedent fact of Lucas
Burch: "Then he heard the child cry. Then he knew . . . that there
had been something all the while which had protected him against
believing, with the believing protected him. . . . he thought . . . *she
is not a virgin. . . . It aint until now that I ever believed that . . .
there ever was a Lucas Burch*" (p. 380). But Byron, learning to face
the evil he has been fleeing, faces it completely because he loves Lena.
When Burch flees from Lena's cabin, Byron confronts him at the
railroad tracks and fights him although the conflict is hopeless. Thus he
earns the right to go with Lena, like another Joseph going with Mary,
as she continues her journey on into Tennessee, but without real hope
of other pleasures than those of serving her.

Lena Grove herself is almost an earth-mother symbol. She moves
with tranquil ease and unflagging faith through the world. "She
advanced in identical and anonymous and deliberate wagons as
though through a succession of creakwheeled and limpeared avatars,
like something moving forever and without progress across an urn" (p.
5), Faulkner tells us, and she thus becomes a third aspect of the urn or
vase image, one neither removed and inhuman like Hightower's or
horribly imperfect and repulsive like Joe's, but simply right and
natural and combining both.[20] When she senses the child within her,
"she sits quite still, hearing and feeling the implacable and immemorial
earth, but without fear or alarm" (p. 26). At the birth of her child,
Hightower observes, "More of them. Many more. That will be her life,
her destiny. The good stock peopling in tranquil obedience to it the
good earth; from these hearty loins without hurry or haste descending
mother and daughter" (p. 384). Faulkner has recently said of her, "It
was her destiny to have a husband and children, and she knew it and
so she went out and attended to it without asking help from anyone.
. . . She was never for one moment confused, frightened, alarmed. She
did not even know that she didn't need pity" (*Paris Rev.*, p. 50). In

---

[20] Norman H. Pearson, in "Lena Grove," *Shenandoah,* III (Spring 1952), 3–7,
has the provocative idea that Lena is the "leaf-fringed legend" and the "foster-
child of silence and slow time" of Keats's "Ode to a Grecian Urn."

one sense she symbolizes the basic natural order in a way very like Whitman's "placid and self-contain'd" animals in "Song of Myself."[21] But in another sense she is the "Queen Goddess of the World," whose rightness in the order of things stands in religious contrast to the Dark Temptress, the symbol and source of sin. In some form or other both always exist in religions.[22] In traditional Christian symbolism they are the Virgin and the Whore of Babylon.

To the degree that Lena Grove symbolizes this earth-mother, Byron Bunch, the simple, good, and unthinkingly religious man, symbolizes the loving service of this natural order which the mass of mankind renders. Together they form a religious symbol of a stable order.

This elemental and eternal aspect of Lena is further enhanced by Faulkner's presenting her [164] story and that of Byron Bunch largely in the present tense. The bulk of the stories of Joe Christmas and of Gail Hightower come to us through elaborate patterns of retrospect and character narration, so that they are in the past tense, and Faulkner is, as we have already noted, anxious to maintain a distinction between present action and antecedent action. Yet the use of the present tense for most of the Lena Grove story and for comparatively little of the other stories, gives her narrative a special quality; for the present tense is the tense of eternal truths, of continuing and forever reduplicating actions; the past tense stamps the action with tragic finality. Faulkner has recently said, "Time is a fluid condition which has no existence except in the momentary avatars of individual people. There is no such thing as *was*—only *is*" (*Paris Rev.*, p. 52). Lena belongs in the world of eternal truths, in the world of *is*.

With the birth of her son she becomes the Virgin of religion. As Malcolm Cowley notes, "The title of the novel . . . refers to Lena Grove and her baby. In the Mississippi backwoods, it is sometimes said of a pregnant woman . . . that she will be *light* in August or September."[23] "Light in August" then is another annunciation, declar-

---

[21] The passage reads:

I think I could turn and live with animals, they're so placid and self-contain'd,
I stand and look at them long and long.
They do not sweat and whine about their condition,
They do not lie awake in the dark and weep for their sins,
They do not make me sick discussing their duty to God,
Not one is dissatisfied, not one is demented with the mania of owning things,
Not one kneels to another, nor to his kind that lived thousands of years ago,
Not one is respectable or unhappy over the whole earth.

(ll. 684–691)

[22] See Campbell, *The Hero with a Thousand Faces*, pp. 109–126, 297–302.

[23] *Portable Faulkner*, p. 652. It has been called to my attention by several people that Faulkner is said orally to have questioned Cowley's Mississippi folklore. However, the reading here given is physically appropriate to the action of the story and to the broad meaning of the theme, whether such a folk saying does

ing in Mississippi folk terms, "Unto us a child is born; unto us a son is given."

This serene and calm and eternally hopeful mother who comes a journey to give birth to her fatherless child in a strange place has similarities, too, to Joe's mother Milly Hines. Both are unwed; both suffer from family disapproval, although in differing degrees; both have lovers who are disreputable betrayers. But their similarity is most apparent in the children they bear. Lena's son is presented as a new Joe. When he is born, old Mrs. Hines confuses him with Joe Christmas as a baby, saying, "It's Joey. . . . It's my Milly's little boy" (p. 376), and she settles down grimly to protect him against Eupheus, lest he be stolen away again. The child sets into motion again what Gavin Stevens calls her "hoping machine" (p. 421). He says, "I dont think that it ever did start until that baby was born out there this morning, born right in her face, you might say; a boy too. And she had never seen the mother before, and the father at all, and that grandson whom she had never seen as a man; so to her those thirty years [since she had seen Joe] just were not" (pp. 421–422). Lena herself gets confused as to the parentage and identity of the child. She says, "She [Mrs. Hines] keeps on calling him Joey. When his name aint Joey. And she keeps on . . . talking about— She is mixed up someway. And sometimes I get mixed up too, listening, having to . . ." (p. 387). For Hightower the birth is a rejuvenating act. He goes home thinking, "Life comes to the old man yet . . ." Usually he sleeps a great deal. "He goes to the door [of his bedroom] and looks in, with that glow of purpose and pride, thinking, 'If I were a woman, now. That's what a woman would do: go back to bed to rest.' He goes to the study. He moves like a man with a purpose now, who for twenty-five years has been doing nothing at all between the time to wake and the time to sleep again" (p. 383). Lena's child is indeed a "newer hope."

Faulkner recently commented on the "trinity" represented in *A Fable* "by the young Jewish pilot officer who said, 'This is terrible. I refuse to accept it, even if I must refuse life to do so,' the old French Quartermaster General who said, 'This is terrible, but we can weep and bear it,' and the English battalion runner who said, 'This is terrible, I'm going to do something about it'" (*Paris Rev.*, p. 42–43). In one sense Hightower is like the Jewish pilot who refused life; Joe Christmas is like the Quartermaster General who could weep and bear

---

or does not in fact exist. Cottrell (*Modern Fiction Studies*, II, 213), has an excellent discussion of the complex meanings of the title: "The light is certainly two things in connection with Joanna Burden—the light in her bedroom which brings about her ruin and the subsequent blaze of her home. The same light is seen by Lena as ominous but she does not understand its full implications. . . . Lena's baby is born in the light of dawn, and the birth makes her, in the country phrase, 'light' again in the month of August. Joe Christmas' skin is light—neither black nor white. . . ."

it; and Lena's son bears the eternal hope that this one is the one who will do something about it. Thus Faulkner's threefold Christ is complete: the Christ who is "a matchless example of suffering and sacrifice and the promise of hope" (ibid., p. 42). Hightower is a symbol of suffering, however impotent and inward; Joe Christmas is a symbol of sacrifice, however private and ineffectual; and Lena's child is a symbol of hope.

This son of Lena has almost no plot relation to Joe; their links are temporal and accidental; their life lines never cross. More binds them, however, than the accident of Mrs. Hines's confusion or the similarities between their mothers. Both are the volitionless inheritors of a social [165] stigma transmitted through their parents: in Joe's case the suspected taint of Negro blood, in the baby's case the fact of his being born out of wedlock. These facts are stigmata that isolate their bearers from their fellowmen, distinguishing them as in some sense "guilty," because of the attitudes of society; and in the puritanical and race-conscious Yoknapatawpha County in which the novel is laid they are blots that have the implication of immitigable evil. It is in order that Lena's son may not achieve the social acceptance of having a legal father that Byron Bunch must go with the mother and the young child as an unwed rather than a wed Joseph as they leave Jefferson and Mississippi. Both Joe and the child bear the social stigmata that are the outward signs of inward states. And Faulkner has so juxtaposed them that they suggest that everyman, like Joe, like Lena's son, has laid upon him the intolerable burden of human institutional coldness and inadequacy (here represented by the church and the atrophy of the religious spirit), the obligations and the abuses of the natural order (here represented by sex), and the accumulated human guilt or original sin (here represented by the bastardy and the tainted blood). And they suggest, too, that everyman is charged with rebelling against these oppressions, and that it is this rebellion, this refusal to accept which is the divine in man, the secret of his hope, the key to "a spirit capable of compassion and sacrifice and endurance," the qualities that assure that "he will prevail."[24]

The three concluding chapters, drawing together the three main strands of the story, suggest by their content and method this same threefold view. Chapter xix tells, belatedly from a narrative sense, of the death of Joe Christmas, ending as his yielding-up of the black blood in death imprisons him in the spectators' "memories forever and ever" (p. 440); thus we see Joe last in his sacrificial dying. Chapter xx shows us Hightower, whose understanding of the situations has been sharp but whose sympathy has been too frail to support action, as he views the world, himself, and his ministry honestly in the moments

---

[24] Faulkner, speech accepting the Nobel Prize for Literature, quoted from *Ten Modern Masters,* ed. Robert G. Davis (New York, 1953), p. 506.

before he dies; thus we see him last in his awareness that he has failed the church (and implicitly that the church has thus failed) because he failed in the primary human relations, that the religious spirit must express itself in service to those like Joe and Lena. In Chapter xxi Lena, Byron, and the child move toward Tennessee, and the narrative comes to us through the detached, comic report of a furniture dealer; thus the child of hope and the earth-mother are seen at last, as Lena had been at first, moving serenely and dispassionately through the world of men and seasons, remote and somehow eternal, preserved in the amber of the comic spirit.

None of these characters are in themselves alone adequate representations of the Christ story or of those elements in it which have special meaning for Faulkner; but each of them is a representation of certain limited aspects of Christ, so that we may look upon them all and the complex pattern of actions through which they move and see, as it were, the dim but discernible outline of Christ as the organizing principle behind them. Viewed in such terms as these the separate story strands are fused into a thematic whole, and it is a whole unified by Faulkner's extensive use of the Christ story and his application of a nontheological interpretation in which Christ is the suffering servant of *Isaiah*, the archetype of man struggling against the order and condition of himself and his world. In a sense he would have us look upon the impotent, suffering despair of Hightower, the "old disaster" of the sacrificially dead Joe Christmas, and the "newer hope" of Lena's son and to say of them all, with Walt Whitman:

. . . I think this face is the face of the Christ himself,
Dead and divine and brother of all, and here again he lies.[25] [166]

---

[25] "A Sight in Camp in the Daybreak Gray and Dim," ll. 14–15.

The Quest for Failure

WALTER J. SLATOFF

JUDGING SOLELY FROM *The Sound and the Fury* AND *As I Lay Dying*, one might conclude that the complexity, ambiguity, and irresolution in Faulkner's work results chiefly from particular structural and stylistic experiment, that they are, so to speak, accidents of technique. *Light in August* reveals quite clearly that much more than this is involved, for neither the style nor the structure of the book in themselves provide any serious obstacle to comprehension. There are, it is true, numerous flashbacks and numerous shifts in event and point of view, but these are clearly marked. And while one is faced with the problem of relating parts of the book to one another there is little problem of deciphering the parts. The complexities lie elsewhere.

Let me begin with Professor Holman's excellent description of the general contents and organization of the book.

> *Light in August* consists of three major and largely separate story strands, what Irving Howe has called "a triad of actions." These strands are the story of Joe Christmas, his murder of Joanna Burden, and his death, together with long retrospective sections that trace his life in considerable detail from his birth to the night of Joanna's [173] death; the story of Gail Hightower, his reintroduction into life through Lena Grove and Joe Christmas, and his death, together with retrospective and narrative sections on his marriage and his ministry; and the story of Byron Bunch and Lena Grove, of her search for the father of her illegitimate child, and of its birth. These strands are tied loosely together by the accident of time, some interchange of dramatis personae and by the almost mechanical device of having characters in one strand narrate events in another. Lucas Burch, the father of Lena Grove's bastard child, is Joe Christmas' helper and would-be betrayer. Byron Bunch, Lena's loving slave, is a friend of Hightower, narrates much of the Joe Christmas story to Hightower and is himself the retrospective narrator for a good deal of Hightower's early story. Joe Christmas' grandmother attempts, with Bunch's assistance, to persuade Hightower to save her grandson, and Joe turns to Hightower in the last moments of his life. Hightower assists at the birth of Lena's child, and Joe's grandmother confuses Lena with her daughter Milly and Lena's child with Joe as a baby. However, these links are not sufficient to tie the triad of actions into "a single action that is complete and whole."
>
> A certain mechanical unity is imposed upon the novel through Faulkner's establishing the action of the story in the ten days between Joe Christmas' killing Joanna Burden and his being killed by Percy Grimm. However, the significance of these present actions is to be found in the past, and the bulk of the novel actually consists of retrospective accounts of that antecedent action. Faulkner attempts to preserve a sense of present action as opposed to antecedent action by the device of telling in the present tense all events that are imagined to be occurring in a forward motion during these ten days, and in the past tense all retrospective and antecedent events.[1]

There has been considerable debate over the extent to which the three stories or "actions" are unified, and over the nature of that unity. Essays have been written arguing that the unity lies in an opposition between "images of the curve" and "images of linear discreteness," in the emphasis on Southern Protestantism, [174] in the emphasis on man's search for community, in the contrast between "the brooding

---

[1] C. Hugh Holman, "The Unity of Faulkner's *Light in August*," *PMLA,* LXXIII (1958), 156–157.

self-conscious, introverted life imposed by modern civilization on both
Joe and Hightower and the simple normal virtues of a life close to
nature like that of Lena and . . . Byron," and in the analogies and
contrasts with the Christ story.[2] Professor Holman, who urges this last
view, has pulled together a number of these themes and has made
what is probably the best case that can be made for the unity of the
novel. He writes:

> There are three distinct bodies of material in the book: formal Protes-
> tant religion, sex, and the Negro in Southern society. Each of the story
> strands deals predominantly with one of these matters but contains the
> other two in some degree. The story of Joe Christmas is centered on the
> problem of the Negro in Southern society; the Gail Hightower story is cen-
> tered in the Protestant church; and the sex element is the controlling factor
> in the story of Lena Grove, her search for the father of her child, and Byron
> Bunch's love for her. The interplays of these materials among these sepa-
> rate story strands help to knit the parts of the novel into a whole, but these
> bodies of material and the stories constructed from them find their most
> meaningful thematic expression as contrasting analogues of the Christ story.[3]

Certainly the themes and threads these critics have pointed to are
in the novel, and certainly there are connections between them, but the
connections are far more tenuous, the themes and emphases far more
numerous, and the meanings far more ambiguous than any of these
critics imply. Moreover, each of the individual stories raises important
questions which are not resolved. Let us begin with these.

The story of Lena Grove, with which the book begins and ends,
has generally been seen as a pastoral frame for the novel, and Lena
and Byron have usually been viewed as providing a [175] norm of
sanity and natural behavior against which the violence and perversions
of the other stories can be measured. Certainly there is much to
compel such a view. Lena's full-bodied health, serenity, and faith in
the natural order of things, and her pleasure in life, are in sharp
contrast to the fanaticism, barrenness, anguish, or despair that mark
most of the other major characters. Hightower, "remembering the
strong young body from out whose travail even there shone something
tranquil and unafraid" thinks that she will have many more children—
*"The good stock peopling in tranquil obedience to it the good earth;
from these hearty loins without hurry or haste descending mother and
daughter. But by Byron engendered next"* (p. 356)*—and he goes on
to suggest that obedience and relation to earth is perhaps equivalent to
prayer. Byron, until the last chapter of the book at least, is clearly a

---

2 For a list and brief characterization of these essays see Holman, p. 155,
notes 1, 2.

3 Holman, p. 157.

* All quotations from *Light in August* are from the Modern Library edition
(New York: Random House, 1950).

norm, if not an ideal, of generosity and unpretentious decency, perhaps the most clearly virtuous of any of Faulkner's characters. His religion, unlike that of McEachern, Hines, and Hightower, is a peaceful modest affair; each Sunday he quietly and unobtrusively goes to a country church to lead the choir.

On the other hand, there is much which works in opposition to this view. Lena unquestionably has a kind of wisdom, but she is deeply mistaken about the character and intentions of Lucas, whose emptiness and falseness are completely and immediately apparent to everyone else who encounters him. When Mrs. Armstid warns her that Lucas will run away if she finds him, she answers, "I reckon a family ought to be all together when a chap comes. Specially the first one. I reckon the Lord will see to that" (p. 18). About this, too, she is terribly wrong, unless one is to consider as a being together the forced and brief encounter between Lena and Lucas just before he flees.

Numerous critics have seen Lena as a sort of earth-mother symbolizing the basic natural order, and Faulkner has said recently, "It was her destiny to have a husband and children and she knew it, and so she went out and attended to it without asking help from anyone. . . . She was never for one moment [176] confused, frightened, alarmed."[4] There is, however, another, far more trivial side to Lena. One of the first things we learn about her is that on trips to town she would ask her father to stop the wagon at the edge of town so she could walk the rest of the way in "because she believed that the people who saw her and whom she passed on foot would believe that she lived in the town too" (p. 3). After breakfast at the Armstids' she is very proud of the fact that she "et polite." Nor is her treatment of Byron in the last chapter particularly natural or admirable, especially when one remembers her easy acceptance and high valuation of the worthless Lucas. Nor is it true that she was never for one moment confused, frightened, or alarmed. She is distinctly confused and frightened by Mrs. Hines' confusion and her own confusion about the identity of her child and its father (p. 359), and she is very much alarmed when she believes Byron has gone away for good. While it is true that she didn't explicitly ask help from anyone, she is not unlike Anse Bundren in her dependence on others and her expectation that help will be provided. This expectation is not completely unselfconscious, Faulkner suggests several times.[5]

It can be argued, of course, that without some of the characteristics I have just pointed to Lena would lose all verisimilitude and become pure symbol, much as Eula Varner is in *The Hamlet*. This is

---

[4] Jean Stein, "The Art of Fiction XII: William Faulkner," *Paris Review*, no. 12 (Spring, 1956), 50.

[5] See, for example, the description of the way she passes and notes the Armstid wagon and then waits for it (pp. 6–10).

true, but it is important to recognize these aspects of her character when one proposes her as a norm or ideal.

But Faulkner undermines this view of her in a more important way—by reducing her to a flat comic character at two crucial points in the book. At the end of the first chapter as she approaches Jefferson, where she hopes to find the father of her child, her only response is: "My, my, . . . here I aint been on the road but four weeks, and now I am in Jefferson already. My, [177] my. A body does get around" (p. 26). And at the very end of the book, after having tormented Byron terribly with her apparent indifference to him, and seemingly unconcerned about his clearly visible pain, she comments: "My, my. A body does get around. Here we aint been coming from Alabama but two months, and now it's already Tennessee" (p. 444).

We are left finally, I think, with the kind of ambiguity about her which is suggested by the description of her face as having "either nothing in it, or everything, all knowledge" (p. 379), an ambiguity often encountered in Faulkner in the phrase "at once empty and profound."

Even harder to reconcile with the view of Lena and Byron as norm is the reduction of Byron in the last chapter to a purely comic character. Not only has he been presented as the highest representative of man and conscience throughout the book, but in the latter part he has grown in stature by taking more responsibility for the people around him than he ever had before. Moreover, more than any other character, he has been involved in all three stories. Yet in the final chapter Faulkner makes us see him chiefly as an ineffectual and ridiculous little man, so defeated and humiliated by Lena that the narrator of the section becomes "downright ashamed to look at him, to let him know that any human man had seen and heard what happened" (p. 441). It is true that both we and the narrator continue to feel sympathetic toward him, but we can hardly feel respect.

Perhaps better than any other of his creations, Joe Christmas illuminates Faulkner's general methods and intentions. I spoke earlier of Faulkner's tendency to push beyond farthermost limits. His equation of Joe Christmas and Christ is another example of this. For by doing so he has made, so to speak, an oxymoron the center of his book. Many writers, of course, have used themes of redemption through violence, and some have hinted at relationships between criminal outcasts and certain aspects of Christ. Faulkner has gone far beyond this. On the one hand, he compels us by dozens of means, many completely explicit, to [178] think of Joe Christmas as Christ or very much like Christ. On the other, he presents Joe not only as a killer but as an extraordinarily violent man. From the age of fourteen, when he beats up the Negro girl who was to provide his first sex experience, he has physical battles with almost every man and woman with whom he has any relationship. (See above p. 109.) But more than this, Faulkner makes him an exceptionally cold and contemptuous person, remarkably incapable of pity, generosity, or love. It is important to recognize that the equation of Joe and Christ is not chiefly an ironic commentary on his divergence from an ideal, as is, for example, the equation of Bloom and Ulysses in Joyce's book, nor is it simply a grim inversion of the Christ story, for Faulkner makes Joe's battle against the twentieth-century Pharisaic order seem a valid one, suggests divine control of the events leading up to the "crucifixion," implies that Joe in a sense bears our common guilt, and suggests strongly that his "crucifixion" and "ascension" will have a permanent value.

Apart from these two opposed general views of Joe there are several other views and understandings of him we must hold in suspension and seek to reconcile. At times one is led to feel that Joe's primary problem is his Negro blood or belief that he has Negro blood and that it is chiefly this which alienates and destroys him. In the summary of his fifteen years of wandering we are told that he tricked white men into calling him Negro in order to fight them, that he almost kills a prostitute when he discovers she will knowingly sleep with Negroes, and that he becomes "sick" after that and lives with Negroes entirely. During this period he fights Negroes who call him white and lives with a woman "who resembled an ebony carving." Lying in bed with her he tried "to breathe into himself the dark odor, the dark and inscrutable thinking and being of Negroes, with each suspiration trying to expel from himself the white blood and the white thinking and being" (p. 197). But his nostrils "would whiten and tauten, his whole being writhe and strain with physical outrage and spiritual denial" (p. 197). A few hours before he kills [179] Joanna he flees from the Negro section of town as though it were some "thick black pit" (pp. 99, 101) and reaches the white section with a great feeling of relief. We read:

He could walk quiet here. Now and then he could see them: heads in silhouette, a white blurred garmented shape; on a lighted veranda four people sat about a card table, the white faces intent and sharp in the low light, the bare arms of the women glaring smooth and white above the trivial cards. "That's all I wanted," he thought. "That dont seem like a whole lot to ask." [p. 100]

The immediate context leads us to assume that all he wanted was the conventional life of white people, although there is an important ambiguity here, since his statement also follows one he makes a few pages earlier which relates to a quite different theme: *"All I wanted was peace* thinking, 'She ought not to started praying over me'" (p. 97). During his flight after killing Joanna, he equates the Negro shoes he is wearing with "the black abyss which had been waiting, trying, for thirty years to drown him" (p. 289). Perhaps most important, since it is not simply Joe's own perception, is Gavin Stevens' interpretation of

Joe's behavior in terms of white and black blood and his equation of the black blood with violence (pp. 393–394). In the final description of Joe, after the castration, we read that

from out the slashed garments about his hips and loins the pent black blood seemed to rush like a released breath. It seemed to rush out of his pale body like the rush of sparks from a rising rocket; upon that black blast the man seemed to rise soaring into their memories forever and ever. [p. 407]

Clearly, in these passages and many others we are strongly urged to interpret Joe's life chiefly in terms of his mixed blood. When we try to do so, however, we encounter a number of problems. During the years he lives with McEachern his difficulties are in no way related to his Negro blood. The McEacherns apparently never suspect it, and there is no [180] evidence that he himself thinks about it until he speaks of it to the waitress, Bobbie. Even then it does not seem particularly important to him. Nor does Bobbie's violent rejection of him seem sufficient to account for his later obsession with the problem. It is true that she makes much of his Negro blood in her hysterics after the dance hall episode and even calls him "a nigger son of a bitch" (p. 190), but we do not feel it is this which bothers her so much as the fact that he has gotten her in a jam with the police. More important, of course, is how Joe interprets it. But here we get no help from Faulkner, for Joe is never once shown remembering or thinking about the episode. We do not know what it means to him, how crucial it was, and, if it was, in what way. Judging from some of his later reactions and remarks we are likely to assume its chief effect was to add to his general distrust of women, a motif I shall elaborate below, rather than to his sense of his black blood.

Although his Negro blood greatly affects Joanna Burden's attitude toward him, and although there are moments when he resents the fact that she thinks of him as Negro, it does not seem very much involved in his most important responses toward her or in his decision to kill her. He puts away the thought of marrying her with the generalized comment: "No. If I give in now, I will deny all the thirty years that I have lived to make me what I chose to be" (p. 232), and before he kills her what clearly obsesses him is the fact that she prayed over him. One does not feel certain that his relationship with her or his feelings about it would have been appreciably different had he not felt himself to be part Negro.

What makes it most difficult to interpret Joe in terms of his mixed blood, however, is the extent to which Faulkner urges us to look at Joe's problem in other terms. A number of critics have urged that we see Joe essentially as victim of narrow or fanatic Protestantism with its unnatural attitude toward sex. This theme is clearly dominant in the McEachern episodes [181] and is prominent in Joe's experience in the orphanage and in his relationship with Miss Burden. More than any-thing else, probably, Miss Burden's puritan background leads to the actions which make Joe feel he needs to kill her. And I suppose we must believe that it is, in part, a deep resentment of the generally repressive puritan attitude which leads Joe to kill her when she insists that he repent with her for their sexual relations. On the other hand, in each of the sections emphasizing this theme, what upsets Joe most is not the repressive Protestantism so much as the unpredictability and illogicality of the women he is involved with. In the McEachern section this is made completely explicit. Joe resents Mrs. McEachern's secret kindnesses to him much more than he does McEachern's puritanical injustice: "It was the woman: that soft kindness which he believed himself doomed to be forever victim of and which he hated worse than he did the hard and ruthless justice of men" (p. 147).

When we seek to relate the theme of repressive Protestantism to that of Joe's Negro blood, we cannot go very far. Hines' religious and sexual fanaticism is inextricably mixed with a fanatic advocacy of white supremacy; Miss Burden's Calvinism is allied with a fanatic desire to save the Negro. One might link these as more or less comparable perversions, but one can hardly press this relationship as a general theme, since we are told nothing at all about the racial atti-tudes of McEachern, who is the chief representative of fanatic Protes-tantism.

Complicating one's understanding of Joe's story still further is the strong emphasis on still another aspect of Joe's life—one which has so far been largely overlooked by commentators—his generally unsatis-factory experience with women and sex. Early in the book Faulkner describes Joe as "too young yet to escape from the world of women for that brief respite before he escaped back into it to remain until the hour of his death" (p. 106); one could make a good case that Joe's chief problem was not nearly so much his black blood or repressive upbringing as that world of women. [182]

His life is largely a series of disastrous relationships with women. At the age of seven he is shocked and bewildered by the dietitian in the orphanage. During the ten years following he rebels against the secrecy and softness of his foster mother, Mrs. McEachern. He is severely shocked twice by the waitress, Bobbie, with whom he believes himself in love, first by the discovery that she is a whore and then by her furious rejection of him when he comes to marry her after killing McEachern. Later he beats a white prostitute almost to death and becomes "sick" for two years after discovering that she will sleep with Negroes. His body and spirit both rebel when he tries to live with a Negro woman as man and wife. And he suffers repeated shocks from Joanna Burden. More than this, some of his reactions to women and natural female functions are almost pathological. At the age of four-teen, when his turn comes to lie with a Negro girl whom a group of boys have engaged for sexual purposes, he goes berserk, kicks and hits the girl, and fights with the four boys until they run away. "None of them knew why he had fought. And he could not have told them" (p. 138). When he learns that women menstruate, he is so disturbed that he feels a need for some ritual acceptance of it, which he achieves temporarily by killing a sheep and bathing his hands in the blood of the dying animal. Several years later, when on his first date with Bobbie she tells him she is menstruating, he is so horrified that he runs away from her and vomits. Part of what infuriates him about Joanna Burden is his belief that she tricked him by lying about her age and *"about what happens to women at a certain age"* (p. 93). When she wants him to go to college, he beats her and tells her over and over that what is wrong with her is that she has become too old to want sex anymore (pp. 242–243). Twice when women feed him he throws the food on the floor, and at some point in his life he becomes so determined to avoid a woman's services that he cannot stand to wear buttons she has sewed on. He goes to the extent of taking his clothes from the family wash [183] before she could replace the missing buttons. "When she foiled him he set himself deliberately to learn and remember which buttons were missing and had been restored. With his pocket knife and with the cold and bloodless deliberation of a surgeon he would cut off the buttons which she had just replaced" (p. 93). On the night before he kills Joanna he stands beneath her window, curses her, and using his hand as a knife, knocks off the last button on his clothing. He sleeps that night in a stable. On the way to it he thinks aloud: " 'Why in hell do I want to smell horses?' Then he said, fumbling: 'It's because they are not women. Even a mare horse is a kind of man' " (p. 95).

Faulkner also suggests that his discovery that Bobbie was a whore had much to do with determining his nature and fate (pp. 173–174), and it is immediately after her rejection of him that he enters the transient and violent course that he runs for the next fifteen years.

Finally, by persistently tying together Joe's relations with women and the eating and rejection of food, Faulkner seems to be suggesting that much of Joe's problem is that he never had a mother and can find no satisfactory substitute.

To a considerable extent we can relate this general theme with the racial one, for most of Joe's difficulties with women directly or indirectly involve his Negro blood, and we can make connections between his sexual difficulties and his repressive Protestant upbringing, although with some difficulty since Faulkner never clearly suggests a causal relationship between the two and since almost all the characters in the book, including Lena, come from somewhat similar backgrounds. But there is little we can do to relate this view of Joe with the view of him as Christ. We are somewhat troubled, too, by the question of how much weight to put on these various interpretations. In his madness old man Hines easily combines all these views of Joe's experience, and Joe, himself, in the same breath, so to speak, often expresses his consciousness of his tainted blood [184] and his resentment of women and never attempts to distinguish between them. As readers, however, we are groping for some understanding and interpretation beyond this, some way of organizing these various views of Joe, of moving beyond the general feeling, the feeling we have about uninterpreted life itself, that there is a highly complex set of relationships which we cannot quite grasp.

Again, however, Faulkner clearly wishes to prevent such a movement and seeks if anything, in the final chapters of Joe's story, to complicate our responses further. First of all, Joe, himself, remains almost completely opaque. In the final chapter of his story, describing his capture, imprisonment, escape, and execution, we see him only from a distance, and in the chapter describing his flight after the murder of Miss Burden he is never shown thinking directly about the murder or in any but the most general terms about the meaning of his former or present actions. As he enters Mottstown to give himself up, we read that

he is entering it again, the street which ran for thirty years. It had been a paved street, where going should be fast. It had made a circle and he is still inside of it. Though during the last seven days he has had no paved street, yet he has travelled farther than in all the thirty years before. And yet he is still inside the circle. "And yet I have been farther in these seven days than in all the thirty years," he thinks. "But I have never got outside that circle. I have never broken out of the ring of what I have already done and cannot ever undo." [p. 296]

We accept this, I think, but we do not know at all clearly in what sense he has gone farther or how that going farther relates to his previous problems. We know that he has attacked a Negro congregation and cursed God from the pulpit. We can interpret this as a parallel of Christ's cleansing of the Temple and as a general act of defiance, but it does not suggest any kind of progress or change, especially in view of his flippant attitude [185] afterward, as he thinks about cutting a notch in the bench leg he has used as a weapon and flips a cigarette toward the terrified Negroes in the bushes with the comment "Have a butt, boys" (pp. 284–285). We know also that he has felt himself to be outside time, that he was terribly hungry for a while and then no longer hungry, that knowing the day of the week becomes more important than food. We can infer that some kind of softening has taken place when instead of asking for food with the harsh words he can feel "marshalling in his mind" he finds himself asking quietly what day it is and then saying "thank you" (p. 290). An even deeper change is suggested when he is remembering a kind of Last Supper in a Negro cabin and thinks, "And they were afraid. Of their brother afraid" (p.

293), and when he realizes later that the reason he feels at peace is that he doesn't "have to bother about having to eat anymore" (p. 295).

Beyond this there is no illumination or resolution of the previously developed themes. We understand that Joe is tired of running and struggling, but as far as we can tell he has been led to this only by physical weariness and by the compulsive awareness (imposed only by the Christ theme) that on Friday he must give himself up. The suggestion, made by his use of the word "brother," that he has accepted his Negro blood is so fleeting and so undeveloped that we cannot really feel he has achieved any resolution of this problem. This is especially true since the chapter ends with an emphasis on the Negro-smelling shoes which suggest his earlier view of his Negro blood and the Negro world as a black pit.

Our reaction to this chapter is complicated by the tone Faulkner uses to describe the futile activities of the sheriff and his posse and bloodhounds, for his satiric treatment of them gives the whole affair a cops and robbers atmosphere, with a dash of Mack Sennett thrown in, and compels us to delight in Joe's ability to outwit his pursuers.

In the final chapter of Joe's story Faulkner goes far out of his [186] way to prevent us from resolving or ordering our understanding of Joe or of the meaning of his life experience. Throughout the chapter he keeps Joe entirely in the background. We see him only for a moment and then at a distance. We have no direct knowledge of what he is thinking or feeling. Furthermore, Faulkner introduces two new characters, Gavin Stevens and Percy Grimm, and devotes the major part of the chapter to the actions and emotions of the latter. It is true that the chapter opens with various speculations about why Joe ran to Hightower's house after escaping and why, once there, he let himself be executed without fighting back. But these are presented clearly as uninformed speculations and are so general and so unrelated to the specific questions we have about Joe that they offer no real illumination. Their effect, and clearly this is Faulkner's intention, is to leave our questions unresolved. It baffles our imagination, just as it baffles Gavin Stevens (who does not believe that anyone could reconstruct the scene) to see how Mrs. Hines could have convinced Joe that Hightower offered a kind of sanctuary, and Stevens' interpretation of Joe's final actions and whole life in terms of alternately ruling white and black blood is so general and mechanical that it can hardly be taken seriously. Nor can it be related satisfactorily to the view of Joe as Christ. Moreover, like most of Stevens' "explanations," it ceases to be comprehensible or coherent when one reads it closely. Perhaps most important, to the extent that we accept Stevens' equation of the black blood with violent and evil acts and accept Joe's own feeling that the black blood is a tainted part of himself, we are accepting the racial attitudes of all the mad and vicious characters in the book. We face this same dilemma if, as Faulkner sometimes encourages us to do, and as Professor Holman has suggested, we view Joe's black blood as a kind of equivalent of original sin, of man's common guilt.

By devoting the major part of the chapter to Percy Grimm, Faulkner not only preserves the suspension he has established [187] but complicates it further. We can relate Grimm to one theme of the Christmas story by viewing him essentially as another kind of zealot and add him to the list of fanatics who have already contributed to Joe's destruction. But Faulkner also compels us to take a far more complex view of him.

Although his patriotism is bigoted, fanatic, and ambitious, he seems at first to be sincerely interested in providing an orderly and dignified military atmosphere which will symbolize the spirit of the United States as he conceives it. He succeeds to the extent that the town comes to accept him "with respect and a little awe and a deal of actual faith and confidence, as though somehow his vision and patriotism and pride in the town, the occasion, had been quicker and truer than theirs" (p. 400). Had it been left up to him he would have escorted Joe with a squad of men so that he could not escape. Yet it is he who departs completely from all order and rule by castrating Joe.

At the same time we must see Grimm on a symbolic level as Joe's assigned and somehow fitting executioner. Here, too, Faulkner provides several suggestions. He describes Grimm as moving with "the implacable undeviation of Juggernaut or Fate" (p. 403). But he also describes him in Christian terms as running "as though under the protection of a magic or a providence" (p. 404), as exhibiting "that serene, unearthly luminousness of angels in church windows" (pp. 404–405), and as crying out with a "voice clear and outraged like that of a young priest" (p. 406). Finally, he describes him several times as a pawn obedient to "whatever Player moved him on the Board" (p. 405).

The chapter, and the story of Joe, ends immediately after the castration with the suggestion that Joe is finally at peace and that the memory of him will remain forever with those who watched him die. It is an effective ending, and one feels that somehow Joe's life and death were significant. But I do not think we can close in at all on the nature of that significance. Apart from our unresolved questions about Joe's character and [188] motives and about who and what is responsible for his fate, we are left with questions about the execution and castration. How are we to interpret Joe's peacefulness? Simply as relief that he doesn't have to run anymore, or as the achievement of some more full and serious acceptance of his fate? Are we to view the castration as a perversion on Grimm's part or as a fitting and somehow necessary part of Joe's fate and a necessary aspect of the crucifixion ritual? If the latter, how are we to square it with the emphasis elsewhere in the book on the importance of natural sexual attitudes and behaviors? How seriously are we to take Joe's "ascension" and the suggestion that he has performed a redemptive function? The heavy emphasis on the Christ parallels in the last two chapters and the tone of the descriptions of his "ascension" and of the effect on his executioners suggests we give it weight. Yet it is hard to see what in Joe's life or end, apart from the shock of seeing him castrated, would cause him "to rise soaring into their memories forever and ever" (p. 407). We cannot help but see the ending also as a travesty upon meaningful ritual or religious experience, especially since Faulkner chooses to end the scene with the scream of the fire siren.

Perhaps the clearest illustration of Faulkner's desire to provide ambiguity is provided by the ending of the Hightower story. Up until that point the character of Hightower and the meaning of his story are reasonably clear. The only serious problem we have had is to understand and accept his obsession with his dead grandfather and the galloping cavalry. What makes it hard to understand and accept is that it does not, except in the retrospect passages and at isolated moments, seem to play any part in his conversation or thought. At no point in his numerous conversations with Byron or in his thought about the problems Byron presents, do we see any evidence of the obsession. Yet we must believe—Faulkner is perfectly clear on this point (pp. 53–56, 65)—that it was the obsession that prevented him from succeeding either as a minister or a husband. [189] As the story progresses, however, we tend to forget about the obsession almost completely, since there is no evidence of it between pages 66 and 408. We come to see Hightower as a man who has abdicated not only his obligations as a minister but all human responsibilities, a man who wants only peace and seclusion and, as he himself puts it, is "not in life any more" (p. 263). His problem, clearly, is to come back into life. All Faulkner's emphasis is on this, on his fright and resistance as Byron becomes involved and seeks to involve him, on his own recognition that he does have obligations, and on his gradual acceptance of those obligations.

The story appears to reach a climax and resolution as Hightower achieves a sense of "purpose and pride" after having taken the responsibility of delivering Lena's child and then goes so far as to perjure himself in an effort to save Joe Christmas.

But Faulkner adds one more chapter. In it he describes Hightower's memories and thoughts several hours after the killing of Joe Christmas. It opens with the suggestion that Hightower has not really changed, for he is waiting at the window just as he had in the past for the vision of the galloping cavalry. We then learn something about Hightower's family background, which explains to some extent why he came to idealize and identify with his dead grandfather, a lusty, swaggering man on the order of Sutpen or Colonel Sartoris, and which ties in somewhat with the opposition of natural versus fanatic or distorted attitudes which has informed other parts of the book. I say "somewhat" because Hightower's father, although initially a fanatic abolitionist and unduly zealous minister, becomes, before Hightower's birth, a reasonably sane and practical man and because the action of the grandfather which obsesses Hightower is hardly a natural or unself-conscious one. Nor is it even clearly a heroic one, for it ends with the grandfather being shot while stealing a chicken in a hen house. [190]

The main weight of the chapter is on Hightower's growing realiza-tion of the extent of his failure and guilt as minister and husband, a failure due primarily, he recognizes more and more clearly, to his obsession with his grandfather. He seems to accept that it is he, himself, who is responsible for the shame and death of his wife: "After all, there must be some things for which God cannot be accused by man and held responsible" (p. 427). As the chapter progresses, Faulkner suggests by his imagery that Hightower is drawing closer and closer to some final realization about himself. Immediately follow-ing the passage just quoted we read that "thinking begins to slow now. It slows like a wheel beginning to run in sand, the axle, the vehicle, the power which propels it not yet aware" (p. 427). As he continues to trace his failure, the wheel slows further, then even more: "Thinking is running too heavily now; he should know it, sense it. Still the vehicle is unaware of what it is approaching" (p. 429). He is described as feel-ing a gathering "as though for some tremendous effort" (p. 429). We are given a fragment of his thought: ". . . revealed to my wife my hunger, my ego . . . instrument of her despair and shame . . ." (p. 429, ellipses Faulkner's). Then "a sentence seems to stand fullsprung across his skull, behind his eyes: *I dont want to think this. I must not think this. I dare not think this*" (p. 429). The sweat begins to pour from him.

Surely no writer could do more to prepare for and promise illumination and resolution. Finally, it seems to come:

Out of the instant the sandclutched wheel of thinking turns on with the slow implacability of a mediaeval torture instrument, beneath the wrenched and broken sockets of his spirit, his life: "Then, if this is so, if I am the in-strument of her despair and death, then I am in turn instrument of someone outside myself. And I know that for fifty years I have not even been clay: I have been a single instant of darkness in which a horse galloped and a gun crashed. And if I am my dead grandfather on the instant of his death, then my wife, [191] his grandson's wife . . . the debaucher and murderer of my grandson's wife, since I could neither let my grandson live or die . . ."

The wheel, released, seems to rush on with a long sighing sound. He sits motionless in its aftermath, in his cooling sweat, while the sweat pours and pours. The wheel whirls on. It is going fast and smooth now, because it is freed now of burden, of vehicle, axle, all. [pp. 429–430, ellipses Faulk-ner's]

The released wheel suggests that there has been resolution and makes us feel it. The diction and syntax of the quotation suggests it: the "then, if this is so . . . then . . ." suggests a cause-and-effect relation-ship. But the second clause is a *non sequitur.* The "and I know" suggests self-understanding, but it is followed by a highly fanciful metaphor which, if anything, contradicts the suggestion that he is an "instrument." Another logical sequence is suggested by "and if . . . then. . . ." This time the logic is indeed unassailable, but it is used to extend the highly figurative and alogical equation of himself with his own grandfather, an equation which both he and we have already established. We wonder now whether we have observed a moment of tragic illumination or an escape into fantasy and confusion. The re-mainder of the chapter complicates our impressions further. The released wheel image, "freed now of burden, of vehicle, axle, all," has suggested strongly that whatever the nature of his final resolution, Hightower is empty and at peace. But apparently he is not, because a moment later we read "then it seems to him that some ultimate dammed flood within him breaks and rushes away" (p. 431). Yet even then there is still conflict within him, for he thinks he should pray but does not try, and there is still self-pity and even more surprising, self-deception. "I wanted so little. I asked so little. It would seem . . ." And there is apparently honor and pride, for the final paragraph begins:

It is as though they [the phantom galloping Confederate soldiers] had merely waited until he could find something to pant with, to be [192] re-affirmed in triumph and desire with, with this last left of honor and pride and life. [p. 431]

He has his vision of the galloping figures thundering past. The tone is excited and triumphant, seeming to suggest that the vision is a kind of final reward, and it seems to be equated with strength and honor and life. But this vision, and the obsession that brings it, has been clearly associated with Hightower's failure to come to terms with himself and his world, and in his presumable recognition of his guilt before the final release of the wheel, he himself has recognized this.

We are left puzzled, therefore, not only about the nature and degree of Hightower's self-realization but about how to feel about it. The rhetoric and placement of the final vision compel us to view it as an affirmative and triumphant end for Hightower. It is, after all, what he has been waiting for. At the same time it seems anything but triumphant and affirmative when we consider that this very vision is a kind of madness which has emasculated and destroyed him and that his welcoming of it means he has again retreated from himself and the world.

This final chapter of the Hightower story is puzzling, too, in that it does not, except most indirectly, develop or extend the theme of detachment and involvement which governs the body of his story. At no point does Hightower think about the return to life he experienced previously, nor is there any evidence that that return was of any consequence. The story ceases to be about a man whose chief problem is to find a way back into life and becomes essentially the story of a man with an obsession. True, the obsession is what led him away from life, but the emphasis here is on the obsession itself, and we feel finally that we are viewing a pathological figure rather than a tragic one.

Each of the stories then is ambiguous or unresolved in certain important respects, and none focuses clearly or consistently on a single theme. Obviously it will not be easy to grasp the [193] relationships between them, especially since Faulkner makes no effort to pull the stories together at the end of the book. In fact, he is careful to keep them separate. At the end of the book we read in order the endings to the Christmas story, the Hightower story, and the Lena Grove–Byron Bunch story. These endings are in separate chapters, and each is clearly and distinctly an ending to only one of the stories. More than this, except for the ending to the Christmas story, which does include an important action of Hightower, none of these endings either involve characters from the other stories or make any direct comment on the other stories or in any direct way illuminate the meanings of the other stories. In the Hightower ending, apart from the brief note that the faces of Byron, Lena, Joe, and Grimm are among those Hightower sees in his dying moments, there is no mention even of the recent events in Hightower's life which connect him to the other stories. Clearly Faulkner is seeking to achieve this separation, is willing even to sacrifice verisimilitude, for this ending is set just a few hours after Joe has been shot in Hightower's house, and it is difficult to believe that Hightower would so completely ignore that event. The ending of the Lena Grove story, which ends the book, is even more detached from the other stories. Indeed, were it not for the furniture dealer's passing comment that Lena must have been in Jefferson when "they lynched that nigger," there would be nothing whatsoever even to remind us of the other stories. Again it would seem that Faulkner is being very careful to keep the endings separate. Faulkner, no doubt, has several reasons for presenting the final chapter from the point of view of the furniture dealer; surely one of them is that he has no knowledge of any of the events which have taken place in the book, and this makes it easy for Faulkner to leave them in suspension.

As in *The Sound and the Fury* and *As I Lay Dying*, Faulkner complicates our final responses further by juxtaposing varied [194] tones as well as varied kinds of material: the tone of the first two endings is serious and intense; the tone of the third is largely playful.

As in *The Sound and the Fury* and *As I Lay Dying* we are left with highly mixed feelings about the significance and worth of the human agony and struggle we have witnessed. We are encouraged to see Joe's crucifixion as both a meaningful apotheosis and a parody of one. We must feel that Hightower's suffering has led to ennobling self-knowledge and that it has led nowhere but back into his obsession. And if at first glance the final chapter seems to provide a kind of comic affirmation, the final effect is far more complex than that. In the first place, the comic tone puts the "affirmative" material in a realm completely sealed off from the world of the other events we have witnessed, a realm which none of the other major characters could possibly enter, and one therefore largely irrelevant when we consider their plights. It does not in any sense provide an alternative way of life or alternative set of attitudes for Joe, Hightower, or Joanna Burden; and even Byron in that realm becomes a comic figure. Moreover, the ideal or norm that Lena represents is hardly a full or adequate one. For one thing, her virtues are almost inseparable from her intellectual limitations; for another, she is too much like Anse Bundren in her self-absorbed and ruthless pursuit of her objectives. Hightower is not simply expressing his own fear of life when he thinks of Byron as her husband and says "Poor boy" (p. 356). The final words in the book, her "My, my. A body does get around. Here we aint been coming from Alabama but two months, and now it's already Tennessee" are delightful, but they are delightful partly because they are such an absurdly inadequate commentary on her experience, to say nothing of the other experiences in the book. These complexities in our view of Lena are especially important, because no matter how one interprets the book one must use Lena as a kind of measuring [195] rod for the other characters. As such she is a provocative but hardly constant instrument.

Finally, as in *The Sound and the Fury* and *As I Lay Dying* we are left with a suspension too varied and complex to organize into any clear pattern. We can, of course, discover a great many relationships between the three stories and between parts of the individual stories, and we can, as a number of critics do, trace various themes which recur with some frequency throughout the book. None of these themes, however, as I hope this analysis makes evident, governs enough of the book or resolves enough of the problems in the book to provide any over-all sense of unity. They, too, come to form part of the insoluble suspension, for they cannot be clearly related to one another.

For example, we cannot quite bring together the strong suggestion in the Hightower section that man fails when he retreats from the world or ignores the needs of his fellows and the celebration of Lena's detached, self-centered, and sometimes hardhearted pursuit of her personal destiny. Whatever one thinks of her, surely her detachment from the world is as great as Hightower's. Nor does the theme of responsibility relate very closely to Joe's story, for it is when Joanna does for the first time become concerned about Joe's welfare that she destroys him and herself. Indeed, much in Joe's story would seem to suggest that zealousness or too great concern with the welfare of others is the chief evil. If we push the theme of Protestant rigidity and intolerance, what are we to make of Joe's, and I think Faulkner's, preference for the ruthless McEachern over his soft and generous wife. Nor can the theme of Protestant bigotry be closely related to Joe's obsessive concern with his Negro blood or to his execution by Percy Grimm. If we try to understand Joe and Joanna and Hightower in relation to their loveless or empty or distorted family backgrounds, we discover that Lena's origin was hardly more promising. If we try to see the Lena [196] story as celebrating healthy sex and fecundity in opposition to the guilt-ridden and barren passion of Joanna or see her as representing the virtues of plain ordinary unalienated people, "the good stock," we must contend with the largely unsympathetic treatment of the ordinary unalienated population of Jefferson. And we must contend with the bleak description of the world from which Lena comes, a "labor- and childridden" world in which her sister-in-law "for almost half of every year . . . was either lying in or recovering" (p. 5), a world which has sweated out of her brother all "softness and gentleness and youth . . . and almost everything else except a kind of stubborn and despairing fortitude and the bleak heritage of his blood-pride" (p. 5). Concurrent with whatever particular theme we explore, we must hold in suspension the feeling that what dominates much of the book is sheer inexplicable madness and obsession. Hightower, Joanna, McEachern, Hines, Grimm, and Joe himself are all people with pathological obsessions, while both the dietitian and the waitress react to Joe with a hysteria bordering on madness. I do not think it is going too far to see a kind of madness even in Lena's stubborn and single-minded search for the father of her child. But at the same time one cannot escape the feeling that Faulkner is also saying that the characters do have free will and the obligation to choose more wisely than they do.

One can loosely group a considerable number of the themes and events in terms of a broad antithesis between rigid, perverted, or distorted attitudes toward religion and sex on the one hand, and on the other, natural attitudes more or less exemplified by Lena Grove and Byron and given a degree of explicit expression by Hightower. Or one can group them in terms of their relation to a broadly conceived image of Christ, as Professor Holman has done. But such groupings are so general and so removed from the actual effects of the structure and rhetoric of the book that they are not particularly helpful. They provide [197] a way of side-stepping rather than ordering the actual complexities of the book. For they stand up only so long as one ignores most of the ambiguities and varied and conflicting emphases which provide the essential character of the book; that is, they provide a possible framework for ordering certain aspects of the book, but they do not illuminate the book itself. [198]

The Achievement of
William Faulkner

MICHAEL MILLGATE

By COMPARISON WITH *The Sound and the Fury* AND *As I Lay Dying*
the opening pages of *Light in August* display a much closer approxi-
mation to the techniques and progressions of "conventional" fiction.
The first chapter, with its image of Lena Grove pursuing her tranquil
way steadily across the face of Mississippi, immediately recalls the
opening of such Hardy novels as *The Mayor of Casterbridge* or *The
Return of the Native,* and even the abrupt transitions to apparently
unrelated material in the second and third chapters will not disturb
anyone familiar with Dickens—with, say, *Bleak House,* or *Our Mutual
Friend.* Throughout *Light in August,* indeed, we are aware of an
essential affinity with the major traditions of the nineteenth-century
novel and especially with the work of Hardy and Dickens, and the
initial impression of the relative conventionality of *Light in August* to
some degree remains to the end of the book. But the demands the
novel makes of its readers are by no means of a wholly conventional
nature; this is especially true of the kind of moral and emotional
engagement which Faulkner extorts, but it is also true of the narrative
technique, which is much less straightforward than might appear at
first sight.

The "time present" of the novel, as defined by the opening
account of Lena's meeting with Armstid, begins on a Friday afternoon.
In a sense, however, Lena's relationship with Armstid and his wife lies
outside the action of the novel proper; it is a framing episode, a
prelude, linked with the epilogue or coda provided in the final chapter
of the book. The point at which the main action of the novel is
engaged is at the very end of the first chapter, when Lena arrives on
the outskirts of Jefferson and sees the smoke rising from the ruins of
Miss Burden's home. This is about midday on the Saturday, and it is
important to note that, for all the novel's abundance of narrative
incident, many of the major events have by this time already taken
place. One major event—indeed, it is one of the three crucial events in
the immediate action of the novel—has taken place during the night
which Lena spent at the Armstid's: this is the death of Joanna Burden.
The two other crucial events both take place on the ninth day following Lena's arrival in Jefferson; that Monday morning Lena gives birth

to her child, and that afternoon Percy Grimm hunts down Joe Christmas and kills him. A very considerable proportion of the novel is taken up with extended "flashbacks" which recount [124] the history of various characters up to the point at which they become involved in the present action. The longest of these retrospections, telling the story of Christmas himself, occupies Chapters six to twelve inclusive, and the others, though much shorter, may even so occupy several pages or almost the whole of a chapter. These passages are introduced and deployed very much as the long sentences in later novels such as *Go Down, Moses* and *Intruder in the Dust:* the immediate action is quite simply held in suspension for the duration of the flashback, rather as the action in *Moby Dick* is sometimes arrested while some essential point of background information is supplied. Faulkner practises no particular subtlety or concealment in introducing these flashbacks, and there even seems to be a touch of deliberate crudeness in the introduction at a late stage of the novel of characters who are to play an important part in its events, or in our interpretation of these events: "In the town on that day lived a young man named Percy Grimm" (p. 425); "Gavin Stevens though had a different theory. He is the District Attorney, . . ." (p. 419)*

It is almost as though, in his passionate need to tell the tragic story of Christmas, Faulkner scorned mere literary finesse, and in answer to a question about the style of *Light in August* he once said:

I don't know anything about style. I don't—I think a writer with a lot to—pushing inside him to get out hasn't got time to bother with style. If he just likes to write and hasn't got anything urging him, then he can become a stylist, but the ones with a great deal pushing to get out don't have time to be anything but clumsy, like Balzac, for instance.

Faulkner had a great deal "pushing inside him" when he wrote *Light in August,* but he was himself a much more deliberate writer than these remarks might seem to imply, and, despite the apparent crudity, he undoubtedly achieves powerful emotional effects by his techniques of delayed revelation and delayed introduction of characters. We first see Christmas, for example, as he appears to Mooney, the foreman at the planing mill, to Byron Bunch, and to the people of Jefferson generally: only later are we given those details of Christmas's birth and upbringing which force us radically to amend our judgment of a man whom we, like the people of Jefferson, have already condemned on sight as inherently vicious and worthless. Similarly, it is only at a very late stage in the book that we are allowed to see Hightower's situation to some extent from his own point of view. If, on the other hand, we are given Lena Grove's history the moment she appears, that

---

* All quotations from *Light in August* are from the Modern Readers Series edition (Norfolk, Conn. New Directions, 1947).

is primarily because she and her background are so simple and so easily explained, and because she seems not so much a character in the book, with possibilities of development and unanticipated variety, as a kind of impersonalised catalytic force, effecting change but [125] itself unchanging. She provides a steady imperturbable groundnote, an onward linear progression that offers a constant contrast to the desperate contortions—moral, emotional, and physical—of the other characters.

It seems possible to speak almost in diagrammatic terms of this novel, rich as it is in symbolic potentialities, disposed in large and readily distinguishable blocks of material, and with whole scenes presented almost in the form of tableaux, as formalised, even frozen, action: Lena traversing the face of Mississippi "like something moving forever and without progress across an urn" (p. 5); Christmas and McEachern waiting in rigid immobility during the intervals of their hourly ritual of command, refusal, and punishment; Percy Grimm pursuing Christmas "with that lean, swift, blind obedience to whatever Player moved him on the Board." (p. 437) It is remarkable that a great deal even of the present action of the novel is not directly recounted but reflected in the minds and memories of witnesses who were not themselves involved in the action: Gavin Stevens giving his interpretation of the events leading to Christmas's death; the furniture dealer telling his wife of his encounter with Lena and Byron Bunch; the impersonal "they" of the latter part of Chapter 15, recounting "about supper tables in electrically lighted rooms and in remote hill cabins with kerosene lamps" (p. 330) the story of Christmas's arrest in Mottstown and the curious behaviour of Doc Hines and his wife. It is almost as though Faulkner were seeking to "domesticate," to incorporate within the structure of a conventional novel, the technique of multiple reflection which he had earlier employed in *As I Lay Dying*, and it is certainly clear that in *Light in August* he is concerned not merely to tell the stories of Joe Christmas, Lena Grove and Gail Hightower but also, and perhaps primarily, to show the impact of these stories upon the people of Jefferson.

One cannot avoid speaking in the plural of the stories of Christmas, Lena and Hightower, for there are quite unmistakably three distinct strands in the novel. They are not, however, entirely separable strands, and critics have become steadily more aware of the essential unity of the novel, a unity secured through various forms of thematic interrelation and ironic reflection rather than through the more familiar kinds of narrative link—though even these links are stronger and more numerous than has often been allowed, as Malcolm Cowley discovered when he attempted to separate one of the strands for inclusion in *The Portable Faulkner*. Joanna Burden, in the corruption of a sensuality discovered too late and pursued too far, offers an obvious contrast to the healthy animality of Lena Grove; Lena herself, travelling down her "peaceful corridor paved with unflagging and tranquil faith and peopled with kind and nameless faces and voices," (p. 4) is at the opposite pole from Joe Christmas, who for fifteen years has travelled down a street which "ran on in its moods and phases, always empty: he [126] might have seen himself as in numberless avatars, in silence, doomed with motion, driven by the courage of flagged and spurred despair." (p. 213) Faulkner himself spoke of Hightower as the antithesis of Christmas, in that he "escaped into his past," presumably an allusion to the way in which Christmas, bereft of all certainty about his past, cannot rest from his passionate engagement with the present. On a more comic level, there is the utter dichotomy between the conscientious Byron Bunch and his shiftless "rival" and near-namesake, Lucas Burch. There are also subsidiary patterns of contrast between these characters and among the minor characters, as well as patterns of irony operating through the recurrence of similar acts in different contexts: when Byron Bunch fights with Lucas Burch, for example, we may remember Joe Christmas's similar defeat following his final chivalric gesture towards Bobbie Allen, the prostitute; in view of Byron's pathetic adventures in the final chapter, we ought perhaps to think also of Joe's earlier experience with the Negro girl and Faulkner's comment about "that spontaneous compulsion of the male to fight with or because or over the partner with which he has recently or is about to copulate." (p. 148) There is irony of a more bitter kind in that Percy Grimm and Hightower, the one ruthlessly pursuing Christmas, the other in a supreme though belated moment of abnegation trying to defend him, are essentially akin in their obsessive allegiance to a dead past.

Running throughout the book is that fundamental irony which Faulkner explores to a greater or lesser degree in almost all of his novels: the gulf between appearance and actuality, the contrast between the public and the private self. We have already noted the contrast between the outward face of Joe Christmas and the inner reality with which the reader becomes increasingly familiar as the book progresses. Another character whom we apprehend on two levels in this way is Joanna Burden, inwardly a chaos of sensuality, outwardly a woman of mature wisdom, dispensing "advice, business, financial and religious, to the presidents and faculties and trustees, and advice personal and practical to young girl students and even alumnae, of a dozen negro schools and colleges through the south." (p. 20) Hightower and Byron Bunch are other characters in whom we become aware of such a duality, while again and again we realise that the characters themselves are seeing their fellow men and women not as they actually are but as they wish them to be: so Miss Burden sees Christmas as "negro"; so Hightower discerns in his wife, as Joe Christmas discerns in Bobbie Allen, a non-existent quality of love.

These ironic patterns are clearly related to that theme in the novel which critics have often, and rightly, identified as being of major significance: the demand of organised society and organised religion that the human individual act in strict accordance with prescribed [127] abstract patterns. At the hands of religious authoritarians such as Hines and McEachern, Christmas has suffered all his life from this demand, and it is in response to the same rigid requirement that he is finally hunted down according to the rules prescribed in Jefferson for the treatment of "nigger murderers." There are, too, several passages in the novel which seem to imply a general social denunciation. After the death of Miss Burden, for instance, the people of Jefferson refused to let her body lie in peace but preferred to believe that it "cried out for vengeance":

Because the other made nice believing. Better than the shelves and the counters filled with long familiar objects bought, not because the owner desired them or admired them, could take any pleasure in the owning of them, but in order to cajole or trick other men into buying them at a profit; and who must now and then contemplate both the objects which had not yet sold and the men who could buy them but had not yet done so, with anger and maybe outrage and maybe despair too. Better than the musty offices where the lawyers waited lurking among ghosts of old lusts and lies, or where the doctors waited with sharp knives and sharp drugs, telling man, believing that he should believe, without resorting to printed admonishments, that they labored for that end whose ultimate attainment would leave them with nothing whatever to do. And the women came too, the idle ones in bright and sometimes hurried garments, with secret and passionate and glittering looks and with secret frustrated breasts (who have ever loved death better than peace) to print with a myriad small hard heels to the constant murmur *Who did it? Who did it?* periods such as perhaps *Is he still free? Ah. Is he? Is he?* (p. 273)

It is interesting, however, that Faulkner's criticism of Jefferson is relatively mild. After the arrest of Christmas it is the peace and quiet of the town which is insisted upon: Percy Grimm walks across "the quiet square empty of people peacefully at suppertables about that peaceful town and that peaceful country," (p. 430) and Faulkner makes it entirely clear in this deeply imagined and superbly evoked episode that it is Percy Grimm alone who provokes the town to that course of ritual action of which he himself inevitably becomes the final instrument. The men who share Grimm's pursuit of Christmas do not necessarily share his savagery, for one of them vomits at the sight of the castration, and it is clear that, in his presentation of Grimm, Faulkner was not especially concerned to portray a specifically Southern type of violence: years later he wrote to Malcolm Cowley of having created a Nazi before Hitler did. Although it would be an exaggeration to say that in its conduct towards Christmas the society of Jefferson appears at its collective worst, it might at least [128] be said that the occasion permitted the worst elements in Jefferson to emerge and take command. But in any case a counterbalance is supplied by Lena Grove: she brings out—not always readily, but eventually—the best in Jefferson, and it is with Lena, in her familiar role as the calm recipient of kindness, that the book begins and ends.

There is, however, little qualification or amelioration of the book's rejection of organised religion and religious fanaticism. The bigotry of several characters, in the past as well as the present, is closely examined and shown to be self-condemned by its own rigidity and inhumanity, and it is a final astringent touch in Faulkner's treatment of this theme that as Percy Grimm hunts down Joe Christmas his face displays "that serene, unearthly luminousness of angels in church windows," (p. 437) and his voice sounds "clear and outraged like that of a young priest." (p. 439) All these characters, so assured in their narrow faith, are in contrast to Joe Christmas himself, a man engaged in unceasing introspection, a persistent and desperate search for personal identity and for a meaning in life. He is several times likened to a monk, and Faulkner, answering a question put to him at the University of Virginia, spoke revealingly of Christmas's self-isolation from the world:

> I think that was his tragedy—he didn't know what he was [i.e. white or Negro], and so he was nothing. He deliberately evicted himself from the human race because he didn't know which he was. That was his tragedy, that to me was the tragic, central idea of the story—that he didn't know what he was, and there was no way possible in life for him to find out. Which to me is the most tragic condition a man could find himself in—not to know what he is and to know that he will never know.

For all his confusion, however, it is Christmas who discovers one of the two forms of religious and moral experience which Faulkner appears to offer as valid. Christmas, who becomes godlike in his last agony, discovers the way of suffering, of passive acceptance, the path of crucifixion. The opposite but complementary figure in the novel is Lena Grove, who, in her simple and unquestioning acceptance of a kind of natural religion, seems to embody those simple and permanent values which Faulkner so frequently and so powerfully affirmed, the values of endurance, patience, fecundity, and simple faith. "*That will be her life, her destiny,*" Hightower recognises: "*The good stock peopling in tranquil obedience to it the good earth; from these hearty loins without hurry or haste descending mother and daughter.*" (p. 384)

The opposition, and indeed counterpoint, of Lena Grove and Joe Christmas is clear and apparent throughout the novel, and its validity [129] is readily acceptable. The disturbing figure, morally and structurally, is that of Hightower. He has seemed to many critics a shadowy and indeterminate figure, lacking a sufficiently substantial stake in the plot or an adequately defined role in the moral or symbolic patterns of the book as a whole. But such a judgment may result from a failure to distinguish Hightower's functions from Faulkner's deliberate characterisation of him as a non-participator, a man withdrawn from life and its sufferings. He is clearly a character with a special significance for Faulkner, a type who had long haunted his imagination. No clearly identifiable forerunner of Hightower appears in any of Faulkner's published works, though we may detect several points of similarity with Mr. Compson, but in the unpublished story "Rose of Lebanon" he is directly prefigured in the central character, Gavin Blount, a bachelor doctor with a run-down Memphis practice, of whom his friend Randolph Gordon thinks "with tolerance and a right smart of affection and a little contempt. Because the life he led was no life for a man, . . . He had inherited from his father what practice he had. Or rather, he had inherited from his father a practice which, by 20 odd years of unflagging endeavour, he had reduced to the absolute minimum." Blount is utterly devoted to a local social organisation, the Guards, of which he has been chairman for seventeen years, inheriting the post ultimately from his great-uncle, also called Gavin Blount, who had died on the field of Chickamauga, and his obsession with this Civil War past leads him to consider marriage with a survivor of that period. When Gordon asks Blount why, at the age of 43, he has not married, Blount replies:

> ". . . She wouldn't have me."
> "Who wouldn't have you?"
> "Lewis Randolph."
> Lewis Randolph is my mother, she is 82 years old.

The second section of the story ends at that point. In the third section Blount himself tells the story of Lewis Randolph, who had kissed all one hundred and four men of her husband's regiment in December 1861, just before the battle of Shiloh, and whose husband, Charley Gordon, had eventually been killed the night Van Dorn burned Grant's stores at Holly Springs, shot at point-blank range by someone with a shotgun during the raiding of a chicken-roost. The story has a comic ending and the treatment of Blount is quite different from the presentation of Hightower in *Light in August*, but the death of Charley Gordon has clearly been taken over into the novel, as have many aspects of Blount, the man to whom Randolph Gordon says, "You cant live then and now too," and who replies, "I can die trying."

Blount reappears in another unpublished story, "The Big Shot," in [130] which he becomes a representative of "the old sense of honor dead everywhere else in America except in the south and kept alive here by a few old ladies who acquiesced in '65 but never surrendered." Dal Martin, the "big shot," has social pretensions for his daughter and persuades Dr. Blount to allow her name to be included on the list for the Guards ball, bribing him by the offer of an art gallery to be named after his grandfather who had died in Forrest's cavalry in 1864. Blount later feels he has betrayed his honour and begs Martin to release him from their agreement, offering to find the money for the art gallery himself; Martin refuses, and Blount commits suicide. In addition to the appearance of a Hightower type in these two unpublished stories, there exist at the University of Texas a few pages of what appears to be an early draft of *Light in August;* this version opens with a description of Hightower in his study and continues with material that was eventually absorbed into the published novel, partly into the third chapter, where Hightower first appears, and partly into the penultimate chapter, in which Hightower's life story is told.

Hightower appears in *Light in August* as the final expression of a conception which had long been present in Faulkner's mind. What is wrong with Hightower, the source of the general uneasiness about him, is that he has remained in the novel the haunting conception which Faulkner tried unsatisfactorily to embody in the unpublished stories. The actions and obsessions of Gavin Blount in "Rose of Lebanon" and "The Big Shot" are grotesquely in excess of the conceivable demands of the human situation in which Faulkner presents him. So, we may well feel, are the actions and obsessions of Gail Hightower. The "idea" informing Faulkner's presentation of Hightower is clear; it is, indeed, sufficiently implied in the obvious symbolism of his name. But Hightower is not a fully realised character, though he might have become so if Faulkner had told the story of his life at an earlier stage in the novel and had treated that story with a higher degree of dramatisation. On the other hand, it may in one sense be very much to the point that Hightower is not completely realised—obsessed with the past, he does not live in the present where realisation can occur—and he is, in any case, more closely integrated into the novel than critics have sometimes suggested. In that rich opening chapter the way is prepared for him in the elaborate image of discarded machinery:

. . . gaunt, staring, motionless wheels rising from mounds of brick rubble and ragged weeds with a quality profoundly astonishing, and gutted boilers lifting their rusting and unsmoking stacks with an air stubborn, baffled and bemused upon a stumppocked scene of profound and peaceful desolation, unplowed, untilled, gutting slowly into red and choked ravines beneath the long quiet rains of autumn and the galloping fury of vernal equinoxes. (pp. 2–3) [131]

Almost all the images associated with Hightower in succeeding chapters are already present in this passage.

Hightower has, too, more than a merely narrative connection with the Byron Bunch-Lena Grove relationship. He is more than once described as an eastern idol, and for Byron Bunch he is initially a repository of wisdom; it is Byron who interprets the stale smell of Hightower's house as the odour of goodness. Byron at the opening of the book is Hightower's disciple, his imitator in silence, withdrawal, isolation from life; but Byron is converted by his love for Lena to a new concern for humanity which soon extends beyond his relationship with Lena herself and overflows into a compassionate if hopeless attempt to aid Joe Christmas. What vitiates so many of the relationships in the novel—between Joanna Burden and Joe Christmas, for example, between Christmas and his various women, between Hightower and his wife—is their selfishness and lack of generosity: the partners use those whom they claim to love primarily as a means of attacking some personal problem. As Hightower comes eventually to realise of his own married life, such relationships remain on an abstract level rather than a human one, and they are effectively criticised in terms of the warm, humane, and outward-going quality of Byron's love for Lena. Byron not only breaks with his earlier discipleship but actually becomes his master's teacher, showing him the way to that recognition of value in life, in human involvement, which Hightower finally achieves. It is, however, too late for Hightower to be effectively reborn. Lena does not name her baby after him, and his mind cannot rest in the vision of human solidarity and interdependence which he has with such agony achieved but returns ineluctably to that obsessive image of his grandfather which has haunted him throughout his life—though Faulkner himself reminded us that this image was not in itself an ignoble one: "[Hightower] had to endure, to live, but that was one thing that was pure and fine that he had—was the memory of his grandfather, who had been brave."

Faulkner said more than once that he began *Light in August* with nothing clearly in mind save the image of Lena Grove—"knowing no more about it than a young woman, pregnant, walking along a strange country road." The Hightower image presumably became associated with this basic image at a fairly early stage in the writing of the book, although it is just conceivable that the manuscript pages at Texas represent the remains of an attempt on Faulkner's part to write a novel with Hightower as its central figure. The suggestion that "Light in August" is a countryman's expression used of a cow or mare due to drop her calf or foal in that month might tend to confirm the primacy of the Lena Grove element, but it seems unlikely that in choosing a title for so various a novel Faulkner would have such a narrow range of relevance in mind. In any case, discussion of this point has to some extent diverted attention from other substantial [132] justifications for the title which appear within the book itself. Many critics have noticed the frequency in the novel of images of light and dark, for example, and Faulkner spoke very interestingly of a special quality of light which he had in mind:

[I]n August in Mississippi there's a few days somewhere about the middle of the month when suddenly there's a foretaste of fall, it's cool, there's a lambence, a luminous quality to the light, as though it came not from just today but from back in the old classic times. It might have fauns and satyrs and the gods and—from Greece, from Olympus in it somewhere. It lasts just for a day or two, then it's gone, but every year in August that occurs in my country, and that's all that title meant, it was just to me a pleasant evocative title because it reminded me of that time, of a luminosity older than our Christian civilization.

It is this light which shines on the day of Christmas's death and at the moment when Hightower finally recognises the truth about himself and the extent of his responsibility both for his own suffering and for that of his dead wife: "In the lambent suspension of August into which night is about to fully come, it [the wheel of his thinking] seems to engender and surround itself with a faint glow like a halo." (p. 465) but Faulkner seems to hint at some wider meaning in his references to "the old classic times . . . fauns and satyrs and the gods" and the "pagan quality" of Lena Grove. The "earth-mother" qualities in Lena Grove are clearly hinted at in her name, and have long been recognised. But given Faulkner's undoubted familiarity with the stories of classical mythology and with the works of Joyce and Eliot, and his probable acquaintance with Frazer's *The Golden Bough,* it would not be surprising if he had further analogies in mind: not necessarily a complex and carefully articulated pattern of analogy such as Joyce evolved in *Ulysses,* but perhaps some slightly opportunistic exploitation of an available source such as he had shown in his allocation of three sections of *The Sound and the Fury* to the dates of Easter 1929 or in the various hinted analogies in *Light in August* itself between Joe Christmas and Jesus Christ, between Lena Grove and the Virgin Mary, and between Byron Bunch and Mary's husband, Joseph.

Any search for underlying patterns in *Light in August* might well begin with a consideration of the extensive series of parallels and substitutions which appear in the course of the novel and which again and again establish thematic and even narrative links between its different strands. An obvious example is Mrs. Hines' confused identification of Lena's baby with Joe Christmas when he was a child, and her further reference to the baby as being actually Christmas's son. One thinks also of the similarities between the apparently opposed [133] backgrounds of Hightower and Miss Burden, fanatics of the South and of the North; of the parallelism between the tragic encounter of Joe Christmas with Percy Grimm and the primarily comic encounter of Byron Bunch with Lucas Burch, which takes place at the same moment in time; of the reverberations set up in the reader's mind by the incident of Christmas breaking into a Negro church like an impersonation of the devil, recalling as it does both the mad forays into Negro churches made by his grandfather, Doc Hines, and the moment of Satanic glee caught by the camera as Hightower leaves his empty church.

Most important of all, however, is the relationship between Miss Burden and Lena Grove and Lena's replacement of Miss Burden at the plantation after the latter's death, and there are reasons for thinking that Faulkner may have intended a series of allusions to the goddess Diana and to the sacred groves where she was worshipped. Lena Grove's name is an obvious hint leading in this direction, and the Burden house itself is several times described as standing almost hidden among a grove of trees, a grove which still stands even when the house itself has gone; the place, too, is one to which Negro women have come for many years as to a shrine or to a "wise woman"—"approaching the house in a manner not exactly secret, yet purposeful, . . . emerging again and returning down the radiating paths not fast and yet not loitering." (p. 243) Miss Burden, the original mistress of the grove, is not on the face of it an especially Diana-like character, but she has certain characteristics in common with the Roman Diana—notably her masculinity, her reputation for virginity, and her moon-like ebb and flow of passion as she and Christmas pass through all the different phases of their relationship—and it is she whom the Negro women have consulted in their troubles, especially, it appears (p. 251), in those troubles of pregnancy and childbirth which were Diana's special province. Lena Grove, on the other hand, with her name, her air of timeless permanence, and her fecundity, has much in common with that Ephesian Diana who was specifically an earth-mother, fertility figure.

Is there, perhaps, some sense in which Faulkner intended the ritualistic murder of Joanna Burden, carried out as Lena Grove pauses overnight on the outskirts of the town, to be an act preparatory to the replacement of Miss Burden's alien, outmoded, and sterile influence by the natural vitality and fecundity embodied in Lena? Certainly something more than the mere establishment of a weak narrative link seems to be involved in Lena's occupation of the cabin on the Burden estate and the birth there of her child. Hightower, in particular, makes it clear that new life has come to the run-down plantation, the "ruined garden," (p. 264) that some kind of symbolic rebirth has been enacted: [134]

He emerges from the woods at the far side of the pasture behind the cabin. Beyond the cabin he can see the clump of trees in which the house had stood and burned, though from here he cannot see the charred and mute embers of what were once planks and beams. 'Poor woman,' he thinks. 'Poor, barren woman. To have not lived only a week longer, until luck returned to this place. Until luck and life returned to these barren and ruined acres.' It seems to him that he can see, feel, about him the ghosts of rich fields, and of the rich fecund black life of the quarters, the mellow shouts, the presence of fecund women, the prolific naked children in the dust before the doors; and the big house again, noisy, loud with the treble shouts of the generations. (p. 385)

Hightower sees the pathos of Miss Burden's passing, but the reader may sense that her death has in some way been a precondition of the rebirth which is here so eloquently evoked. The death seems fated, like so much else in the novel, and, like the death of Joe Christmas nine days later, it is certainly executed in ritualistic fashion: Miss Burden herself prepares for it in prayer and Christmas prepares for it by performing what can perhaps be best described as the quasi-rituals of stripping himself of the last woman-sewn button and showing himself naked in the lights of a passing car, by shaving at the spring, and by temporarily immersing himself in the "thick black pit" (p. 107) of the Negro district.

Immediately before Christmas goes in to kill Miss Burden, at midnight on the Friday, we are given this insight into his thoughts:

Now it was still, quiet, the fecund earth now coolly suspirant. The dark was filled with the voices, myriad, out of all time that he had known, as though all the past was a flat pattern. And going on: tomorrow night, all the tomorrows, to be a part of the flat pattern, going on. He thought of that with quiet astonishment: going on, myriad, familiar, since all that had ever been was the same as all that was to be, since tomorrow to-be and had-been would be the same. Then it was time. (p. 266)

This is as precise a verbal definition as can be found in the novel of the kind of representative significance embodied by Lena Grove: Christmas here realises, in a flash of insight, the fundamental permanence of the earth and of human experience which lies beneath and beyond the immediate present of agonised searching and violent experience in which he is himself so inextricably engaged. Also significant, however, is the final statement: "Then it was time." This is the moment on which, in a very real sense, the whole novel turns, the moment of midnight on the Friday night which Lena spends at the Armstids'. It is on this point of time that the entire long flashback [135] recounting Christmas's previous experiences is poised, and since the flashback begins on page 111 and occupies only a few pages short of a third of the novel, it must be considered one of Faulkner's most extended experiments in suspended time.

The statement, "Then it was time," may thus be in the nature of an announcement that the moment has been released from its suspension, that the action is henceforward immersed once more in the flow of time. This is, however, a novel in which the course of present events is very carefully charted and in which many of the characters display an extraordinary awareness of time: Byron meticulously keeps his own time when working alone; Hightower always knows the time although he has no clock; while Christmas is being pursued he is driven to speak to people not by any need for food but by his need to know what day it is. It seems probable that Faulkner had some kind of deliberate time scheme in mind as he wrote the book, and since the ancient festival of

Diana used to be celebrated in August it is conceivable that he intended some allusion to it. The fact that fire was especially important in the celebration of the festival would then give additional significance to the fire at the Burden house and to the title of the novel itself. There are several more hints of this kind, and there are even a number of features in the account of Christmas's pursuit and murder by Percy Grimm—most notably, the comparison of Grimm to a young priest—which tempt one to wonder whether Faulkner's imagination may not initially have been seized by Frazer's description in the opening pages of *The Golden Bough* of the "barbarous custom" followed in Roman times to decide the succession to the priesthood of Diana's sacred grove and sanctuary at Nemi.

These suggested correspondences between *Light in August* and the mythology and anthropology surrounding the figure of Diana may be entirely accidental. Alternatively, such correspondences, like those linking characters in the book with the members of the Holy Family, may represent only one among several patterns of analogy which Faulkner pursued in the course of the novel, and it is possible that he intended a symbolic substitution of Lena as a Holy Mother figure (an aspect in her presentation which is particularly stressed in the final chapter) for the barren Diana figure of Miss Burden. But one thing is clear: the structure of *Light in August* cannot be adequately defined as a loose combination and conflation of three separate stories. As other critics have argued, there are in effect three quite distinct conclusions to the novel, each containing a bare minimum of references to the other two, and it would have been extremely simple for Faulkner, had he so wished, to establish a much closer texture of purely narrative links between the three strands. He did not so choose, however, and the structure of *Light in August* which we have already remarked as harking back in certain important respects [136] to *As I Lay Dying* may also be said to look forward to the divided "double-novel" structure of *The Wild Palms*. But in reading *Light in August* we are not especially aware of the discreteness of the different narrative strands. Much of the novel's cohesion derives from its interconnecting patterns of reflection, repetition, substitution, and contrast. Something is also gained by Faulkner's use of recurrent images, such as that of the circle, and of analogical patterns. But the great and unifying strength of the book remains its most obvious one: the sheer force and passion of its presentation of Joe Christmas, the quintessential victim, and the way in which we, like all the characters in the book, are irresistibly swept into the vortex of Christmas's restless life and agonising death. [137]

The Puritan Sinner

PETER SWIGGART

IN *Light in August* FAULKNER CONTINUES HIS EXPLORATION OF THE South's puritan mentality; at the same time he introduces racial miscegenation as a central dramatic issue. As a white Southerner convinced that he has Negro ancestry, Joe Christmas directs his racial prejudice inward, against himself, and the resulting torment commits him to a path of lonely violence. He is driven by a strong sense of guilt and a need for some kind of punishment or moral expiation. Faulkner fits Joe's pattern of self-destruction into a dramatic context that establishes it as an exploration of the central moral and social problem of the racially divided South. Joe assumes unwittingly the role of a sacrificial victim who accepts the white South's own burden of past sin and present injustice. His characterization brings out into the open issues that lie deep within the [131] Southern mind, and his death suggests a personal atonement for the racial crime of his region.

Joe Christmas's early life is associated with a number of fanatical Protestant Christians. His grandfather, Euphues (Doc) Hines, kills Joe's father, a dark-skinned circus man, and allows Joe's unmarried mother to die in childbirth. Hines believes that Joe represents the very "teeth and fangs" (338) of Satan's evil, and he becomes convinced that God wants him to wait for this evil to bear fruit. "I have put the mark on him, and now I am going to put the knowledge" (325).* Hines finds a job as the janitor of an orphanage and abandons the infant Joe Christmas at its doorstep. As Joe grows up, the other children respond to the grandfather's malignant influence and begin to call Joe a "nigger," a charge which the boy convinces himself must be true. Hines's religious mania is introduced not only to explain Joe's obsession, but to call the reader's attention to the internal puritan force which oppresses the boy and against which he reacts.

Although Joe escapes the religious fanaticism of his grandfather, he finds a similar figure in McEachern, the Presbyterian farmer who adopts him. Through his relation with the farmer, who is characterized by a Bible or catechism held in one hand and a strap in the other, Joe is given a taste of the expiating punishment for which he uncon-

---

* All quotations from *Light in August* are from the Modern Library edition (New York: Random House, 1950).

sciously yearns. He rebels against the grim farmer, but the two are symbolically joined by their mutual "stubbornness" and "rigid abnegation of all compromise" (130). The salient feature of their common puritanism is its abstract or impersonal nature. McEachern's voice is "not unkind," but it is inhuman and impersonal. "It was just cold, implacable, like written or printed words" (130).

The repressed emotions of Faulkner's puritans are usually associated with a masklike facial expression. Such figures are described as looking simultaneously calm and rapturous, and terms like "fury," "outrage," and "implacable urgency" are combined with those implying outward repose or immobility. Doc Hines and his wife are excited at finding their grandson still alive, but to the Reverend Hightower they appear transfixed by "frozen and mechanically moved inertia," as if they were puppets "operated by clumsy springwork" (323). Hines appears oblivious and indifferent to his surroundings, "and yet withal a quality latent and explosive, paradoxically rapt and alert at the same time" (323). When Joe's mistress, (132) Joanna Burden, tries to shoot him, her eyes are described as "calm and still as all pity and all despair and all conviction" (247). The implication here is not merely that Joanna's eyes appear calm in spite of her emotion, but that such emotions as pity and despair are associated with calm and still facial expressions.

In the narrative world of *Light in August* emotion itself seems to adopt the posture and pose of impersonal rapture and martyrdom. Hearing the sound of church singing, the Reverend Hightower describes the Southern mind and heart as being "expiated by the stern and formal fury" of its Sunday morning service. Whereas the voices of the singers adopt "the shapes and attitudes of crucifixions, ecstatic, solemn, and profound," the music itself is "stern and implacable, deliberate and without passion" (321). That is to say, puritans tend to express their emotions, if at all, within the framework of rigid social conventions.

Puritan emotion occasionally breaks out in unrestrained violence, as in the mass fury of a lynching mob, but such violence is not a spontaneous expression of pent-up emotions. According to Faulkner the puritan mind avoids natural expression of feelings. "Pleasure, ecstasy, they cannot seem to bear: their escape from it is in violence, in drinking and fighting and praying." By forcing human emotions into the service of abstract convictions, these Southerners transform themselves into moral fanatics. Hightower explains that a mob of Southern churchgoers will lynch Joe Christmas in order to stifle their own consciences. They will crucify him gladly, "since to pity him would be to admit selfdoubt and to hope for and need pity themselves" (322). In other words the whole town will resort to a stylized and traditional act of violence rather than admit emotional realities.

This combination of moral conviction and ruthless violence is succinctly characterized by the desire of Calvin Burden, Joanna Burden's grandfather, to "beat the loving God" (213) into his four children. This staunch figure stands for a tradition of New England Puritanism that is related in both spirit and doctrinal roots to the more evangelical Presbyterian sects dominating the American Middle West and Deep South. It is significant that he reads the Bible to his children in Spanish, a language which they cannot understand. What they do understand is a series of impromptu sermons, [133] composed half of "bleak and bloodless" New England logic and "half of immediate hellfire and tangible brimstone of which any country Methodist circuit rider would have been proud" (212). The result is the Protestant blend of emotionalism and abstract morality which Faulkner consistently satirizes.

Faulkner's aim in introducing Calvin Burden and his New England heritage is to show the relation between the attitude of the abolitionist Burdens toward the Southern Negro and the racial hatred of a man like Doc Hines. Whereas Hines sees his grandson's Negro ancestry as a token of the Devil, the Burdens look upon Negroes as the sign and symbol of the white man's moral sin. Joanna Burden sees the curse of slavery as a "black shadow in the shape of a cross" (221) falling upon all white children. The curse of the black race is the irrevocable fate of being held in bondage, "but the curse of the white race is the black man who will be forever God's chosen own because He once cursed him" (222). The Burdens take up social work among the Negroes in the postwar South as a step toward expiating the curse which has fallen upon their own white blood. Their abstract approach to the race problem is comparable to that of Hines, who reacts in hatred to his similar belief that the Negro race is a curse upon the white. Joe Christmas inherits the prejudice of his grandfather, but he is also influenced by Joanna Burden and presumably by the doctrines which her family represents. Faulkner's references to the religious heritages of both New England and the South link social and political issues involving all of America to the racial obsession underlying Joe's violence.

At the heart of Joe Christmas's puritanism is a strong sense of moral guilt. At the orphanage where his grandfather has placed him the five-year-old boy is caught eating toothpaste in the dietician's bathroom and naturally expects extreme punishment. But the frightened woman believes that Joe has witnessed an assignation, and instead of punishing him she tries to bribe his silence with a gleaming silver dollar. The boy associates the money with his memory of guilt and the sensation of being sick from the toothpaste. "He was still with astonishment, shock, outrage. Looking at the dollar, he seemed to see ranked tubes of toothpaste like corded wood, endless and terrifying; his whole being coiled in a rich and [134] passionate revulsion. 'I dont

want no more,' he said. 'I dont never want no more,' he thought"
(109).

This episode symbolizes the main currents of Joe's adult life. His
consciousness of unexpiated guilt becomes involved with the belief
that he is part Negro and in need of moral absolution. His experience
with the dietician, herself a food symbol, confirms his revulsion against
food, money, and women.

Upon leaving the orphanage Joe encounters a series of symbolic
repetitions of this same traumatic experience. He does not mind the
brutality of McEachern, his stepfather, so much as the "soft kindness"
of Mrs. McEachern. When she washes Joe's feet upon his arrival, he
keeps waiting for something unpleasant to take place, and he is upset
because it never does. Later on he imagines the woman standing
between himself and the punishment from McEachern which, "deserved or not, just or unjust, was impersonal, both the man and the
boy accepting it as a natural and inescapable fact" (146). When
McEachern sends him to bed without any supper, the boy feels "weak
and peaceful" (134). But the woman spoils his martyrdom by secretly
bringing him a tray of hot steaming food. Joe throws it on the floor,
but an hour later he is on his knees devouring the food resentfully,
"like a savage, like a dog" (136).

Joe's early hatred of food anticipates a later disgust at his own
sexual needs. His first traumatic experience is with a Negro girl, a
"womanshenegro," who waits for the boy and his friends in a dark
shed where her eyes glint like "dead stars" reflected at the bottom of a
"black well" (137). Instead of doing what is expected, Joe kicks the
girl and fights with the other boys as they rush in. His resort to
violence is an effort to escape a primitive force far stronger than his
male puritanism: "it was as if a wind had blown among them, hard
and clean" (137). A similar incident takes place when Joe first learns
about the menstruation of women. Unable to live with his knowledge,
he buys immunity, as Faulkner puts it, by killing a sheep and dipping
his hands in its blood. But Old Testament ceremonies cannot help Joe
when the information is repeated by Bobbie, his first mistress. "In the
notseeing and the hardknowing as though in a cave he seemed to see a
diminishing row of suavely shaped urns in moonlight, blanched. And
not one was perfect. Each one was [135] cracked and from each crack
there issued something liquid, death-colored, and foul" (165).

This blanched and cracked world in which Joe Christmas finds
himself trapped is a projection of his own puritan thinking. Joe learns
to hate his own body as well as its physical and emotional needs, and
to him hunger and desire seem oppressive forces associated with
darkness and evil. Food is always something "hot and fierce," prepared
by women, which he must eat hurriedly and with a vague feeling of
self-betrayal. When Joe steals into Joanna Burden's kitchen in des-

perate hunger, "he seemed to flow into the dark kitchen: a shadow returning without a sound and without locomotion to the allmother of obscurity and darkness" (200). Since food and sex are closely related in Joe's mind, it is no accident that he rapes Joanna that same night.

Opposed to these dark forces is the power of abstinence, which is associated in Joe's mind with calm certainty and the hard clean air of masculinity. As a boy he feels weak and peaceful because of the lack of food; and once more, before his death, he is able to rise above such human needs. Before surrendering to a society that he knows will crucify him, Joe has a feeling of peace and unhaste and quiet. He wonders why, "until suddenly the true answer comes to him. He feels dry and light. 'I dont have to bother about having to eat any more,' he thinks. 'That's what it is' " (295).

Christmas's guilty hatred of sex is illustrated most strongly in his relations with Joanna Burden, the product of a puritan heritage similar to his own. At first Joe is drawn toward his alter-ego (Joanna) because she acts more like a man than a woman. She combines a woman's body with "the mantrained muscles and the mantrained habit of thinking born of heritage and environment" (205). When Joe attacks her, she seems to resist as a man might, "as if he struggled physically with another man for an object of no actual value to either, and for which they struggled on principle alone" (205). But Joanna soon reveals a split personality, becoming a mannish old maid by day and a nymphomaniac by night. This transformation is explained in terms of her religious heritage as "the abject fury of the New England glacier exposed suddenly to the fire of the New England biblical hell" (225). He watches in passive disgust as his mistress seeks to compensate for the "frustrate and irrevocable years" [136] by "damning herself forever to the hell of her forefathers" (226). Two creatures seem to struggle within her for mastery. "Now it would be that still, cold, contained figure . . . who, even though lost and damned, remained somehow impervious and impregnable; then it would be the other, the second one, who in furious denial of that impregnability strove to drown in the black abyss of its own creating that physical purity which had been preserved too long now ever to be lost" (228).

During this period Joe Christmas discovers in Joanna the epitome of the primitive forces of nature which he has tried to escape. Her nymphomania is described in terms of darkness and lust, her eyes "in the dark glowing like the eyes of cats" and her body caught in the wild throes of passion. "She would be wild then, in the close, breathing halfdark without walls, with her wild hair, each strand of which would seem to come alive like octopus tentacles, and her wild hands and her breathing: 'Negro! Negro! Negro!' " (227). She desperately seeks to drown her long-preserved purity in a morass of corruption. To his own horror Joe finds himself drawn into this quagmire. He imagines himself lying "at the bottom of a pit in the hot wild darkness" (235) and watching his own body "turning slow and lascivious in a whispering of gutter filth like a drowned corpse in a thick still black pool of more than water" (93).

Joe's puritan hatred of women and the physical desire they represent is consistently involved with his hatred of the Negro blood which he seems to hold responsible for the terrifying world in which he must live. He imagines relations with women as a pit or pool of glimmering darkness out of which he cannot extricate his own lost and damned mulatto body. The religious and sexual agony of Joanna Burden reflects, as in a distorted Beardsley drawing (the comparison is Faulkner's), Joe Christmas's own tormented self.

Joanna's late burst of passion comes to a sudden end as she passes through her change of life and resumes her spinster's role. Now she tries to send Joe to a Negro college where he can learn enough law to become her secretary and carry on her social work. When Joe indignantly refuses, she tries to make him kneel down with her and pray. By these twin demands she crystallizes both Joe's racial obsession and his hatred of orthodox Calvinist piety. He recalls the bowed head of McEachern and the latter's ruthless morality. [137] Imagining the print of his own knees beside Joanna's bed, he jerks his eyes away "as if it were death that they had looked at" (244). Joe is bound to his former mistress just as he is bound to his own destiny. Their conflict over his future becomes a stalemate in which neither party can surrender or escape. "They would stand for a while longer in the quiet dusk peopled, as though from their loins, by a myriad ghosts of dead sins and delights, looking at one another's still and fading face, weary, spent, and indomitable" (244).

The main difference between Joe and Joanna lies in their response to comparable racial, religious, and sexual dilemmas. Joanna finds that her old maid's "virginity," which she sought to destroy, is returning with her change of life. Before this happens, she asks God to let her be damned a little longer before having to pray. "She seemed to see her whole past life, the starved years, like a gray tunnel, at the far and irrevocable end of which, as unfading as a reproach, her naked breast of three short years ago ached as though in agony, virgin and crucified; 'Not yet, dear God. Not yet, dear God'" (231). This "crucifixion," which parallels the more serious one of Joe Christmas, is only temporary, and Joanna does return to the religion of her forefathers, accepting its spiritual complacency along with its doctrines.

In her inverted religious feeling, in her obsession with the Negro race, and in her sexual masochism, Joanna Burden mirrors the important features of Joe Christmas's destiny. This is the meaning of Joanna's surname: it suggests Joe's burden as well as her own. However, in submitting to spiritual piety she rejects the demonism, the raging puritanism, that characterizes Joe's life. Her function in the novel's structure is first to reveal to Joe what he is, then to abandon him to his solitary path.

Because of their intractable opposition, the two ex-lovers decide that both of them must die. Joanna tries to kill Joe with her grandfather's antique pistol, but the pistol misses fire. Joe then kills her with his razor. After the crime, he spends a week wandering through the country and preparing himself for death. During this time he makes more "progress," the reader is told, than in all the preceding thirty years of unremitting anguish. This progress is toward a realization of what his sense of guilt means and how it can be expiated. Refusing to identify himself as either white or Negro, and refusing [138] to live any longer in two contradictory worlds, he drives on, knowingly, to his self-created fate.

Throughout *Light in August* the Negro blood that Joe imagines surging within him is associated, along with hunger and sexual desire, with the hot, savage, and dark forces of nature. Between Joe's flight from McEachern and his arrival in Jefferson, a period of at least twelve years, he tries to unite himself with that primitive force by crossing the color line. Living with a Negro woman in a northern city, he lies in bed, sleepless, breathing hard and deep: "trying to expel from himself the white blood and the white thinking and being" (197). But Christmas cannot escape his puritan hatred of nature, and even as he tries to make the "dark odor" of Negroes his own, he writhes and strains "with physical outrage and spiritual denial" (197).

A comparable struggle takes place the night of Joe's crime, when he takes a walk in both the white and Negro sections of Jefferson. In the white man's world he resembles "a phantom, a spirit, strayed out of its own world, and lost" (99). Then he passes down the hill into Freedman Town, the Negro quarter. In sharp contrast to "the cold hard air of white people," it lies "lightless hot wet primogenitive Female" (100) and assumes the shape of a "black pit" about to engulf him. With "drumming heart and glaring lips" (101) Joe races back to the white man's part of town. In symbolic terms he walks both racial streets at once, with "his steady white shirt and pacing dark legs" (101). His primary allegiance is to the white world, even though the dark one, as he conceives it, draws him to his death.

The few actions associated with Joe Christmas between the time of the murder and his surrender at Mottstown represent his violent acknowledgment of the primitive force which he has equated with Negro blood. He bursts into a Negro cabin and gorges himself on the occupants' prepared food. He invades a Negro church during a night service and stands in the pulpit cursing God, while the congregation flees in terror. These actions indicate Joe's realization that his racial guilt can be expiated only through death. He affirms his white nature but accepts the burden which his puritan training has imposed. The climax occurs when Joe exchanges his shoes for those of a Negro woman. The shoes are a symbol of the death which he [139] now accepts: "the black shoes smelling of Negro: that mark on his ankles the gauge definite and ineradicable of the black tide creeping up his legs, moving from his feet upward as death moves" (297).

The central chapters of *Light in August,* dealing with Joe Christmas's life and death, are preceded and followed by chapters devoted to less important characters. The opening chapter describes the arrival of Lena Grove in Jefferson, and the closing one describes her departure. The other chapters concern the actions and perceptions of such figures as Gail Hightower, Byron Bunch, and Lucas Burch, alias Joe Brown. These characters establish the Yoknapatawpha environment and provide a series of perspectives in which Christmas's violent life and sacrificial death are viewed. The reader is led from Lena's indifference through Byron's absorbed interest into the heart of the story, and back out again by virtually the same route in reverse. The result in many cases is a series of multiple views of the same events. When Joe frightens a Negro congregation or surrenders to the Mottstown authorities, the reader is given in quick succession the incident from Joe's point of view and the same incident as it affects the community.

As the novel opens, Lena Grove unhurriedly searches for the father of her unborn child. Like other Faulkner primitives she takes life as it comes without trying vainly to understand it. The "peaceful corridor" of time in which she lives is opposed symbolically to Joe Christmas's "savage and lonely street." Joe believes that an unshakable fatality is pursuing him, but his narrow destiny is shaped by his own puritan imagination. "He thought that it was loneliness which he was trying to escape and not himself. . . . But the street ran on in its moods and phases, always empty . . . driven by the courage of flagged and spurred despair; by the despair of courage whose opportunities had to be flagged and spurred" (197).

The opposition between the attitudes represented by Lena and by Joe is modified when the latter accepts the certainty of coming death. The day opens peacefully for him, "like a corridor, an arras, into a still chiaroscuro without urgency" (97). As Joe reads a magazine, he permits each separate word, devoid of meaning, to hold his attention as if his entire being were suspended in space: "so that hanging motionless and without physical weight he seemed to [140] watch the slow flowing of time beneath him" (97). Like Lena Grove he is free of the pressure of space, time, and physical needs. "He is not sleepy or hungry or even tired. He is somewhere between and among them, suspended, swaying to the motion of the wagon without thought, without feeling" (296).

For the first time in his life Joe Christmas feels no contradiction between his human emotions and his moral convictions. This fact explains the "progress" which he is described as making during his week of spiritual retreat. His destiny has always been a "flat pattern" (246), but for the first time he stops trying to avoid it; he realizes that with approaching death he has no need to escape the raging paradox within himself.

Although Lena's undeviating faith is non-Christian and obtained at the cost of near-imbecility, her placidity prefigures Joe's "peace and unhaste and quiet" (295) when he is captured at Mottstown and, later on, when he is brutally castrated. The relation between Joe Christmas and Lena Grove may be compared to that between a point on the circumference of a moving wheel and the wheel's center or hub. The outside point moves faster and covers a larger area, but at the end of the trip it has advanced no further than the central point. Joe and Lena travel in the same direction, yet their paths never meet. They are joined only in the confused mind of Joe's grandmother, who believes that Lena is Milly, Joe's mother, and that the baby is Joe. Lena even thinks for a moment that the "Mr Christmas" (359) she hears about is the baby's father.

The lives of Joe Christmas and Lena Grove are both associated with that of the cowardly Lucas Burch, or "Joe Brown" as he is known in Jefferson. After abandoning Lena because she is pregnant, Brown flees to Jefferson, where he becomes the companion and foil of Joe Christmas and sells the latter's bootleg whiskey. Brown's irresponsible behavior emphasizes by contrast Joe's "brooding and savage steadiness" (34). Even though he imitates Christmas's movements, Brown "merely contrived to look scattered and emptily swaggering where the master had looked sullen and quiet and fatal as a snake" (39). He is a fatalist like Joe Christmas, yet of a different kind: "it seemed to him now that they were all just shapes like chessmen—the Negro, the sheriff, the money, all—unpredictable and without reason moved here and there by an Opponent who [141] could read his moves before he made them and who created spontaneous rules which he and not the Opponent, must follow" (383). The key phrase here is "unpredictable and without reason." The force that determines Joe's chessboard moves does not operate according to "spontaneous" rules but rather, in the words applied to Percy Grimm, "with the delicate swiftness of an apparition, the implacable undeviation of Juggernaut or Fate" (403). There is no deviation from purpose, however blind Joe's actions may seem, because the compelling force is within, and the arbitrary "rules" are constant and devised by will.

Whereas Brown is driven here and there by life's unpredictable forces, the Reverend Gail Hightower tries to avoid the complexities of life altogether. He identifies his own life with his grandfather's, and tries to convince himself that since his grandfather is dead he no longer has any responsibility toward the living. As a divinity student, confusing religion with this effort to escape into the past, Hightower imagines "his future, his life, intact and on all sides complete and inviolable, like a classic and serene vase, where the spirit could be born anew sheltered from the harsh gale of living and die so, peacefully, with only the far sound of the circumvented wind, with scarce even a handful of rotting dust to be disposed of" (419). This "serene vase" is an echo of the grecian-urn image associated with Lena Grove, but Lena's rejection of the spatial and temporal world is instinctive rather than deliberate and rational. Moreover Hightower's vision is projected onto an elusive past and bears comparison with the urn of death and not the ideal one of beauty and truth.

Although Hightower represents a serious moral fault, he is treated almost comically. When the minister's wife commits suicide in a Memphis brothel, his congregation becomes enraged. Already angered by Hightower's confusion between the Civil War and the gospel, the elders drive him from the pulpit and expect him to leave town in disgrace. He refuses to do so and accepts with delight a mock "crucifixion" at the hands of a town mob:

He seems to watch himself, alert, patient, skillful, playing his cards well, making it appear that he was being driven, uncomplaining, into that which he did not even then admit had been his desire since before he entered the seminary . . . allowing himself to be persecuted, to be dragged from his bed at night and carried into the woods and beaten [142] with sticks, he all the while bearing in the town's sight and hearing, without shame, with that patient and voluptuous ego of the martyr, the air, the behavior, the *How long, O Lord* until, inside his house again and the door locked, he lifted the mask with voluptuous and triumphant glee: *Ah. That's done now. That's past now. That's bought and paid for now* (428–429).

In treating Hightower's martyrdom as burlesque, Faulkner contrasts it to Joe Christmas's subsequent death—at the hands, no doubt, of the same Jefferson mob. The minister's gesture is exposed as false and hypocritical because he wants to live to enjoy his sacrifice. Hightower has looked forward to this moment all his life because it provides him with an excuse for rejecting the present world and retreating into the past.

Another figure who has tried to escape reality is the minister's only friend, Byron Bunch. Byron takes refuge from human emotion by working hard during weekdays and preaching in the country over the weekend. As the novel develops he slips away from Hightower's influence and is taken in tow by Lena Grove, whom he is presumably destined to marry. Byron's false sanctuary is symbolically demolished, and he is forced into the mainstream of conventional existence. This is why the minister counsels his friend to escape Lena's orbit, to "leave this place forever, this terrible place, this terrible, terrible place. I can read you. You will tell me that you have just learned love; I will tell you that you have just learned hope. That's all; hope" (275–276).

Hope becomes a terrible thing for Byron because his new personality, anticipating his future role as husband and father, represents a
disruptive force. Believing that Lena is returning to her former lover,
Byron at first takes Hightower's advice and prepares to flee. He
imagines the future—a future without Lena—as a state of nothingness
where trees would not be trees, men would not be men, "and Byron
Bunch he wouldn't even have to be or not be Byron Bunch" (371). He
is about to re-enter his past sanctuary where he was sheltered from
ordinary responsibilities. But when Byron sees Joe Brown fleeing town
he knows that Lena will now need him. Thinking of their future life
together, he is aware of becoming "Byron Bunch" again. For a moment
the moving train carrying Brown away seems like a barrier between
Byron and the world: "a [143] dyke beyond which the world, time,
hope unbelievable and certainly incontrovertible, waited, giving him
yet a little more of peace" (386–387).

Hightower is also affected by the life force which Lena Grove's
mere presence seems to generate. When her time comes and no doctor is available, he officiates at her delivery and afterwards feels an
unaccustomed surge of energy, a "glow of purpose and pride." When
he chooses a book from his library, it is not the usual Tennyson, but
Henry IV, "food for a man" (355). But the minister cannot sustain his
new mood, and he surrenders to inertia. "I am not in life any more," he
has stated earlier. "That's why there is no use in even trying to meddle,
interfere" (263). At one point Byron finds in the sleeping figure of
Hightower "a quality of profound and complete surrender," as if his
friend "had given over and relinquished completely that grip upon
that blending of pride and hope and vanity and fear, that strength
to cling to either defeat or victory, which is the I-Am, and the relin-
quishment of which is usually death" (345). Hightower's absorption
in the past is thus defined as a loss of personality, of self, the equivalent of death.

This theme is further emphasized, after the death of Joe Christmas, when Hightower sits at his window reviewing his life's pattern.
As sundown approaches, he tries to retreat as usual into his vision of
his grandfather galloping with General Forrest's cavalry down what
was once the main street of town. This fusion between past and present is concentrated for Hightower upon a moment of "*soon*ness," just
before dusk, when he can look out and actually see the riders "sweep
into sight, borne now upon a cloud of phantom dust" (431).

This moment of fusion, when the past becomes real, is called the
soon rather than the *now* because once the galloping horses do appear
the timeless moment of Hightower's vision will have pushed present
reality entirely from his mind.

Prior to the culmination of Hightower's vision the old man's
"wheel of thinking" is described as turning "with the slow implacability of a mediaeval torture instrument, beneath the wrenched and
broken sockets of his spirit, his life" (429–430). This remarkable image

indicates Hightower's realization that he has failed to avoid responsibility for present events. Projecting the face of an accusing [144] God before him, Hightower hears himself blamed for his wife's death. The argument is strange: "And if I am my dead grandfather on the instant of his death, then my wife, his grandson's wife—the debaucher and murderer of my grandson's wife, since I could neither let my grandson live or die—" (430). Even though he identifies himself with his own grandfather, the minister cannot avoid self-accusation. Hightower is defeated by his own sophistry, and in this sense his wheel of thought makes a destructive cycle as it rushes on, "going fast and smooth now, because it is freed now of burden, of vehicle, axle, all" (430).

After Hightower's wheel of thought or destiny has been released, "it seems to engender and surround itself with a faint glow like a halo" (430). This halo is filled with faces, "peaceful, as though they have escaped into an apotheosis" (430), his own among them. Among the faces seen by the minister is that of Joe Christmas, whose features appear superimposed upon those of the mob leader who pursues and castrates him. The two "seem to strive (but not of themselves striving or desiring it: he knows that, but because of the motion and desire of the wheel itself) in turn to free themselves one from the other, then fade and blend again" (430–431).

The fusion of the faces of Joe Christmas and Percy Grimm helps to define for the reader the meaning of Joe's sacrificial role. The two characters are driven by the same excess of puritan zeal even though the one figure is consistently self-righteous and the other marks himself as a deserving victim. Grimm becomes an unwitting instrument of Christmas's yearning for self-expiation in blood. At the same time the castration scene reveals dramatically the guilt and self-hatred that are locked within Grimm's intolerant fury. Together they act out the drama of the Southern puritan mind and its tragic dilemma. Because they both represent a South divided against itself, they are pursued by the same sense of guilt. Thus Joe Christmas becomes his own pursuer and Percy Grimm his own victim.

Faulkner's effort to create for Joe Christmas this highly complex and symbolic role is responsible for the lavish use of Christian imagery. Joe gets his last name because he is found on the steps of the orphanage on Christmas Eve. The name follows him, as Byron Bunch puts it, like an augur or sign, as if "he carried with him his [145] own inescapable warning, like a flower its scent or a rattlesnake its rattle" (29). He has the mark of God or Satan upon him, according to Doc Hines, and his name suggests the nature of this mark. Throughout the novel Joe is treated in terms which combine Old Testament moral severity with references to the life of Christ. Upon arriving in Jefferson, Joe is thirty-three years old. In one passage his feet are ceremoniously washed, he is betrayed for a thousand-dollar reward by a disciple, Joe Brown, and so on. He commits his crime on a Friday and surrenders a week later, having spent the intervening time in retreat and mental preparation. In this respect the symbolism is at odds with the chronology, for Joe is described as surrendering on "Friday" to a "Saturday" crowd of farmers.

Other less detailed references to Christianity or to religious ceremony and ritual may be found. Faulkner's typical manner of describing puritan qualities is to compare the faces of his characters to the rapt and inscrutable ones of monks or hermits. When Joe is whipped by his stepfather, his body seems "a post or a tower upon which the sentient part of him mused like a hermit, contemplative and remote with ecstasy and selfcrucifixion" (140). Such language is sometimes extended to the physical scene, as when countrymen in overalls move "with almost the air of monks in a cloister" (364). Faulkner often describes Southern puritans as if they always wore a stylized mask, expressive of moral certitude, in confronting the complex and shifting facts of human experience. Such a mind will insist upon formalized behavior, ranging from group worship to mob violence. Racial intolerance or any other kind of moral prejudice is a natural outlet for this attitude just as a Christ-like expression is a natural posture. The Christian imagery of *Light in August* dramatizes puritan intensity of mind and also defines the central meaning of Joe's sacrifice.

Faulkner's effective use of religious imagery may be illustrated by the several references to the glint of handcuffs above Joe Christmas's head as he runs before his pursuers. Joe's "bright and glittering hands" (406) are compared to "the flash of a heliograph" (404), to the glint of fire, and finally to "lightning bolts" (406). Although Joe's face has "that serene, unearthly luminousness of angels in church windows" (404–405), his "raised and armed and manacled hands" give him the appearance, as he strikes the Reverend [146] Hightower down, of a "vengeful and furious god pronouncing a doom" (406). The symbolic meanings are almost too numerous for expression. In Christian terms the handcuffs function as a combined halo and crown of thorns. In terms of the tragic action of the novel they represent Joe's manacled destiny and the inevitability of his death. The images by which the cuffs are described suggest punishment or judgment. As a "vengeful god," Christmas pronounces judgment upon Hightower and by implication upon the society whose divided conscience he embodies.

The religious imagery as well as the temporal mysticism associated with Joe Christmas prepare the reader for an understanding of his death and its significance. In his flight from the mob Joe seeks refuge in the Reverend Hightower's home and is there shot down and castrated by Grimm:

But the man on the floor had not moved. He just lay there, with his eyes open and empty of everything save consciousness, and with something, a shadow, about his mouth. For a long moment he looked up at them with peaceful and unfathomable and unbearable eyes. Then his face, body, all, seemed to collapse, to fall in upon itself, and from out the slashed garments about his hips and loins the pent black blood seemed to rush like a released breath. It seemed to rush out of his pale body like the rush of sparks from a rising rocket; upon that black blast the man seemed to rise soaring into their memories forever and ever. They are not to lose it, in whatever peaceful valleys, beside whatever placid and reassuring streams of old age, in the mirroring faces of whatever children they will contemplate old disasters and newer hopes. It will be there, musing, quiet, steadfast, not fading and not particularly threatful, but of itself alone serene, of itself alone triumphant. Again from the town, deadened a little by the walls, the scream of the siren mounted toward its unbelievable crescendo, passing out of the realm of hearing (407).

The symbolism of this passage is emphasized by the narrative point of view which soars, like Joe's pent blood, to a transcendent theme. The dark blood which leaves his white body stands both for mortality and for the final expiation of guilt. Joe's eyes are "peaceful and unfathomable" because he is free at last from his own divided nature. Yet his eyes are "unbearable" to others, just as the "black blast" which leaves his body becomes a part of their conscience. The burden of guilt, no longer tormenting Joe, becomes public property. [147]

The crucifixion image which dominates this climactic scene derives its meaning less from Joe's martyrdom than from the violence of society's retribution. The men who watch the scene are confronted with their own need for violent expiation. They see Joe's death as a mirror of the "old disasters and newer hopes" from which their victim is now absolved. Joe's martyrdom, like its Christian counterpart, is a deliberate self-sacrifice. Yet Faulkner's hero is barely aware, if at all, of society's existence. Among the townspeople he alone, the crucified, is the one that is saved. [148]

The Community and the Pariah

CLEANTH BROOKS

. . . NEARLY ALL THE CHARACTERS IN THIS NOVEL ARE DRAWN FROM THE ranks of the plain people and most of them exhibit a Puritan ethic. They are in tension with nature, and some have even been deformed and perverted in a struggle against it. The theme of man strained away from nature, however, is only one of several significant Faulknerian themes to be found in *Light in August*. . . . *Light in August* also provides examples of the typical difficulties that many people experience in reading Faulkner.

One of the most characteristic is that of finding a principle of unity. No novel of Faulkner's exhibits more brilliant writing or abounds in a greater number of memorable individual scenes, and no reader would fail to respond to most of them. There is, for example, the very touching scene at the orphanage in which a young girl named Alice, who is departing for the home of her [47] new foster parents, wakes the sleepy child Joe Christmas to tell him good-bye. She has mothered the little boy and now she weeps. "He didn't know that she was crying because he did not know that grown people cried, and by the time he learned that, memory had forgotten her. He went back into sleep while still suffering her, and the next morning she was gone. Vanished, no trace of her left, not even a garment, the very bed in which she had slept already occupied by a new boy" (119).*

There is the scene in which the boy Joe Christmas and his foster father McEachern face each other, both of them silent and obstinate, over the Presbyterian catechism. There is the scene in which Joe as an adolescent confesses, shyly but almost proudly, to Bobbie the waitress-prostitute, his belief that he has some Negro blood. There are the several scenes in which Joe faces Joanna Burden, among them the one in which she tells Joe about her father and grandfather and relates the incident in which her father showed her, a four-year-old child, the secret graves of her grandfather and her brother. There is the equally wonderful scene—but so different in tone—in which the grim and damned woman, clutching the old cap-and-ball pistol, demands that Joe kneel down with her and pray. There are the quietly charged scenes in which Byron sits opposite the Reverend Gail Hightower in Hightower's little cottage and tells him about Lena and her plight, and later calmly makes the terrible proposal that Hightower should save the murderer Christmas with a lie. He tells Hightower that if he will only say that Joe Christmas spent the night of the murder with him at his house: "Folks would believe you. They would believe that, anyway." There is the account of Percy Grimm running lightly and surely with the automatic in his hand and suddenly discovering what it is that he wants. These are only a few of the tremendously moving and exciting scenes to be found in the novel.

The difficulty has never been that such individual segments of the narration lacked vividness and power. The difficulty has always come with the attempt to relate the various episodes so as to show a coherent pattern of meaning. . . . [48]

---

* All quotations from *Light in August* are from the Modern Library edition (New York: Random House, 1950).

As for typical misreadings, two in particular seem to recur. Since either can affect the meaning of this novel, it may be well to dispose of them at the outset. The first has to do with Joe Christmas' alleged Negro blood. Most commentators refer to his mixed blood and several call him a mulatto (technically, one-half Negro), though Joe easily "passes" as white. But what is the evidence for Joe's mixed blood? Two special passages seem to have fostered this supposition. The first is Joe's flaunting of his alleged Negro blood—as when he tries to shock the white prostitute by telling her that he is a Negro. The second is the hypothesis put forward by Gavin Stevens as he tries to account for the events that occur just before Joe's death. Stevens sees Joe's last actions as involving a clash between his white blood and his black blood: the "black blood drove him first to the Negro cabin. And then the white blood drove him out of there, as it was the black blood which snatched up the pistol and the white blood which would not let him fire it" (393), etc. Because many readers are disposed to consider Stevens Faulkner's mouthpiece in the novel, his comments about Joe's Negro blood may seem endowed with special authority. But Faulkner says specifically in the interviews he gave at the University of Virginia[1] that the scholarly and somewhat romantic Stevens is not his mouthpiece. Stevens, who evidently has no more facts than we have, is merely spinning a theory.

What do we really know about Joe's ancestry? The fanatical old Doc Hines is quite certain that his daughter, Joe's mother, is lying when she tells him that her lover is a Mexican. But that conviction is part and parcel of his fanaticism. He "knows" that the man is a Negro just as he knows many other things—by a special revelation that short-circuits any need for evidence. It is true that Mrs. Hines admits that after her husband's trial for his murder [49] of Joe's father, "the circus owner come back and said how the man really was a part nigger instead of Mexican, like Eupheus said all the time he was. . . ." But she adds, a sentence or two later, "it was just that circus man that said he was a nigger and maybe he never knew for certain" (330).

Is Mrs. Hines here allowing hope to warp her judgment? Or was the circus owner, in admitting that Joe's father was part Negro, simply humoring the *idée-fixe* of the old monomaniac? At any rate, we are never given any firm proof that Joe Christmas possesses Negro blood, for the sufficient reason that Joe would have become what he became whether he had an infusion of Negro blood or not. The pressures that mold him into an Ishmael have, as Faulkner knows, nothing to do with

---

[1] "Question: Sir, if he . . . does not definitely have Negro blood, well, what is the significance of Gavin Stevens's surmise at the end . . . that there's a conflict of blood? . . . Answer . . . That is an assumption, a rationalization which Stevens made." *Faulkner in the University,* p. 72.

biology as such. The decisive factor is the attitude that the world takes toward Joe and the attitude that he takes—toward other men and toward himself.

Faulkner has made this point very powerfully in a number of scenes. There are those in the orphanage in which old Hines as janitor watches the child Joe and broods over him in malignant hate, silently gloating when the children begin to call Joe "nigger." The author tells us that the child, with "more vocabulary," might have thought "That is why I am different from the others: because he is watching me all the time" (121). There is the scene in which the child follows a Negro workman around, fascinated by him, "until at last the nigger said, 'What you watching me for, boy?' and he said, 'How come you are a nigger?' and the nigger said, 'Who told you I am a nigger, you little white trash bastard?' and he says, 'I aint a nigger,' and the nigger says, 'You are worse than that. You dont know what you are. And more than that, you wont never know. You'll live and you'll die and you wont never know'" (336). Or there is the scene in which Joe is talking with Joanna Burden. To her question whether he has any idea who his parents were, he tells her only that "one of them was part nigger." (It is significant that he says "one of them," not "my father" as he might have done had he even as much information as Old Hines believed that he had.) When Joanna asks him how he knows that, he "didn't answer for some time. Then he said: 'I dont know it'" (222). [50]

The Negro workman's reply touches the matter of real importance. Joe does not know what he is. Throughout his life, he lashes out at both the white community and the Negro community. But the warping of his mind and spirit—Faulkner has been at great pains in this book to show just how it has been done—is the result of the way in which he has been reared from infancy. The biological matter is quite irrelevant.

The second misreading that recurs in comments on *Light in August* is less important but betrays a bias worth noting. Many readers assume that Joe Christmas is lynched at the end of the novel. Joe is killed by Percy Grimm when, during his trial, he breaks away and tries to escape. Percy sees him enter Hightower's house, finds him in the kitchen armed with a pistol, barricaded behind an overturned table, and shoots him five times with his automatic. Then with a knife picked up in the kitchen he emasculates Christmas.

Grimm is unaided. Three men who had been deputized to prevent disorders and who had joined in the chase followed Grimm into the house, but they evidently do not participate in the violence, and when they see what Grimm is doing, one of them cries out and begins to vomit.

A lynching is defined as the concerted action by private individuals who execute summary punishment outside the forms of the law. Can a lynching be carried out by one person? The jurists who framed the proposed federal statute on the subject evidently did not think so. Christmas is murdered, not lynched, and even the charge of murder would seem to be obviated insofar as Grimm was a properly deputized officer, attempting to apprehend a fugitive from justice who turns out to be armed. Grimm could have claimed (doubtless later he must have claimed) that he had to fire first, since he had every reason to believe that this desperate man did not mean to be taken. What gives away Grimm's storm [51] trooper mentality is what he says to the dying man and his act of mutilation.

Something more than a mere quibble about a term is involved. If we use the word "lynching" loosely and carelessly, we shall be in danger of missing the relation of Joe Christmas to the community he has defied, and more importantly, that of Percy Grimm to the community he claims to represent. There is, in fact, every reason to think that Grimm's whole *conscious* motivation is to ensure that the good name of the town not be marred by a lynching—even though the community itself is not apprehensive of a lynching. The Commander of the American Legion post to whom Grimm appeals does not think that a special force is needed to preserve order and frowns upon vigilante tactics, even in a good cause. Even if force were needed, he tells Grimm, "We would all have to act as civilians. I couldn't use the Post like that" (396). And the sheriff is just as emphatic in opposing Grimm's idea. There has been no hint of trouble and he can't have fifteen or twenty people "milling around the square with pistols in their pants" (398). But Grimm's utter seriousness and complete dedication to the concept of order prevails against these counsels. Obviously, the sheriff does not know what Grimm's real motivaton is; but then, Grimm does not himself know what it is until, with his blood up, his pistol ready, fired by the excitement of the chase, he faces Joe Christmas across the overturned table. I shall have something to say later in this chapter about Grimm's relationship to Joe and to the community. But Grimm's action does not commit the community, and although it involves the community powerfully it does so only in a very special way.

The community demands special consideration at this point, for the community is the powerful though invisible force that quietly exerts itself in so much of Faulkner's work. It is the circumambient atmosphere, the essential ether of Faulkner's fiction. But for many a reader, the community is indeed invisible and quite imperceptible: it exerts no pressure on him at all—and lacking any awareness of this force, he may miss the meaning of [52] the work. Such readers find *Light in August* quite baffling simply because they are unaware of the force of community that pervades it and thus miss the clue to its central structure.

Yet a little reflection will show that nearly all the characters in *Light in August* bear a special relation to the community. They are outcasts—they are pariahs, defiant exiles, withdrawn quietists, or simply strangers. Miss Burden, the daughter of carpetbagger intruders, has lived for years within what can be described only as a kind of cultural cyst. The community has tried its best to expel the Reverend Mr. Hightower, though having failed in the attempt it has finally accorded him a sort of grudging acceptance. Joe Christmas is, of course, Ishmael himself, actively defying the community. Even Byron Bunch fits into this pattern of alienation. Byron, with his methodical earnestness and his countrified asceticism, is regarded as a kind of eccentric—a "character." For "seven years [he] had been a minor mystery to the town" (369).

But the community itself, the great counterforce to which these characters are attracted or against which they are reacting, has no special representatives in the novel and need have none. For the community, everywhere in the novel, is visible to the reader who is prepared to see it. It expresses itself through Mrs. Armstid emptying her china bank and knotting the coins into a sack for Lena; through the sheriff kicking the ineffectual bloodhounds or ordering the thrill-seekers away from his examination of the Negro witness; through the second-hand furniture dealer who relates the closing episode of the novel; and through a dozen other minor or anonymous characters.

Sometimes the author makes an explicit comment upon the community, as he does in the long and brilliantly handled account of Gail Hightower in chapter 3. After Mrs. Hightower's shameful death, the community is sure that Hightower will resign his church. When he does so at last, after persistent moral pressure, the town is glad. "Then the town was sorry with being glad, as people sometimes are sorry for those whom they have at last forced to do as they wanted them to" (60). But Hightower still would not leave the town, and the community was furious with him for his stubbornness. Finally, some men took him out and [53] beat him, and the townspeople, now horrified, offered "to prosecute the men who had done it" (62). But Hightower refused to tell who his assailants were. "Then all of a sudden the whole thing seemed to blow away, like an evil wind. It was as though the town realized at last that he would be a part of its life until he died, and that they might as well become reconciled." Neighbors once more began to leave baskets of food upon his porch—"though they were the sort of dishes which they would have sent to a poor mill family. But it was food, and wellmeant" (63).

One way in which to gauge the importance of the community in this novel is by imagining the action to have taken place in Chicago or Manhattan Island, where the community—at least in Faulkner's sense —does not exist. As far as the general plot is concerned, everything in the novel could be easily accounted for: The frustration and rage of Joe Christmas, the murder of the lonely old maid, Miss Burden, and the moral impotence and isolation of Hightower are situations and events that occur frequently enough in the setting of our great modern world cities. The plight of the isolated individual cut off from any community of values is of course a dominant theme of contemporary literature. But by developing this theme in a rural setting in which a powerful sense of community still exists, Faulkner has given us a kind of pastoral—that is, he has let us see our modern and complex problems mirrored in a simpler and more primitive world. *Light in August* is, in some respects, a bloody and violent pastoral. The plight of the lost sheep and of the black sheep can be given special point and meaning because there is still visible in the background a recognizable flock with its shepherds, its watchdogs, sometimes fierce and cruel, and its bellwethers.

Yet the reader of *Light in August* may still question the relation of the fact of community to the meaning of the novel. Granted that the community is a living force, what does that have to do with the meaning of the novel? And he can scarcely be blamed if he goes on to ask whether *Light in August* is a novel at all. What possible relation is there between the two main characters, Lena and Joe Christmas, who never meet and who go their separate ways, the one placidly, the other violently? There is obviously the [54] bare fact of contrast; but is there anything more? Do not these characters between them rend the book in two?

Both questions are in order. A proper answer to the first (the relation of the community to the meaning of this novel) will suggest an answer to the second (the unity of the novel). But the answer to the first cannot be succinct, and in any case we must begin by considering more fully the relations of the various characters—to each other and to the world around them.

Lena and Joe Christmas, as everyone has seen, stand in obvious contrast to each other. Their very likenesses stress their basic differences. Both are orphans; both escape from home by crawling out a window; both are betrayed by their first loves; both in the course of their wanderings come to Jefferson. But how different they are in relation to society! Every man's hand is sooner or later lifted against Joe Christmas; he demands that it be so. But Lena, heavy with child, on an obviously ridiculous quest to find the father of her child, leads a charmed life. Even the women who look upon her swollen body with evident disapproval press their small store of coins upon her, and the community in general rallies to help her. As Mrs. Beard remarks to Byron Bunch: "Aint you and that preacher and ever other man that knows about her already done everything for her that she could think to want?" (368). In the person of Bunch, her quixotic errand actually raises up for her an authentic though clumsy knight-errant, who becomes her protector and fights her battles.

Joe repels, Lena attracts the force of the community into which they both come as strangers. But the point is not that Lena is "good" and Joe "bad." Joe's alienation from the community is not simply "willed"—there are deep-seated reasons for it, and, moreover, his is only the most extreme of a whole series of such alienations.

Faulkner has documented each history of alienation rather carefully, and has done so in great detail with those of Joe Christmas and Gail Hightower. Hightower, because of certain warping influences in childhood, becomes fettered to the past. Because of [55] certain traumatic experiences in childhood, Christmas is cut off from any meaningful past. Hightower toward the end of the novel comes to the bitter realization that he has hardly lived at all. The son of middle-aged parents (his father fifty, his mother forty), brought up in an austere house, he came as a child to dote upon the memory of his Confederate cavalryman grandfather, who represented all that his father was not. Hightower regards his father as an enemy. As he puts it, "I skipped a generation" (418). He is able to invest his grandfather's death (he was shot while robbing a henhouse on some foraging expedition) with romantic glamour. His sermons mix up in an incredible farrago the charging cavalry with the word of God. Late in the novel he comes to admit to himself that "for fifty years" he has "not even been clay: I have been a single instant of darkness in which a horse galloped and a gun crashed. . . . my dead grandfather on the instant of his death" (430). But his friend Byron Bunch has realized the truth about him long before, thinking to himself: "it's the dead folks that do him the damage. It's the dead ones that lay quiet in one place and dont try to hold him, that he cant escape from" (65).

But Christmas has no "dead ones" to hold him, no family, no past. The orphanage, where he was conscious that the grim old man was watching him "all the time," and life with his foster father, the dour Calvinist McEachern, lock him into himself. He is cut off from ties of any sort, and he learns to suspect and resent any appeal to sentiment or tenderness. Part of that suspicion of tenderness comes from his experiences with sex. Faulkner has most skillfully traced this development through the well-known toothpaste episode, the experience with the Negro girl, and the affair with the prostitute-waitress Bobbie, but he has not forced the development to extremes. Joe is not made into an overt homosexual. But his distaste for women and his fear of them is accounted for, and this antifeminine attitude becomes, as we shall see, a meaningful part of the novel. It is parallel to the attitude of Hightower, who does not understand women and comes to shrink from them and all that they represent. Doubtless the community was viciously wrong in accusing Hightower of homosexual practices; yet there is a latent tendency in him just as there is in [56] Christmas. There is this much justice in Grimm's bitter accusation when Hightower, attempting to give Christmas the alibi for which Bunch had pleaded, says, "He was with me the night of the murder" (406).

It is Joe's latent homosexuality that involves him with Joanna Burden. When he forces himself upon her, there is "no feminine vacillation, no coyness of obvious desire. . . . It was as if he struggled physically with another man for an object of no actual value to either, and for which they struggled on principle alone" (205). It is when Joanna's masculinity finally dissolves into nymphomania and that in turn gives way to feminine religiosity that Joe kills her. He cannot bear having her pray over him.

Joanna Burden is one of the most interesting of Faulkner's characters. Some years ago Maxwell Geismar protested that Faulkner had made "this decent and well-meaning abolitionist spinster" the "special object of his venom." He accused Faulkner of hating her because she is a modern woman and a "Northern" woman and of subjecting her to humiliations that he spares the Southern women in his novels. This comment is obviously silly. Faulkner endows Joanna Burden with pathos and even tragic dignity. She is lonely, cut off from her kind, shunned by the community; and she has been crippled (very much as Hightower has been) by her personal inheritance. But she has courage, a quiet power of endurance, and a remarkable lack of bitterness at her plight.

Joanna is one of Faulkner's masculinized women, but Faulkner is no harder upon Joanna than he is on his other masculinized women including Drusilla Hawk, the Southern girl who rode with a Confederate troop of cavalry. It is inaccurate to say that Faulkner is hard on either of them: he thinks, rather, that life has been hard on them. He has treated both Drusilla and Joanna with great sympathy and understanding.

Joanna has been warped by the pressure of events away from the fulfillment of her nature. She has been forced to bury a part of herself; but the needs and desires are there, and when they are awakened too late for normal fulfillment in children and a home, something very terrible happens to her. Joe Christmas is [57] perceptive enough on this point. He says to himself early in their relationship: "At least I have made a woman of her at last" (207), though later, less certain of the fact, he thinks: "She's trying to be a woman and she dont know how" (210). But Joe is not prepared for the torrent that is released when the "New England glacier [is] exposed suddenly to the fire of the New England biblical hell" (225). Later he observes, when she sometimes stares at him "with the wild, despairing face of a stranger," that "she wants to pray, but she dont know how to do that either" (228).

Faulkner is pitiless in recounting the details of Joanna's sexual discovery of herself and in indicating the man's revulsion from her—his feeling that he was "being sucked down into a bottomless morass" (227). But there is never any question that Joanna is essentially the victim—of sex too long repressed, of sex driven up into the head—or of her being compelled to her actions by a self that she had scarcely known existed. To witness Joanna's one love affair is like watching a stunted autumnal plant frantically trying to bloom and seed itself before the killing frosts—"something of dying summer spurting again like a dying coal" (228). Compare also: "hair just beginning to gray drawn gauntly back to a knot as savage and ugly as a wart on a diseased bough" (241).

At the end, Joanna reverts to her ancestral religion—as in some sense she has known all the time that she must. "Don't make me have to pray yet," she prays. "Dear God, let me be damned a little longer, a little while" (231). When she becomes once more the religious woman, the solicitous mother figure, the woman who would counsel the child and do him good, Joe finds that he has to kill her, and does—though not before Joanna has tried to kill him, for she serves a just God who will not be mocked, whose judgments are very sure, and she is ready to be that God's instrument. The last point is very important: Joanna's final gesture is not the spiteful reaction of a jilted woman. There is something almost impersonal about it. As she has told Joe when she asked him for the last time to kneel and pray with her, "It's not I who [58] ask it" (247). She is the dedicated instrument of her God, whether in saying "kneel with me" or in pulling the trigger.

Joanna Burden's frantic exploration of sex contrasts with Joe's attitude toward sex. Joe's life, as the author observes, had been, "for all its anonymous promiscuity . . . conventional enough, as a life of healthy and normal sin usually is" (227). And on another level, Joanna is contrasted with Lena in her attitude toward sex, for Lena, with her uncomplicated urge to foster life, is not so much normal as an embodiment of the very norm itself.

Most of all, however, Joanna invites comparison with Hightower. Faulkner has pointed to the parallels between these two characters in a number of ways. Both are recluses. Both have been rejected by the community for good and sufficient reason. Both are dominated by the past, since the family past has impinged upon both of them in a special way. Because of all this, the incautious reader might even leap to the conclusion that it was something in the personal heritage of these two people that destroyed them, leaving them unfulfilled and incomplete. In contrast to Joe Christmas, who has no roots in anything, Joanna and Hightower may seem too deeply rooted, helplessly fettered by their personal traditions—the one of militant abolitionism, the other of the galloping Confederate cavalry leader. But neither's is a live tradition. It does not connect past with present. It is absurdly doctrinaire and abstract or absurdly romantic. That, incidentally, is how the community judges both these obsessions.

The ancestors of both Gail Hightower and Joanna Burden were able to fulfill themselves. Calvin Burden, Joanna's grandfather, was lusty, full-blooded, completely alive. He was a fire-eating abolitionist, coming home "especially on Saturday nights . . . still full of straight whiskey and the sound of his own ranting. . . . [But he] was no proselyter, [no] missionary" (212). His peer is Hightower's grand-father, a "hale, bluff, rednosed man with the moustache of a brigand chief" (412), triumphantly at home in his world.

Joanna's father Nathaniel, after an exciting youth spent in the Southwest, becomes an austere grizzled man who settles in [59] Jefferson immediately after the Civil War. There his father and his son are shot down in a Reconstruction period election. But with all his justification for bitterness, and though isolated as a hated alien, he has an understanding of the values of the community. As Joanna herself reconstructs it: "We were foreigners . . . that thought differently from the people whose country we had come into without being asked or wanted. And [father] was French, half of him. Enough French to respect anybody's love for the land where he and his people were born and to understand that a man would have to act as the land where he was born had trained him to act" (223).

Like Joanna's father, Hightower's father was an abolitionist, though a Southern abolitionist. But he entered the Confederate army and "took an active part in a partisan war and on the very side whose principles opposed his own" (414). He taught himself surgery during the war, retained his idealism, and, as Faulkner puts it, "the other part of him, which lived in the actual world" (415), was as successful as any man and more successful than most. Thus, though Joanna's and Hightower's fathers were as unlike their own fathers as they could be, they too were able to fulfill themselves. Both the grandfathers and the fathers of Joanna and Hightower were whole men, fully related to the world outside them, fully alive. The issue is not that of a Northern or Southern heritage or even that of a sensual or ascetic temperament: both traditions and both temperaments are represented in their an-cestors. The real issue is whether one's relation to one's heritage permits participation in life or isolates one from life—whether it connects past with present or is simply a private obsession.

The most fascinating instance of the alienated person that occurs in the novel is that of Percy Grimm. Faulkner says: "I wrote [*Light in August*] in 1932 before I'd ever heard of Hitler's Storm Troopers,"[2] and thus had described a storm trooper without knowing it. Faulkner's claim that he had described the breed without help from the news-papers is quite justified; but because of hazy and inaccurate notions of the rise of Nazism, some readers will not realize just how accurate Faulkner's account is. In the [60] first place, it may seem strange to them that one should regard Percy Grimm as an alienated character at all. Yet Faulkner has gone to great pains to show that Grimm is cut off from the community and is thoroughly conscious of being cut off from

---

2 *Faulkner in the University*, p. 41.

it. Indeed, Faulkner has been almost as careful in working up the background of Percy Grimm's spiritual starvation and alienation as he has with that of Gail Hightower.

Grimm had been born too late to take part in the First World War. Because he had missed out on being a soldier, the boy had received a kind of psychic blow. As Faulkner puts it: "The boy was suffering the terrible tragedy of having been born not alone too late but not late enough to have escaped first hand knowledge of the lost time when he should have been a man instead of a child" (394). At another point, Faulkner makes the comment that Grimm had no one "to open his heart to." In short, Percy Grimm is a man who needs desperately to be felt a part of the community. He needs it so much that he attempts to seize the community values by violence. He yearns to wear a uniform marking him as the community's representative and defender. Whereas Christmas repudiates the customs and institutions of the community, Grimm insists upon seeing them in peril and demanding the right to take up arms in their defense. We shall miss the point badly if we entertain any doubts as to Percy Grimm's sincerity of motives in trying to prevent a lynching. He wants to ensure that Joe Christmas, murderer though he be, shall have a fair and proper trial.

So much for Grimm's conscious motives. What his unconscious motives are becomes plain enough when he confronts Joe Christmas at the end of the chase. Faulkner makes it clear that only in the heat of the chase does Grimm suddenly feel released, happy, fulfilled. Grimm runs "with a kind of fierce and constrained joy." Later, "above the blunt cold, rake of the automatic, his face had that serene, unearthly luminousness of angels in church windows" (402). It is probably only at the very end that the dammed-up sadism is revealed even to Grimm himself, bursting forth in a full tide as he fires the shots into the overturned table and seizes the butcher knife. [61]

A lesser artist would have made of Grimm a kind of caricature, merely brutalized and bestial. It is a mark of Faulkner's insight that even in his "Storm Trooper" he sees lurking beneath the fury and brutality the emotionally starved, lonely, terrified little boy.

In a sense we may say that Joe Christmas and Percy Grimm are closely akin—mirror images of each other in their relation to the community. This is why it makes good artistic sense that the stricken and wounded Hightower, in a final moment of truth about himself, should see the faces of Christmas and Grimm blurred together. In this vision there appear to him the faces of his wife, the townspeople, the members of his congregation, and those of Byron Bunch, Lena, and Joe Christmas. But one "face alone is not clear. It is confused more than any other, as though in the now peaceful throes of a more recent, a more inextricable, compositeness. Then he can see that it is two faces which seem to strive . . . in turn to free themselves one from the other, then fade and blend again" (430). Suddenly, he realizes whose the second face is: " 'Why, it's . . .' he thinks. 'I have seen it, recently . . . Why, it's that . . . boy. . . . who fired the . . .' " (431).

The theme of alienation from the community is in this novel closely connected with an emphasis on a kind of hell-fire Protestantism. In much of his work Faulkner reveals himself to be a Protestant anticlerical, fascinated and also infuriated by some of the more violently repressive features of the religion that dominates his part of the country. But in *Light in August* his criticism of the harsher Protestantism is not a gratuitous gesture that disturbs the work of art: it is absorbed into the total pattern of meaning.

Many of the characters in *Light in August* are doctrinaire by temperament and by training. The specific doctrines that they hold are forms of "Calvinism," but naturally there is a wide variation in content and stress. For McEachern the doctrines are quite literally those of the Westminster Confession, though McEachern overstresses the self-regarding and repressive virtues and conceives of God primarily as a god of wrath who administers an inexorable justice. In old Doc Hines there is definite distortion and [62] perversion. His fury at "bitchery and abomination" is the fury of a crazed man. What is particularly bloodcurdling is Hines' confidence that he is privy to God's plans and purposes. There is the wonderful passage in which he relates how God "said to old Doc Hines, 'You can go too now. You have done My work. There is no more evil here now but womanevil, not worthy for My chosen instrument to watch.' And old Doc Hines went . . . But he kept in touch with God" (338).

In her conversation with Bunch and Hightower, Mrs. Hines states quite precisely what has happened to her husband: he began "then to take God's name in vain and in pride to justify and excuse the devil that was in him" (326). His attribution of his furies to God is quite literally a taking of God's name in vain, blasphemy. The tendency to call one's own hates the vengeance of a just God is a sin to which Protestantism has always been prone. But not merely Southern Protestantism and not merely Protestantism as such. Norman Cohn's *The Pursuit of the Millennium* shows how deep-rooted is this element in our culture. In fact, most of the millennial movements, including the revolutionary movements, of the West share in this tendency to attribute the desires and hates of an individual or a group to God or to the dialectic of history or to the nature of reality. Doc Hines' distortions of this aspect of some of the Protestant sects, though they are those of a madman, are meaningful, for they constitute a serious caricature of views held by people who are quite "normal."

Joanna Burden's grandfather should be mentioned in this company. He was the son of a Unitarian minister, but when he ran away to the West he became a Catholic and lived for a year in a monastery. On his marriage he repudiated the Catholic Church, choosing for the scene of his formal repudiation "a saloon, insisting that every one present listen to him and state their objections" (211). But in repudiating Catholicism, he did not repudiate religion. Though he could not read the English Bible—he had learned from the priests in California to read Spanish—he began to instruct his child in the true religion, interspersing his readings to the child in Spanish with "extemporized dissertations composed half of the bleak and bloodless logic which he [63] remembered from his father on interminable New England Sundays, and half of immediate hellfire and tangible brimstone" (212). Perhaps he differs from the bulk of doctrinaire hellfire and brimstone Protestants in not being a proselyter or a missionary. But everything else marks him as truly of the breed: his intensity, his stern authoritarianism, and his violence. He has killed a man in an argument over slavery and he threatens to "frail the tar" (212) out of his children if they do not learn to hate what he hates—hell and slaveholders.

Hightower's father differs sharply from Calvin Burden, but the doctrinaire element in him is also unmistakable. He "was a man of Spartan sobriety beyond his years" (414). His bibulous father, the Confederate cavalryman, teases him a little for being a "sanctimonious cuss" who requires for a wife only somebody who "can sing alto out of a Presbyterian hymnbook" (413), though Faulkner also makes it plain that the father has a great deal of respect for his sober-minded son and that the son is in many respects an admirable man. But to the neurotic boy, Gail Hightower, this man of principle, his father, is more than a stranger, he is an enemy. To the child he seemed to "fill the room with rude health and unconscious contempt" (416). The relation between them makes a certain parallel with the relation between Joe Christmas and his foster father McEachern. The parallel is far from exact, but it is discernible. It is only another of the several ways in which Hightower and Christmas resemble each other.

Gail Hightower, of course, is the only one of these Protestants who has had formal theological training. Because of that fact, one might expect him to be the most doctrinaire of all. He is not. He seems at the beginning of the book the most tolerant and pitying of all the characters, the one who recoils in horror at man's capacity for evil and man's propensity to crucify his fellows, the man whose only defense against violence is nonresistance. One may be inclined to say, therefore, that Hightower has rebelled against his Calvinist training and repudiated its jealous and repressive God; and certainly, there is truth in this notion. [64] Hightower is a disillusioned man and a man who has learned something from his sufferings. But there is a sense in which he has never broken out of the mold: he still stresses a God of justice rather than a God of mercy, for his sincerest belief is that he has somehow "bought immunity." He exclaims: "And after all, I have paid" (429)—in confidence that God is an honest merchant who has receipted his bill and will honor his title to the precious merchandise he has purchased at such cost. But although he cannot entirely free himself from his intellectual heritage, he has broken with his earlier Calvinism, and his indictment of the Church is an indictment of "the professionals who control it" because they have seen to it that its steeples are "skypointed not with ecstasy or passion but in *adjuration, threat,* and *doom*" (426; italics mine).

Lastly, there is Joe Christmas, the most violent rebel of all against hellfire Protestantism. As a child, he is conscious that he is being hounded by the fanatically religious old Doc Hines; he resists stubbornly the discipline imposed by his foster father McEachern, whom he finally brains with a chair; and when his paramour, Joanna Burden, threatens him with hell and insists that he kneel with her and pray for forgiveness, he decapitates her. Yet there is a most important sense in which Joe Christmas is the sternest and most thoroughly dedicated "Calvinist" in the book.

He has imbibed more from the training of his foster father than he realizes. For all that he strains in fierce resistance against him, he "could depend" on "the hard, just, ruthless man." It is the "soft kindness" of the woman, his foster mother, that he abominates. If one mark of the "Calvinists" in this novel is their fear and distrust of women and their hatred of the female principle, then Joe Christmas is eminently qualified to take a place among them. He even has affinities with his old childhood ogre, Doc Hines, and with Hines' fury at the bitchery of women and abomination of Negro blood. Joe, hearing the "fecund-mellow" voices of Negro women, feels that he and "all other man-shaped life about him" had been returned to the "lightless hot wet primogenitive Female" (100) and runs from the scene in a kind of panic. [65]

Christmas too wants not mercy but justice, is afraid of the claims and obligations of love, and yearns only for a vindication of his identity and integrity—a vindication made the more difficult by his not knowing precisely what he would vindicate. When he puts aside the temptation to marry Joanna and win ease and security, he does it by saying: "If I give in now, I will deny all the thirty years that I have lived to make me what I chose to be" (232). Finally, Joe is something of a fatalist, and his fatalism is a kind of perversion of Calvinist determinism. On his way to murder Joanna, "he believed with calm paradox that he was the volitionless servant of the fatality in which he believed that he did not believe" (244). But so "fated" is his act of murder that he keeps saying to himself "I had to do it" (245)—using the past tense, as if the act had already been performed.

In *Light in August* some of the characters who have become cut off from the community—and from life—become reintegrated with it, fully or partially. Such a character is Byron Bunch. He has suffered no traumatic experience in his youth; he has received no special conditioning from the past; nor has he violently rebelled or been violently rejected by the community. He is rather the methodical little "settled" man with no vices, the perpetual bachelor, who is somewhat withdrawn from the tides of life. We are told how he came to fall in love and, through this love, became involved in matters of life and death, crime and scandal. We are also told how Hightower, who had tried so desperately hard to avoid involvement ("I have bought immunity") is also drawn back into decision and responsibility. Hightower, as Bunch's confidant and in some sense his spiritual adviser, fears that Bunch is risking his "freedom," and counsels him to avoid involvement. But finally, through Bunch, he himself once more becomes involved in life and death; he delivers Lena's baby, since the doctor has not got to her in time, and he makes a desperate last-minute attempt to save Joe Christmas just before he is shot to death in the next room.

The involvement of Bunch comes through a woman, and that [66] fact itself is significant. For the alienation of many of those separated from the community has come about through their attitudes toward woman and sex—or at least reveals itself in those attitudes. It is so with Christmas, with Hightower, and with Byron Bunch. One might include Joanna Burden here, for though she is a woman, her masculinization is the badge of her loneliness and the means through which she is destroyed. Hightower makes the connection very definitely. As he passes the charred timbers of her house he says: "Poor, barren woman. To have not lived only a week longer, until luck returned to this place. [Lena's child has just been born in a cabin on her place.] Until luck and life returned to these barren and ruined acres" (357). Joanna's own barrenness is precisely to the point, and conversely Lena's fertility is connected not only literally with life but also with luck, good fortune.

Lena, by the way, is the only one of the strangers—the outsiders who have come into the community—who does not suffer from frustration and alienation. The others suffer from the characteristic disease of modern life, its sick hurry and divided aims. One can recognize in the situation of Christmas or Hightower themes characteristic of other writers of our time such as Eliot and Joyce. To all of them one might apply John Crowe Ransom's telling description of modern man as a being unable "to fathom or perform his nature." Since Christmas does not know who he is, he can express himself only in fits of compulsive violence. Gavin Stevens thinks that perhaps just before his death, Christmas did come to know who he was, and there are rather clear indications that Hightower fathoms his nature at the end, but this knowledge comes very late. Lena is almost alone in not suffering from this modern defect. She can perform her nature because she does not need to fathom it: she *is* nature.

Lena (along with Eula of *The Hamlet*) has sometimes been called an "earth goddess." The description does have a certain aptness when applied to Eula, especially in some of the more rhapsodic passages of *The Hamlet*. But it is a little highfalutin for Lena. It is more accurate to say that Lena is one of Faulkner's several embodiments of the female principle—indeed, one of the [67] purest and least complicated of his embodiments. Her rapport with nature is close. She is never baffled as to what course of action to take. She is never torn by doubts and indecisions. There is no painful introspection. This serene composure has frequently been put down to sheer mindlessness, and Lena, to be sure, is a very simple young woman. But Faulkner himself undoubtedly attributes most of Lena's quiet force to her female nature. Faulkner may indeed have had a rather romantic idea of woman. He certainly had an old-fashioned idea of her. In the Faulknerian world men have to lose their innocence, confront the hard choice, and through a process of initiation discover reality. But women are already in possession of this knowledge, naturally and instinctively. That is why in moments of bitterness Faulkner's male characters—Mr. Compson in *The Sound and the Fury*, for example—assert that women are not innocent and have a natural affinity for evil. It would be more accurate to say that Faulkner's women lack the callow idealism of the men, have fewer illusions about human nature, and are less trammeled by legalistic distinctions and the niceties of any code.

In *Light in August*, however, the male-female contrast is stressed in a rather different way. Here, the principal male characters suffer alienation. They are separated from the community, are in rebellion against it—and against nature. But Lena moves serenely into the community and it gathers itself about her with protective gestures. Its response to her, of course, is rooted in a deep and sound instinct: Lena embodies the principle upon which any human community is founded. She is the carrier of life, and she has to be protected and nurtured if there is to be any community at all.

A basic theme in *Light in August* is man's strained attempt to hold himself up in rigid aloofness above the relaxed female world. Many of the men in the novel take up this stance, notably Hightower and Christmas. The crazed fanatic Doc Hines and the dour Presbyterian McEachern are to be numbered here too; perhaps also, though with an obvious difference, Hightower's father, [68] Joanna Burden's father, and Joanna (as masculinized woman) herself. Byron Bunch, when we first see him, is aligned with this group. He is timid with women, and his religiousness has just a hint of the anchorite in it. Even Lucas Burch ought to be mentioned in this company—if only for comic relief (though he does have a quite literal claim to be admitted: in his own terms, he is not the marrying kind, and we last see him frantically escaping from Lena and her baby and his responsibilities to them).

Lena's function in the novel ought now to be clear. Faulkner uses her to affirm a kind of integrity and wholeness by which the alienated characters are to be judged. But Lena has more than a symbolic function. She is the means through which Byron Bunch is redeemed from his pallid half-life and brought back into the community. And she is the indirect means through which Hightower is redeemed. This coming back into the community is an essential part of their redemption. Unless the controlling purposes of the individual are related to those that other men share and in which the individual can participate, he is indeed isolated and is forced to fall back upon his personal values, with all the risk of fanaticism and distortion to which such isolation is liable.

The community is at once the field for man's action and the norm by which his action is judged and regulated. It sometimes seems that the sense of an organic community has all but disappeared from modern fiction, and the disappearance accounts for the terrifying self-consciousness and subjectivity of a great deal of modern writing. That Faulkner had some sense of an organic community still behind him was among his most important resources as a writer.

If in Faulkner's work the community can still serve as a positive norm, does that mean that in his fiction there is no room for the roles of the prophet and the saint? Can one ever find implicit approval of the individual's effort to amend or transcend the values held by the community? The answer is yes, and often. Faulkner was always fascinated by rebels and has usually accorded them a full measure of dramatic sympathy. But his fiction also reveals keen awareness of the perils risked by the individual who attempts to run counter to the community. The divergent individual may [69] invite martyrdom; he certainly risks fanaticism and madness. In *Light in August* Faulkner's emphasis is primarily on the distortion and perversion and sterility which isolation from the community entails, though even here there is a clear recognition of a heroic element in Hightower, Joanna Burden, and Joe Christmas.

The term "redemption" may seem to claim too much for Hightower. Yet by the end of the novel he has been powerfully changed. After he has successfully delivered Lena's baby, he feels "a surge of something almost hot, almost triumphant" and thinks "I showed them! . . . Life comes to the old man yet" (355). And he goes home to read not Tennyson but *Henry IV*, "food for a man" (355). When he hears that Byron has left, he says to himself: "So he departed without coming to tell me goodbye" (363). And then, with a conscious and purposed inversion of the usual phrase, "After all *he* has done for *me*. Fetched to me. Ay; given, restored, to me" (italics mine). Later, it is true, Hightower has to experience Christmas' attack upon him, the futile attempt to stop Grimm with a lie offered too late to save Christmas' life, and the blood-letting in his own house. But he has dared the opprobrium and told the generous lie, and in the long reverie which closes Faulkner's account of him he has admitted to himself that he "was the one who failed" (426), that he was responsible for his wife's death, that he has been "a charlatan preaching worse than heresy" (427), and that, bound by his romantic fixation on his grandfather's death, he has himself been neither dead nor alive. In this hour of truth he has his vision of the faces, and sees them for what they are, and he hears once again the phantom cavalry, the mystic experience with which he has sustained himself in the past, but this time he hears with a difference "the clashing sabres and the dying thunder of hooves," for he himself has finally dared something and has broken out of his self-centered dream.

Most readers have assumed that Hightower, old and exhausted, his head bandaged after Christmas' blows, dies as he hears "the dying thunder of hooves." But Faulkner, in his University of Virginia discussions, indicated that Hightower "didn't die."[3] This is obviously highly interesting; but as far as the larger scheme of [70] the book is concerned, it hardly matters: whether Hightower died or lived on, he had broken out of the circle in which we find him at the opening of the story.

And what of Byron Bunch? Is he also "redeemed?" Can we say so in view of the curious and somewhat ambiguous ending of the novel in which Lena has not accepted marriage with Byron but, with Byron in tow, pursues her ridiculous quest for the father of her child, the unspeakable Lucas Burch? An answer to this question necessarily brings up for consideration Faulkner's attitude—not only to the characters in this episode but to all the happenings in the book. What shall we call the predominant mode? Tragic or comic or neither?

Finally and generally, I believe, the mode is that of comedy. To say so in the light of some of the terrible episodes may seem perverse. But Faulkner's comedy is frequently a makeweight to the terrible. The tender-minded reader may feel that Faulkner frequently uses a savage humor; but his is never a cynical and nihilistic humor. Its function is to maintain sanity and human perspective in a scene of brutality and horror. For example, there is the wonderful passage in which the countryman who has discovered the fire in Miss Burden's house enters and finds her body with the head almost severed, a condition which presents him with a problem in getting the dead woman downstairs. He is afraid to try to pick her up and carry her out "because her head might come clean off." But the fire forces the issue and he has to pick her up and bring her out as best he can. When he deposits the body on the ground, however, the cover in which he had hastily wrapped her "fell open and she was laying on her side, facing one way, and her head was turned clean around like she was looking behind her. And he

---

3 *Faulkner in the University,* p. 75.

said how if she could just have done that when she was alive, she might not have been doing it now" (80).

This is comic and we may call it a grotesque and savage comedy, but we miss the point if we think that the countryman is being rude or cynical. It does not occur to him to leave the body in the burning house, and he has done his best under the circumstances to observe the decencies. His wry and sardonic humor is not [71] disparaging or irreverent, though it speaks to the issue and keeps, amid the horror, a tenacious grip on common sense. Faulkner's work is full of this kind of comedy. *The Hamlet* and *As I Lay Dying* abound in it, and there is not a little of it in *Light in August.*

One can look at Faulkner's comedy in still another way. We may say that Faulkner tends to take the long view in which the human enterprise in all its basically vital manifestations is seen from far off and with great detachment. If the view is long enough and the perspective full enough, the basic attitude is almost inevitably comic. James Joyce comes to mind. His *Ulysses,* though it has much pathos and horror in it, is also finally a comic work. In *Light in August* Faulkner observes even the tragic events that involve Joanna Burden with detachment and in a full perspective. It is Lena and her instinct for nature, Lena and her rapport with the community, Lena as a link in the eternal progression from mother to daughter who provides the final norm for our judgment. In this connection Faulkner's abiding concern with man's endurance and his ability to suffer anything— compare the Nobel Prize speech—is worth remembering. Tragedy always concerns itself with the individual, his values, his tragic encounter with the reality about him, and the waste which is suffered in his defeat. Comedy involves, on the other hand, the author's basic alignment with society and with the community.

In calling *Light in August* a pastoral we have already suggested something of the comic mood. The pastoral, on the whole, aligns itself with comedy, not with tragedy. The suggestion made earlier that *Light in August* is a kind of pastoral has not been made whimsically. The last chapter of the book, with the adventures of Byron Bunch and Lena, is almost conventionally pastoral, and pastoral with an authentic comic note, for Byron is comically balked of his reward. The little man has done quite nobly. He has befriended and protected Lena, and now Lena obviously should marry him; but as the book closes, Lena is still hitchhiking across Tennessee in pursuit of Lucas Burch. Yet Byron finds it impossible to abandon her.

Our last glimpse of Lena is given through the eyes of a character whom we have not met before in the novel. Faulkner [72] introduces him most casually. The last chapter simply opens to the statement that there lives in the eastern part of the state a furniture repairer and dealer "who recently made a trip into Tennessee to get some old pieces of furniture which he had bought by correspondence." On this trip the furniture dealer picked up the hitchhikers, Lena, her baby, and her strange little bachelor companion. The oddity of the group piques his curiosity. Later he senses what is going on and the situation stirs his amusement, though it is an amusement not without insight into Lena's coquetry and not without a trace of pity for Byron's abashed devotion.

The reader may resent the casual and last-minute introduction of the new narrator and he may be disposed to dismiss this incident as simply another of Faulkner's tricky fictional devices. Yet if he has been able to see the importance of the community in this novel, he should have little difficulty in hearing and recognizing the voice of the community once more in the furniture dealer's narration. It is not important that we do not know his name or that we have not met him before or that we shall not meet him again. He can be for us the anonymous, earthy, genial, experienced, tough-minded representative of a corporate body of values, insights, and beliefs.

As such a representative, he finds Byron's plight amusing, and he obviously enjoys having so good a story to relate to his wife when he gets home. But his humor is not cruel and his insights into the relation of man and woman, the nature of chivalry, and the connection of love with honor are not untouched by a certain wisdom. In any case, we can observe that this last chapter of *Light in August*, with its comic overtones, does not really represent an abandonment of the theme that I ventured earlier to characterize in a phrase borrowed from John Crowe Ransom. For Byron Bunch too is a man unable "to fathom or perform his nature"—still unable, that is, in our last glimpse of him, to bring Lena to terms. He has acted unselfishly and gallantly, but he cannot do now what the furniture dealer knows that he ought to do: force the issue and persuade Lena to accept him as lover and husband.

On the first night they camp out together, the furniture dealer thinks that Byron has nerved himself to the act. He watches [73] Byron quietly entering the truck where Lena is sleeping and, as he observes to his wife, "I says to myself, 'Old boy, if you'd a just done this last night, you'd a been sixty miles further south than you are now, to my knowledge" (440). But Lena repels Byron's advances with the exclamation: "Why, Mr. Bunch. Aint you ashamed. You might have woke the baby, too." And the furniture dealer tells his wife: "I be dog if I dont believe she picked him up and set him back outside on the ground like she would that baby if it had been about six years old" (441).

Byron had retired in confusion, but when the furniture dealer started the next day's journey with the imperturbable Lena and her child, Byron was waiting around the next curve in the road, and got back in the truck with the explanation: "I done come too far now. . . . I be dog if I'm going to quit now." Lena answers him with: "Aint nobody never said for you to quit" (443).

The furniture dealer evidently has no doubt that eventually Lena will marry Byron. He says to his wife, in explaining Lena's continuation of her obviously foolish quest, "I think she was just traveling. I dont think she had any idea of finding whoever it was she was following. I dont think she had ever aimed to, only she hadn't told him [Byron] yet. . . . I reckon she knew that when she settled down this time, it would likely be for the rest of her life. That's what I think" (444).

Gail Hightower, too, had earlier made the same prophecy when he imagined that Lena would continue to bear children, fulfilling her nature, but, in the future, children sired by Byron. Eventually, one supposes, Byron came to realize that Lena wanted to be possessed and mastered. For though Faulkner counsels that man should stand in awe of nature, and, loving and respecting it, should forbear to violate it, he does not expect man to stand perpetually aloof from nature, completely passive and lacking a field for action. Byron needs to learn the mean between a rape and Platonic love. But Faulkner did not choose to give us here the story of the marriage of Byron and Lena. He preferred to end his novel on the dominant theme of man's inability to fulfill himself, though the theme is treated here not tragically but with humor and amused irony—even as social comedy. [74]

Myth and Motion

ROBERT P. ADAMS

CRITICS HAVE HAD A GREAT DEAL OF TROUBLE IN EFFORTS TO DEMONSTRATE any general unity in *Light in August,* and have sometimes concluded that it is an inferior book. The great majority, however, feel that, unity or no unity, it is one of Faulkner's greatest works. Evidently there is something in it that has not been adequately explained.

The problem presents itself most obviously in the fact that the stories of Lena Grove, Joe Christmas, and Gail Hightower are not connected logically in such fashion as to account for the degree of unity critics generally expect to find in a great work of art. Attempts to discover thematic and symbolic links among the three stories have met with only partial and unconvincing success. The harder such attempts are pressed, the more they tend to demonstrate that the stories are not meant to be linked in quite that way. A formula is needed that will account for the quality of the novel without compromising the separate identities of the stories within it.

A useful suggestion was made when James W. Linn and Houghton W. Taylor, only three years after the book was published, called it a "counterpoint of stories,"[1] which is what Faulkner later called *The Wild Palms*.[2] Linn and Taylor [84] suggested that an author might compose a novel by placing two or more separate stories in juxtaposition, without close logical connections, and that the novel could be unified by unstated comparisons, involving differences as much as likenesses. This suggestion has not been developed very much in recent criticism of *Light in August*, perhaps because neither Linn and Taylor nor anyone else has succeeded in finding a common denominator in terms of which the structures of the constituent stories could be shown to cooperate in establishing a solid structure of the whole.

The materials for such a demonstration have, however, been made available. Many critics have noticed that Lena's story has parallels with fertility myths and that Christmas's is based (often in ironically reversed terms, to be sure) on the Christ story, and one critic, Beach Langston, has contended that Hightower's story is significantly related to the story of Buddha.[3] If these parallels are valid, and if Faulkner was using the mythical method, in conjunction with a contrapuntal technique, we may find the common denominator we need in the juxtaposition of the three religious stories, each of which carries its own distinct system of ritual symbolism, and each of which may contribute its archetypal structure to help organize the story Faulkner wanted to tell.

In an interview at Virginia, Faulkner said his conception of *Light in August* "began with Lena Grove, the idea of the young girl with nothing, pregnant, determined to find her sweetheart. . . . As I told that story I had to get more and more into it, but that was mainly the story of Lena Grove."[4] Later, in answer to a question about the meaning of the title, Faulkner explicitly associated the book, and particularly Lena, with Greek mythology, saying that "in August in Mississippi there's [85] a few days somewhere about the middle of the month when suddenly there's a foretaste of fall, it's cool, there's a lambence, a luminous quality to the light, as though it came not from just today but from back in the old classic times. It might have fauns and satyrs and the gods and—from Greece, from Olympus in it somewhere. . . . it reminded me of that time, of a luminosity older than our Christian civilization. Maybe the connection was with Lena Grove, who had something of that pagan quality of being able to

[1] J. W. Linn and H. W. Taylor, *A Foreword to Fiction* (New York: Appleton-Century, 1935), p. 157.

[2] *Writers at Work*, p. 133; *Faulkner at Nagano*, pp. 79–80; *Faulkner in the University*, p. 171.

[3] Beach Langston, "The Meaning of Lena Grove and Gail Hightower in *Light in August*," *Boston University Studies in English*, V (Spring 1961), 51–63.

[4] *Faulkner in the University*, p. 74.

assume everything, that's—the desire for that child. . . ."[5] The imagery used and the intention suggested here are strikingly similar to what
Faulkner had been trying for in some of his earliest work, notably
"Twilight" and "The Hill," where the quality of light at sunset is
associated with the dancing of nymphs and fauns. Lena's story is
roughly analogous to the typical myth of the fertility goddess—
Cybele, Aphrodite, Demeter-Persephone—, and it seems to have particular affinities with the account of the Arician Diana given by Frazer
in the opening pages of *The Golden Bough*.[6]

Faulkner seems, however, to have deliberately avoided giving too
firm a structure to Lena's story. She serves as a representative of pure
motion, tranquilly natural, comfortable, and inevitable, completely in
harmony with the motion of life in the earth. She is never stopped or
frustrated, and so her story has no dramatic conflict out of which a
structural system of relations could be developed. She is so defined
that she cannot serve by herself to effect the artificial stopping of
motion at which Faulkner always aimed. Therefore Faulkner had to
bring in at least one other story in order to provide the [86] frictions,
blockages, and tensions needed for the accomplishment of his artistic
purpose.

Joe Christmas is the most direct foil and the most obvious antithesis to Lena. He experiences and represents frustration, denial of
life, and failure to change or develop or, in any meaningful sense, to
move. His situation, conceived in terms of continual conflict, within
himself and between him and others, is rich in drama, and Faulkner
exploits it richly. It occupies so much of the foreground of the book
that most critics have taken Christmas to be the protagonist. Faulkner,
however, according to the statement quoted above, regarded Christmas as only a means to an end. His function in the story is to stand
over against Lena as a static contrast in relation to which her motion
can be seen and her power of life appreciated.

This function defines his role as a Christ figure in a rather special
way. He does not represent the Christ of the New Testament, but
rather the rigid repressiveness which Faulkner had associated with
Southern Protestant morality in *Sanctuary* and *As I Lay Dying*. Christmas is more the helpless victim of a pharisaical society than Christ
was. He is not only persecuted and killed; he is also corrupted by
being made to pattern himself on the models of repression, such as
Doc Hines and Simon McEachern, who impose his alienation from life.

---

[5] *Ibid.*, p. 199.

[6] This similarity is convincingly demonstrated by Millgate, p. 136. Millgate
seems excessively cautious in thinking that "These suggested correspondences
. . . may be entirely accidental"; I prefer his alternative hypothesis that "such
correspondences, like those linking characters in the book with the members of
the Holy Family, may represent only one among several patterns of analogy which
Faulkner pursued in the course of the novel. . . ."

Because the principle of static repression is as much within him as it is about him, he is unable to accept change, or survive disillusionment, without reacting destructively. Therefore he becomes a murderer, and his own death looks like suicide. He is a mirror image of the sterility that kills him. Hightower, meditating with helpless concern on the coming event, defines it as a "crucifixion" to which each of the town's three churches "will raise a cross. 'And they will do it gladly,' he says. . . . 'Since to pity him would be to admit selfdoubt and to hope for and need pity themselves'" (p. 348*). It is the image [87] of such churches that Christmas reflects when, being religiously beaten by McEachern, he looks "like a monk in a picture" (p. 140), and a little later when "The boy's body might have been wood or stone; a post or a tower upon which the sentient part of him mused like a hermit, contemplative and remote with ecstasy and selfcrucifixion" (p. 150). The same expression is seen on the face of that other murderer, Percy Grimm, as he pursues Christmas to kill him: "that serene, unearthly luminousness of angels in church windows" (p. 437). In Hightower's final meditation, the faces of Christmas and Grimm "fade and blend" into one (p. 466). Christmas embodies all the static and sterile intolerance from which he suffers. His death, like his punishment by McEachern, is actually a "selfcrucifixion."

Several other kinds of intolerance are associated with Protestantism in the book, and they are developed in ramifications and subramifications of Christmas's story. The intolerance of Doc Hines is not so much religious as it is racial and sexual. The Burden family's intolerance of slavery is as dogmatic and as violent as the doctrine it opposes. And Christmas's own intolerance of experience, or of life, is demonstrated over and over in his encounters with women: the dietician at the orphanage, Mrs. McEachern, his prostitute sweetheart Bobbie Allen, the anonymous prostitute who is tolerant of Negroes as customers, and Joanna Burden.

The religious parallels in *Light in August* are not used to inculcate any religious belief that Faulkner himself may have had, nor are they intended primarily to express his criticism of other people's beliefs. Their function is to help build the artificial static obstacle to the motion of life that Faulkner needed if he was to succeed in telling the story of Lena. They tell us nothing at all about Faulkner's personal feelings or opinions about anything except the art of fiction, in the exercise of which he made them serve as tools. [88]

Hightower, according to Beach Langston, is an incarnation "of the recurring figure of the Buddha, or, more accurately, of a Bodhisattva."[7] That is, he tries by meditation and passive suffering to emulate the

---

* All quotations from *Light in August* are from the Modern Library edition (New York: Random House, 1950).

[7] Langston, p. 47.

Buddha in spiritual purification, to escape the cycle of life, and to achieve Nirvana, a nothingness or a loss of identity, a static condition in which he can be at peace. Langston's hypothesis is supported in the text by Faulkner's use of the word "avatar" (pp. 5, 213, 244),[8] by the image of "the wheel of thinking" in Hightower's final revery (pp. 462–66), and by the description of Hightower, on two occasions, sitting like "an eastern idol . . ." (pp. 83, 298). [9] Langston notes that Hightower, like a disciple of Buddha, has two possibilities of salvation: the passive way of withdrawal, the Lesser Vehicle, Hinayana; or the way of Mahayana, the Greater Vehicle, a life of responsible action such as the Buddha led after his enlightenment under the Bo-Tree.

In his last session of sunset meditation, Hightower is forced to realize that his effort to escape the responsibilities of present life by a process of passive withdrawal has been disastrously unsuccessful. He sees that, by using his wife as a means of retreating into the past, he has driven her to sexual debauchery and probably to suicide; that he has been " 'her seducer and her murderer, author and instrument of her shame and death' " (p. 462). His withdrawal, instead of being passive and virtuous, has been a negative action, for the results of which he has to acknowledge a criminal responsibility.

He is able to arrive at this realization partly because he has been forced, by the insistence of Byron Bunch, to take an active part in life, after twenty-five years of isolation. It is he who delivers Lena's baby; and for a time he feels that the [89] waste land aspect of his world has been overcome. He is sorry for Joanna Burden chiefly because she has " 'not lived only a week longer. . . . Until luck and life returned to these barren and ruined acres.' It seems to him that he can see, feel, about him the ghosts of rich fields, and of the rich fecund black life of the quarters, the mellow shouts, the presence of fecund women, the prolific naked children in the dust before the doors; and the big house again, noisy, loud with the treble shouts of the generations" (p. 385). The momentum of this feeling carries him to the point of offering the alibi that Byron has asked him to furnish for Christmas, trying to stop Percy Grimm and his followers by telling them, " 'He was here that night. He was with me the night of the murder' " (p. 439). When Hightower acknowledges that he himself is, in effect, a murderer, the tormenting weight of "the wheel of thinking" is lifted. "The wheel, released, seems to rush on. . . . going fast and smooth now, because it is freed now of burden, of vehicle, axle, all. In the lambent suspension of August into which night is about to fully come, it seems to engender and surround itself with a faint glow like a halo. The halo is full of

---

[8] The word "avatar" is never applied directly to Hightower, however.

[9] The probable source of this image in the last paragraph of Conrad's *Heart of Darkness* is more explicit: Marlow "sat apart, indistinct and silent, in the pose of a meditating Buddha."

faces. . . . They are peaceful, as though they have escaped into an apotheosis; his own is among them" (p. 465).

According to Langston, this description indicates Hightower's attainment, by the way of Mahayana, the Greater Vehicle, of the Buddhist "*pari-nirvana*. Hightower has bought his immunity through crucifixion on the martyr's wheel, has worked out his karma, has attained the peace that passeth understanding, has finally on this August night turned the Wheel of the Law and become, momentarily at least, an enlightened Bodhisattva. He has been released from the chain of reincarnations which required that he should continually reenter the world as an avatar of his grandfather and the romantic religion of the Civil War."[10] Faulkner's text confirms the view that Hightower experiences a kind of release: "Then [90] it seems to him that some ultimate dammed flood within him breaks and rushes away. He seems to watch it, feeling himself losing contact with earth, lighter and lighter, emptying, floating. 'I am dying,' he thinks" (p. 466). But the nature of this experience is more dubious, more complex and equivocal, than Langston's account seems to recognize. Faulkner has said in an interview that Hightower "didn't die. . . . He had to endure, to live," and that he still had "the memory of his grandfather, who had been brave."[11]

Hightower's ultimate vision is the same one into which he has been retreating from life for twenty-five years, the vision of his grandfather's cavalry troop charging into Jefferson in a gallant and successful effort to destroy a cache of supplies intended for Grant's army. As his imagination recreates the scene, "They rush past, forwardleaning in the saddles, with brandished arms, beneath whipping ribbons from slanted and eager lances; with tumult and soundless yelling they sweep past like a tide whose crest is jagged with the wild heads of horses and the brandished arms of men like the crater of the world in explosion" (pp. 466–67). This vision hardly seems an appropriate representation of the Buddhist pari-nirvana, which Langston describes as "that infinite and eternal peace into which the enlightened Bodhisattva may enter when he has worked out his karma and thus broken the chain of reincarnation."[12] On the contrary, it is a vision of war and violent action, in which two of Faulkner's favorite images of life in motion, the horse and the flood, are energetically combined.

It seems very probable that Faulkner did use the story of Buddha as a basis for his characterization of Hightower. But he was no more confined by it than he was by the story of Christ, and Hightower is no more like the Buddha than Christmas is like the Savior. Hightower's symbolic value in [91] the structure of *Light in August* lies some

---

[10] Langston, p. 60.
[11] *Faulkner in the University,* p. 75.
[12] Langston, p. 55.

where between those of Lena Grove and Joe Christmas. Hightower is not wholly static, like Christmas, but neither is he wholly dynamic, like Lena. His effort to enter the current of life is too reluctant and it comes too late to be more than partly successful. He falls back on his vision of the past. But it is a dynamic vision, and perhaps now he is able to see it less as a retreat from life and more as an encouragement to help him endure whatever life remains with a better grace than he has had before.

The pattern of individual personal development in *Light in August* is most clearly seen in the experience of Byron Bunch, which has generally been regarded by critics as part of Lena's story rather than a story in its own right, but which nevertheless provides a major element in the structure of the book as a whole. Byron begins by being as isolated as Hightower in his Hinayana phase, and as static as Christmas in his rejection of any fertile relations with women. But Byron falls in love with Lena, and finds himself launched, willy nilly, in the current of life. Unlike Christmas, he falls from innocence into involvement, into acceptance of sin, guilt, responsibility, and all the other burdens of creative activity.

To assume that Christmas is the protagonist of *Light in August*, as critics have generally done, is to classify the story as a tragedy and to find, as many critics have found, that it is lacking in unity, faulty in structure, and full of irrelevancy. Faulkner pointed to the error in an interview by saying that *Light in August* does not argue "for the acceptance of an inevitably tragic view of life" (his questioner's phrase) and by remarking that "the only person in that book that accepted a tragic view of life was Christmas. . . . The others seemed to me to have had a very fine belief in life, in the basic possibility for happiness and goodness—Byron Bunch and Lena Grove, to have gone to all that trouble."[13] On another occasion, in [92] answer to the more general question, "Mr. Faulkner, do you consider human life basically a tragedy?" he said, "Actually, yes. But man's immortality is that he is faced with a tragedy which he can't beat and he still tries to do something with it."[14] Byron Bunch says much the same thing when he sees Lucas Burch, Lena's other lover and the biological father of her baby, running away from the opportunity and the responsibility of marrying her: " 'I took care of his woman for him and I borned his child for him. And now there is one more thing I can do for him. I cant marry them, because I aint a minister. And I may not can catch him, because he's got a start on me. And I may not can whip him if I do, because he is bigger than me. But I can try it. I can try to do it' " (p. 403). If we regard Byron as the protagonist, rather than Christmas, the

---

13 *Faulkner in the University*, pp. 96, 97.
14 *Faulkner at Nagano*, p. 4.

book becomes comedy instead of tragedy, and its structure makes
more sense.

The book is framed, as well as permeated, by the story of Byron
and Lena, and it ends on a note of humorous absurdity which has
been particularly embarrassing to critics of the Christmas-as-
protagonist-of-a-tragedy school. Hyatt H. Waggoner indicates the
proper corrective when he says that the function of Byron and Lena in
opening and closing the novel "seems to me crucial and not to have
been given sufficient weight in most interpretations." But Waggoner
considers the ending "an anticlimax," and reaches out, rather desperately, to suggest that "the final implication of the book is a kind of
Christian existentialism which could be explicated in terms of the
theology of a Tillich or a Bultmann."[15] We need not go so far afield as
that. We need only look at the whole structure to see that the book is
not a tragedy with an inappropriate bit of farce tacked on at the end,
but a comedy which contains a [93] tragedy and assimilates it, as life
assimilates disease and death.

Byron's function is rather like that of Anse Bundren in *As I Lay
Dying*, except that Byron's result is more clearly optimistic. It is not
easy. Byron, having accepted the loss of his innocence, the end of his
friendship with Hightower, the death of Christmas, and Lena's lack of
virginity, must also accept his own weakness and absurdity, as he has
partly done in his unsuccessful fight with Burch. In the final sequence,
as narrated by the anonymous furniture dealer, Byron walks off twice,
once after Lena ignores his roundabout proposal of marriage and
again when she puts him out of the truck " 'like she would that baby if
it had been about six years old . . .' " (p. 477). But he persists, and
his success has been foretold, with misgiving, by Hightower, who says
to himself after delivering the baby, "*She will have to have others,
more. . . . That will be her life, her destiny. The good stock peopling
in tranquil obedience to it the good earth. . . . But by Byron engendered next. Poor boy*" (p. 384). The furniture dealer, whose humor
goes along with a shrewd objectivity of judgment, supports the same
view, concluding that Lena probably has no intention " 'of finding
whoever it was she was following. I dont think she had ever aimed to,
only she hadn't told him yet. . . . I think she had just made up her
mind to travel a little further and see as much as she could, since I
reckon she knew that when she settled down this time, it would likely
be for the rest of her life' " (p. 480).

In assimilating the stories of Lena, Christmas, and Hightower
more or less closely to Byron's experience of change and growth,
Faulkner has been careful not to compromise their identity as separate
stories. They remain distinct, and they represent sharply different
aspects of human nature and the world. Each is insulated from the

---

[15] Waggoner, pp. 113, 114.

others by its own particular mythological ambience; each has its own time dimension, different from and incompatible with the others; and each has its own protagonist, who is not a complete human being but a [94] typical Faulkner caricature, or grotesque. Lena is so fully immersed in the flow of life, and so slightly developed in the dimensions of conscious thought and feeling, as to seem almost subhuman. Christmas, isolated by his refusal either to identify himself in relation to other people and the world or to be content with anonymity, lacking the ties of tenderness and mutual dependency that keep normal people from going beyond the bounds, becomes inhuman. Hightower, retreating from life in the present, exiles himself to an extrahuman region from which even Byron's exigencies cannot quite rescue him. Because they resist a too-complete assimilation, either in Byron's experience or that of the reader, they serve to dramatize the artificial stoppage of motion at which Faulkner aims. The motion, the stoppage, and the artificiality of the dramatic confrontation are all emphasized by the counterpoint. The total impression aroused by the tension between the motion and the stoppage is greatly enhanced by the stubbornly maintained independence of the separate materials. [95]

A Demonic World

WALTER BRYLOWSKI

FAULKNER CONTINUES HIS PORTRAYAL OF A DEMONIC SOCIETY IN THE BACKground of *Light in August*. Here, however, he makes one of his strongest affirmations through the juxtaposition of the story of Lena Grove to that of the sacrificial scapegoat, Joe Christmas. Both stories are centered on quests: Lena's comic search for the father of her child and Joe's more complicated tragic quest. [102]

The primary myth held here in counterpoint is that of Christ as the crucified scapegoat. Stated in its simplest form, the myth as used by Faulkner holds Christ, the god, to have achieved his ultimate identification with humanity only through the suffering of his death. It is only in this broad outline that Joe Christmas is to be thought of as a Christ figure. Both Christmas and Christ are examples of an archetypal pattern with the Christ "legend" used as one of Faulkner's oft explained "tools":

Remember, the writer must write out of his background. He must write out of what he knows and the Christian legend is part of any Christian's background, especially the background of a country boy, a Southern boy. My life was passed, my childhood, in a very small Mississippi town, and that was a part of my background. I grew up with that. I assimilated that, took that in without even knowing it. It's just there. It has nothing to do with how much of it I might believe or disbelieve—it's just there.

Joe Christmas, like the hero of the romantic quest, has origins that are shrouded in mystery. It is only at the end of the novel that Faulkner attempts to solve the "technical problems for making it plausible," the displacement which offers the parentage of Milly and the shadowy circus worker who might have been Mexican or part Negro. Found on the steps of the orphanage on Christmas eve, Joe receives his name. His early youth is spent under the watchful eye of an ogre-like "protector," Doc Hines, his maternal grandfather, who subtly insinuates in the minds of everyone the belief that Joe is part Negro.

Doc Hines, in his madness, partakes of a rabid Calvinist theology that causes him to talk of himself as God's appointed instrument; indeed, he would appear at times to be the figure of god-the-father, a father role he shares toward Joe with McEachern.

It is Hines who establishes the relative values of the Negro-white blood lines: [103]

"I know evil. Aint I made evil to get up and walk God's world? A walking pollution in God's own face I made it. Out of the mouths of little children He never concealed it. You have heard them. I never told them to say it, to call him in his rightful nature, by the name of his damnation. I never told them." (119) °

The name of his damnation is "nigger." In the Calvinist framework of the novel, a framework transposed to the South, the Negro is damned; the white is of the elect. Joe's search for identity can in one sense be likened to the introspection of the Puritan seeking signs of grace.

The center of evil in the novel is in this doubleness of race and religion, the one dividing mankind into black and white, the other into the damned and the elect. In Faulkner's "theology" it is neither *eros*, symbolized by Joe's sexual adventures, nor *agape*, symbolized by the many food offerings, which can overcome this division of mankind; it is only in death that man's essential humanity can be recognized. In the order of society, an order based on the acceptance of this division of mankind, Joe, whose role is ambiguous, who can "pass" for white, represents a threat to the artificial stability. As a social being, Joe must determine his role in society, determine whether he is black or white, determine an identity for himself.

° Page references are to the Harrison Smith and Robert Haas, Inc. edition of *Light in August* (New York, 1932).

After an adolescent "captivity" under McEachern who attempts to impose an identity on Joe, Joe begins to assert himself first through the knowledge of sex. This becomes a mode of self definition, a symbolic means of differentiating himself from a large part of the world, the female part, that would seek to impose an identity—*any* identity upon him. In true Calvinistic fashion, Joe must achieve his own identity. The ultimate rejection of this "enclosement" threatened by the female world is, of course, the murder of Joanna Burden when she attempts to force upon him her relation to the [104] Father with the command, "Kneel with me." His initiation is twice postponed, the first time when he kicks out at the Negro girl in the barn, rejecting the containment threatened, "enclosed by the womanshenegro and the haste . . ." (147). There is a sense of freedom in the male world of McEachern, "as if the whole situation were perfectly logical and reasonable and inescapable. Perhaps he was thinking then how he and the man could always count upon one another, depend upon one another; that it was the woman alone who was unpredictable" (149). But this is a false sense of freedom, a sense equated for Joe with the hard, clean male body, as when he is fighting with the four other boys over the Negro girl in the barn: "There was no She at all now. They just fought; it was as if a wind had blown among them, hard and clean." (147) That night he is late for his chores and McEachern beats him:

The boy's body might have been wood or stone: a post or a tower upon which the sentient part of him mused like a hermit, contemplative and remote with ecstasy and self-crucifixion. . . .
    When he went to bed that night his mind was made up to run away. He felt like an eagle: hard, sufficient, potent, remorseless, strong. But that passed, though he did not then know that, like the eagle, his own flesh as well as all space was still a cage. (150–51)

The only true freedom for Joe can come when the body that creates chains through its appetites is left behind.
    Joe's second attempt at sexual initiation is postponed because the whore Bobbie had forgotten her menstrual cycle. The accent on the demonic imagery of sex throughout the book creates a naturalistic equivalent to the damnations of sin and Negro in the religious and racial images. Along with food which is constantly rejected as an offering but sought out in animal necessity, these motifs create a picture of a world in which no metaphysical truth of the spirit can be realized. When Joe had first learned about menstruation through the [105] juvenile grapevine, he had stalked a sheep, killed it, and washed himself in its blood. Evidently this ritual "blood of the lamb" is an attempt on the level of mythical thought to wash away the "sin" of man's animal nature, to expiate.

Then he knelt, his hands in the yet warm blood of the dying beast, trembling, drymouthed, backglaring. Then he got over it, recovered. He did not forget what the boy had told him. He just accepted it. He found that he could live with it side by side with it. It was as if he said, illogical and desperately calm *All right. It is so then. But not to me. Not in my life and my love.* (174)

But again this sense of security or "immunity" is proved false. When Bobbie is trying to tell him about her mistake in making a date for this night,

He just stood there, with a still downspeaking voice dying somewhere about his ears. He had forgot about the shot sheep. He had lived with the fact which the older boy had told him too long now. With the slain sheep he had bought immunity from it for too long now for it to be alive. (175–76)

His attainment to maturity symbolized by his moral break with the teachings of McEachern is followed by the archetypal break with the father: Joe braining McEachern with a chair, Zeus defeating Cronus, or even Oedipus killing Laius. . . . [106]

Frye suggests in his work that the image of the street may serve as a displacement for the hero's maze. It is in just this way that Faulkner compresses the next fifteen years of Joe's life:

He thought that it was loneliness which he was trying to escape and not himself. But the street ran on: catlike, one place was the same as another to him. But in none of them could he be quiet. But the street ran on in its moods and phases, always empty: he might have seen himself as in numberless avatars, in silence, doomed with motion, driven by the courage of flagged and spurred despair. (213)

Early in the novel, the first presentation of Joe has him moving toward the still center of his "maze." The night before he is to murder Joanna Burden he wanders the town and countryside, a journey which leads him into the underworld:

Then he found himself. Without his being aware the street had begun to slope and before he knew it he was in Freedman Town, surrounded by the summer smell and the summer voices of invisible negroes. They seemed to enclose him like bodiless voices murmuring, talking, laughing, in a language not his. As from the bottom of a thick black pit he saw himself enclosed by cabinshapes, vague, kerosenelit, so that the street lamps themselves seemed to be further spaced, as if the black life, the black breathing had compounded the substance of breath so that not only voices but [107] moving bodies and light itself must become fluid and accrete slowly from particle to particle, of and with the now ponderable night inseparable and one. (106–7)

This accidental descent into the underworld frightens him:

He began to run, glaring, his teeth glaring, his inbreath cold on his dry teeth and lips, toward the next street lamp. Beneath it a narrow and rutted lane turned and mounted to the parallel street, out of the black hollow. He turned into it running and plunged up the sharp ascent, his heart hammering, and into the higher street. He stopped here, panting, glaring, his heart thudding as if it could not or would not yet believe that the air now was the cold hard air of white people. (107)

He passes out of the town and into the surrounding hills:

But he did not look back until he reached the crest of the hill. Then he could see the town, the glare, the individual lights where streets radiated from the square. He could see the street down which he had come, and the other street, the one which had almost betrayed him; and further away and at right angles, the far bright rampart of the town itself, and in the angle between the black pit from which he had fled with drumming heart and glaring lips. No light came from it, from here no breath, no odor. It just lay there, black impenetrable, in its garland of Augusttremulous lights. It might have been the original quarry, abyss itself. (108)

Here again the damnation of "Negro" is established, a damnation Joe still seeks to escape. In the white section of town he had looked about at the whites on their porches. " 'That's all I wanted,' he thought. 'That dont seem like a whole lot to ask' " (108). But it *is* this society's equivalent of election.

After having killed Joanna Burden (whose function within the framework of the romance is the rather minor one of a sexual obstacle in the search of the hero, and within the framework of damnation and election a force attempting to enclose and define Joe's nature), Joe eludes his pursuers, once by trading shoes with a Negro woman to throw off the dogs set on him, thereby symbolically determining his damnation: [108]

It seemed to him that he could see himself being hunted by white men at last into the black abyss which had been waiting, trying, for thirty years to drown him and into which now and at last he had actually entered, bearing now upon his ankles and the definite and ineradicable gauge of its upward moving. (313)

Tired of running, he goes into Mottstown to walk the streets until recognized and apprehended:

Looking [down at Mottstown], he can see the smoke low on the sky, beyond an imperceptible corner; he is entering it again, the street which ran for thirty years. It had been a paved street, where going should be fast. It had made a circle and he is still inside of it. Though during the last seven days

he has had no paved street, yet he has travelled further than in all the
thirty years before. And yet he is still inside the circle. (321)

At the center of his maze lies not the truth of Negro but the truth of
his membership in humanity. There is left but the ritual murder and
castration to complete this pact with humanity and to place him in the
ironic role of scapegoat to this society, a society which insists on black-
white, damned-saved demarkations to assure its own stability. "The
adventure of the hero," says Joseph Campbell, represents the moment
in his life when he achieved illumination—the nuclear moment when,
while still alive, he found and opened the road to the light beyond the
dark walls of our living death." Campbell's description of the hero's
quest posits an end in which the truth is symbolized as the release of
the waters of life and Joe's gushing black blood after his castration
might be remarked as a particularly demonic displacement of this
symbol.

The use of the Christ figure as a counterpoint to the life and death
of Joe Christmas has raised some question about Faulkner's Christianity. The objections are based on Joe's moral and ethical existence:
he is a fornicator, bootlegger, and murderer. How then can Faulkner
expect the reader to take seriously the parallels to the Christ figure and
expect him to [109] regard Joe's death in the realm of the sacred?
Such questions directed at Faulkner's "Christianity" demonstrate the
level at which the myth of Christianity operates in our society, the
level, paradoxically enough, of rational empiricism. "Whereas scientific
thought," says Cassirer,

takes an attitude of inquiry and doubt toward the "object" with its claim
to objectivity and necessity, myth knows no such opposition. It "has" the
object only insofar as it is overpowered by it; it does not possess the object
by progressively building it but is simply possessed by it. It has no will to
understand the object by encompassing it logically and articulating it with
a complex of causes and effects; it is simply overpowered by the object. . . .
The contents of the mythical consciousness form a self-enclosed realm and
possess a common tonality, by which they are distinguished from the contents of common, everyday, empirical existence. . . . It is this characteristic
transcendence which links the contents of the mythical and the religious
consciousness. In their mere immediate existence they all contain a revelation and at the same time retain a kind of mystery; it is this interpenetration,
this revelation which both reveals and conceals, that gives the mythical-
religious content its basic trait, its character of the "sacred."

If we could modify our "scientific" expectations of Faulkner to allow
for some of the mythic force of his thinking, I believe there would be
much less critical frustration in the attempts to explain his "religion."
The same ethical objections which are made to Joe's character are
made toward Lena Grove, who as an earth-goddess figure seemingly

does not fulfill expectations because of her mammalian stupidity, but her role, after all, does not call for any intelligence and we have no vested interest in earth goddesses, so these complaints are not especially loud.

"The basic principle of all mythology," says Campbell,

is . . . of the beginning in the end. Creation myths are pervaded with a sense of the doom that is continually recalling all created shapes to the imperishable out of which they first emerged. The forms go forth powerfully, but inevitably [110] reach their apogee, break, and return. Mythology, in this sense, is tragic in its view. But in the sense that it places our true being not in the forms that shatter but in the imperishable out of which they again immediately bubble forth, mythology is eminently untragical. Indeed, whereever the mythological mood prevails, tragedy is impossible. . . . Herein lies the basic paradox of the dual focus. . . . One breaks into the many, destiny "happens," but at the same time "is brought about." From the perspective of the source, the world is a majestic harmony of forms pouring into being, exploding, and dissolving. But what the swiftly passing creatures experience is a terrible cacophony of battle cries and pain. The myths do not deny this agony (the crucifixion); they reveal within, behind, and around it essential peace (the heavenly rose).

This "basic paradox of the dual focus" lies at the center of my claim for Faulkner's consideration as a writer in the mythic mode. In *Light in August*, he achieves one of the finest resolutions of his "dual focus" in the structural complement to the story of Joe Christmas: the story of Lena Grove which contains the "essential peace" surrounding the crucifixion.

Lena's progress from Alabama to Mississippi "is a peaceful corridor paved with unflagging and tranquil faith and peopled with kind and nameless faces and voices" (4). Pregnant, placid, her role is that of the earth mother. "We still find it said," says Cassirer, "that it is not the earth which imitates women in conceiving and giving birth but women who imitate the earth. But for the original mythical intuition there is here no before or after, no first or second, only the complete and indissoluble involvement of the two processes." Lena's relationship to the story of Joe is somewhat artificial at first. It might be looked upon as a product of displacement, providing us with a credible history of that moment when her giving new birth is required as a mythological counterpart to the death of Joe Christmas.

When Joe is finally caught in Mottstown, on the scene are Doc Hines and his wife who have made this their home [111] for the last thirty years. Mrs. Hines recognizes Joe as her grandson. Dressed in purple suitable to the passion, she takes the old madman in tow and follows Joe to Jefferson where that compound of good Samaritan and St. Christopher, Byron Bunch, takes them under his wing and introduces them to Hightower and then into Lena's cabin. Faulkner was

willing to dare much of his craft to achieve the necessary coincidences
to support the cyclic idea of life which is to soften the passion of the
crucifixion. On that Sunday night, Mrs. Hines tells the story of Joe's
origins to Hightower, leading to her one impossible request:

I am not saying he never did what they say he did. Ought not to suffer for
it like he made them that loved and lost suffer. But if folks could maybe just
let him for one day. Like it hadn't happened yet. (367)

In the sense that Joe is already dead, she is asking for nothing less than
a resurrection. On Monday morning Lena's baby is born with Mrs.
Hines in attendance and, as the old woman's mind wavers, the birth is
equivalent to the resurrection in that time disappears and Joe's life is
somehow revived. At first Lena becomes her dead daughter Milly and
the child becomes Joe; then " 'She keeps on talking about him like his
pa was that . . . the one in jail, that Mr. Christmas' " (387–88), talk
Lena fears because it threatens to mix *her* up as well.

   Gavin Stevens, who puts the old couple on the train for Mottstown, promising to send the body along after them, attempts to
summarize this:

"Very likely that was the first time she had ever told it. And very likely she
learned it herself then for the first time, actually saw it whole and real at
the same time with Hightower. So I don't think it is so strange that for the
time she got not only the child but his parentage as well mixed up, since in
that cabin those thirty years did not exist—the child and its father whom she
had never seen, and her grandson whom she had not seen since he was a
baby like the other, and whose father likewise to her had never existed, all
[112] confused. And that, when hope did begin to move in her, she should
have turned at once, with the sublime and boundless faith of her kind in
those who are the voluntary slaves and the sworn bondsmen of prayer, to
the minister." (422–23)

   The minister. The last phase of romance, the literary form of the
quest, is, according to Frye, marked by the movement from active to
comtemplative adventure. "A central image of this phase, a favorite of
Yeats, is that of the old man in the tower, the lonely hermit absorbed
in occult or magical studies." Hightower, who is introduced in the
chronology of the novel after Joe's murder of Joanna Burden, provides
this contemplative depth of the passion and its optimistic mythical
counterpart, Lena's perpetuation of the cycle of life. While Gavin
Stevens has been introduced to the novels for the first time to provide
the scientific-empiric rationale just quoted, Faulkner is not yet ready to
forego the mythical thinker.
   Hightower is the antithesis of Lena Grove, denying the movement
of life for a sterile regression. We are told that he suffered a psychic
arrest at the age of eight when he discovered his father's patched coat

worn during the War and that from that time "That son grew to manhood among phantoms, and side by side with a ghost" (449), the ghost of his grandfather killed by "a fowling piece, in a henhouse" (459). Hightower's only aim in life becomes the desire to go to the scene of that foolish escapade in Jefferson:

While at the seminary, after he first came there, he often thought how he would tell them, the elders, the high and sanctified men who were the destiny of the church to which he had willingly surrendered. How he would go to them and say, "Listen. God must call me to Jefferson because my life died there, was shot from the saddle of a galloping horse in a Jefferson street one night twenty years before it was ever born." (452)

He had thought that the seminary would afford him a haven, a place where "truth could walk naked and without shame or [113] fear" (453). But his truth is that of an unrecognized myth, the myth of a moment of time in his timeless consciousness. "In the concrete mythical-religious consciousness of time there always lives a specific dynamic of feeling—a varying intensity with which the I devotes itself to the present, past, or future and so places them in a definite relation of affinity to or dependence on one another."

Married to a daughter of one of the ministers in the seminary, Hightower wins his post at Jefferson and on the train going there tries to communicate his truth to her. With his entire psyche funneled into this private myth, his wife turns away toward her own destruction.

Hightower's career in his Jefferson church was as a

figure antic as a showman, a little wild: a charlatan preaching worse than heresy, in utter disregard of that whose very stage he preempted, offering instead of the crucified shape of pity and love, a swaggering and unchastened bravo killed with a shotgun in a peaceful henhouse, in a temporary hiatus of his own avocation of killing. (462)

Turned out from his church and refusing to leave the town, he suffered a beating at the hands of the Klan, a beating he regarded as purchasing his immunity, the price of his refusal to involve himself with mankind in time. Hightower's ultimate error has been the belief that "It is any man's privilege to destroy himself, so long as he does not injure anyone else, so long as he lives to and of himself" (464). Having destroyed himself and his wife, it is his involvement in the birth of Lena's child that gives him the momentary illusion that he is once again alive in a kind of biological and therefore mythic time:

He moves like a man with a purpose now, who for twenty-five years has been doing nothing at all between the time to wake and the time to sleep again. . . . [Thinking,] *More of them. Many more. That will be her life, her destiny. The good stock peopling in tranquil obedience to it the good earth; from these hearty loins without hurry or haste descending mother and daughter.* (383–84)

But this is a false sense of rebirth on his part. Having refused the night before to lie about Joe's whereabouts at the time of the murder in one last attempt to save him, and now having assisted at the birth of Lena's child, "There is one thing more reserved for him" (392). Joe Christmas, pursued by Percy Grimm, runs into Hightower's house where the old man now attempts the lie:

"Men!" he cried. "Listen to me. He was here that night. He was with me the night of the murder. I swear to God—"
"Jesus Christ!" Grimm cried, his young voice clear and outraged like that of a young priest. "Has every preacher and old maid in Jefferson taken their pants down to the yellowbellied son of a bitch?" He flung the old man aside and ran on. (439)

Joe, dying and castrated, the blood rushing "like a released breath," achieves his apotheosis as victim:

. . . upon that black blast the man seemed to rise soaring into their memories forever and ever. They are not to lose it, in whatever peaceful valleys, beside whatever placid and reassuring streams of old age, in the mirroring faces of whatever children they will contemplate old disasters and newer hopes. It will be there, musing, quiet, steadfast, not fading and not particularly threatful, but of itself alone serene, of itself alone triumphant. (440)

Grimm is the tyrant-leader Frye remarks in the sacrifice of the *pharmakos:*

In the sinister human world one individual pole is the tyrant-leader, inscrutable, ruthless, melancholy, and with an insatiable will, who commands loyalty only if he is egocentric enough to represent the collective ego of his followers. The other pole is represented by the *pharmakos* or sacrificed victim, who has to be killed to strengthen the others. In the most concentrated form of the demonic parody, the two become the same.

This most concentrated form of the demonic parody, the identification of slayer and slain is offered through Hightower's reflection: [115]

Byron Bunch's; the woman with the child; and that of the man called Christmas. This face alone is not clear. It is confused more than any other, as though in the now peaceful throes of a more recent, a more inextricable, compositeness. Then he can see that it is two faces which seem to strive (but not of themselves striving or desiring it: he knows that, but because of the motion and desire of the wheel itself) in turn to free themselves one from the other, then fade and blend again. But he has seen now, the other face, the one that is not Christmas. 'Why, it's . . .' he thinks. 'I have seen it, recently. . . . Why, it's that . . . boy. With that black pistol, automatic they call them. The one who . . . into the kitchen where . . . killed, who fired the . . .' Then it seems to him that some ultimate dammed flood within him breaks and rushes away. (465–66)

But Hightower is not the only agent of this movement from active to contemplative adventure which marks the last phase of romance:

On a more popular and social level it takes in what might be called cuddle fiction: the romance that is physically associated with comfortable beds or chairs around fireplaces or warm and cosy spots generally. A characteristic feature of this phase is the tale in quotation marks, where we have an opening setting with a small group of congenial people, and then the real story told by one of the members. . . . The effect of such devices is to present the story through a relaxed and contemplative haze as something that entertains us without, so to speak, confronting us, as direct tragedy confronts us.

And this is the way Faulkner ends *Light in August* for us. "There lives in the eastern part of the state a furniture repairer and dealer who recently made a trip into Tennessee to get some old pieces of furniture which he had bought by correspondence" (468). Lying in bed with his wife, he recounts the final comic adventure of Lena, her child, and Byron Bunch "just travelling."

Light in August may be viewed as a romance, a quest on the part of Joe Christmas for identity in a society that denies [116] identity, setting up various schema of division in opposition to this quest. The central myth is that of the scapegoat and its archetypal representative the Christ who, part divine and part human, achieved his identity with humanity only through the sacrifice of his death. It is the most successful artistic embodiment of Faulkner's dual focus, his rational empiric view of life with its tragic implications and his optimistic, mythic faith with its essentially comic implications. Perhaps because of this success he was able, after the "breather" represented by *Pylon*, to concentrate on the largely historical myth presented in *Absalom! Absalom!* without the necessity of insisting on some kind of apocalyptic resolution to the lingering defeat of the South. [117]

A William Faulkner Chronology

1897	Born in New Albany, Mississippi, on September 25.
1902	Moves with his family to Oxford, Mississippi.
1918	Joins Royal Air Force and goes to Canada for training.
1919–20	Enters and leaves the University of Mississippi.
1924	*The Marble Faun* appears.
1925	Lives and works in New Orleans and France.
1926	*Soldiers' Pay* appears.
1927	*Mosquitoes* published.
1929	*Sartoris* published; later in the year, *The Sound and the Fury* appears; Marries Estelle Oldham.
1930	*As I Lay Dying* appears; buys home.
1931	*Sanctuary* published after revisions in galleys.
1932	*Light in August* appears; first begins to write for the movies in Hollywood.
1933–34	Buys airplane and begins accumulating background for *Pylon*.
1935	Brother killed in airplane accident; more writing in Hollywood.
1936	*Absalom, Absalom!* published.
1939	*The Wild Palms* appears; made member of National Institute of Arts and Letters.
1940	Publishes *The Hamlet*.
1942	Returns to work in Hollywood; *Go Down, Moses* appears.
1948	*Intruder in the Dust* published with commercial success; made member of American Academy of Arts and Letters.
1950	Wins Nobel Prize for Literature and American Academy Medal for Fiction.
1951	Wins National Book Award. *Requiem for a Nun* published; awarded Legion of Honor by the French government.
1954	*A Fable* published; daughter married.
1955	Receives National Book Award for second time followed by a Pulitzer Prize; visits Japan under State Department auspices.
1957	Accepts post as Writer in Residence at the University of Virginia; visits Greece for the State Department.
1959	*The Mansion* appears.
1961	Visits South America for State Department.
1962	*The Reivers* published; dies in Oxford on July 6.

Questions for Study and Discussion

1. How true is Faulkner's comment that he wanted "to underline the tragedy of Christmas's story by the tragedy of his antithesis"? In what sense is Hightower the antithesis of Joe Christmas?
2. To what extent is the narrative presentation of Hightower's grandfather factual and to what extent imaginative? How can one distinguish between the two?
3. What light does the novel throw on Faulkner's statement that he doesn't know anything about style?
4. What evidence in the text is there that Joe Christmas "deliberately repudiated man"?
5. Considering the length of her journey and her persistence, what do you think Faulkner meant by his remark that Lena Grove "didn't especially need any father" for her child?

CULLEN AND WATKINS

1. How close do you find the parallels between Cullen's account of Nelse Patton and the novel's presentation of Joe Christmas? Between his view of the town of Oxford and Jefferson in the novel?
2. If Nelse is in fact his source, why did Faulkner deliberately make Joe's race ambiguous?
3. What similarities and differences do you find in Senator W. V. Sullivan and Percy Grimm?
4. How does our uncertainty about Joe's blood influence our evaluation of Percy Grimm and the lynch mob?
5. Can we reach any conclusions about Faulkner's creative process by comparing a scene as narrated or reproduced by Cullen with its equivalent in *Light in August*?

HOWE

1. Answer the following questions posed by Howe: "How much is gained for Christmas by his juxtaposition to Lena? How bright an illumination does the mind of Hightower shed on the behavior of the other characters?" Do your answers suggest a general view of the structure of *Light in August*? How much light does Faulkner shed on the problem of three rather tenuously connected strands of action?

2. Are the flashbacks for Joanna Burden and Doc Hines in "excess of what the narrative requires"? Would either be convincing as characters without this extension of their lives into the past? Is such an extension a legitimate way of enlarging a major theme?

3. Do you agree that "the murder of Joanna Burden, while explicable through several hints placed by Faulkner, cannot acquire the tragic intensity it should have had"? How would you define Howe's phrase "tragic intensity"? What alternatives to Howe's general assertion do you think there are?

4. Do you think Lena Grove is "an agent of traditional morality" or "the good unruffled vegetable"? Could she be both? In what ways do the views of O'Connor and Waggoner qualify the above alternatives?

5. Is Howe correct when he suggests that considering Lena as "an agent of traditional morality" amounts to thinking that "goodness is contingent upon a low level of intelligence"? Does Gail Hightower's intelligence and substantial uninvolvement better equip him to serve as Faulkner's moral center or norm in the novel?

6. Is Howe correct in assuming that "like all of Faulkner's Negroes, Christmas is seen mainly from the outside?" What basis for this assertion does Howe have? What evidence contradicts him? Would it be legitimate to use Faulkner's own comments, which were published after Howe's work? What does Waggoner have to say that is relevant to this issue?

7. Is Howe correct in contending that *Light in August* suffers from a certain structural incoherence"? What evidence from the novel itself answers this question? What significant points bearing on this issue do other critics present?

O'CONNOR

1. To what extent does Joe Christmas's disruption of the revival meeting document O'Connor's statement that the church, "far from making his life easier, is one of the agents of his destruction"? In what sense is the church or Calvinism an agent of destruction? What is the relationship between O'Connor's position and that of Waggoner?

2. What comparisons can be drawn between Hightower's actions and the views of the church he serves? What does Waggoner have to say on this issue?

3. Do you agree with O'Connor's statement that Lena Grove and Byron Bunch "by what they are and the way they act . . . insinuate powerfully what is wrong with the community"? What specific aspects of character and action bear on this issue?

4. To what extent is Joanna Burden's character explained by O'Connor's observation that she is acting "out of an obligation to carry out God's design in a depraved world"?

5. Is Percy Grimm adequately described as "another of the avatars of self-righteousness"? Do other characters fall into the same category? What form does their self-righteousness take?

VICKERY

1. How much of *Light in August* is explained by Vickery's assertion that Faulkner is examining the relationship between individual consciousness and "the public world of events, statements and mass responses"? Can her concept of the public world be equated with the community stressed by Brooks?
2. Would you defend or refute the notion that Joe Christmas, Reverend Hightower, and Joanna Burden are "both villain and victim"? What scenes would you cite in support of your position? How does Longley's essay bear on this question?
3. Does Vickery's discussion of the novel's circle imagery add or detract from the interest in the narrative itself?
4. Do you agree with Vickery's statement that "Joe is forced into the ritual of pursuit and lynching performed almost casually by a society which has been elaborating it for generations"? In what ways does it conflict with Brooks' view that the community serves as the source of values in the novel? Can these positions be reconciled?
5. What are the main points that Vickery makes concerning the thematic significance of the novel's black-white symbolism? Do these differ markedly from the points made by Longley?
6. What uses of the shadow as image and symbol does Vickery discuss? Do you find other uses not mentioned by her?
7. Does Vickery deal with the use and function of humor in the novel? Do other critics? What measure of agreement is there in their views?
8. Does Vickery's essay suggest a possibility that the central theme in *Light in August* is madness in various forms and degrees? What other critics deal with this possibility? Do they differ?
9. Would you add anything to Vickery's discussion of Joe Christmas's death scene? How pertinent are matters of imagery and symbolism to the scene? How effective is the scene as an ending to Joe's story?
10. Does Vickery regard the final scenes with Hightower, Lena, and Byron as an anti-climax to Joe Christmas's death? Do you? Is it possible to defend either artistically or thematically the seeming progress from the tragic to the pathetic to the comic? What specific contributions to this issue are made by Waggoner, Longley, and Lind?

WAGGONER

1. Is Waggoner correct in saying that *Light in August* "demands nothing less than a withholding of self-righteous negative moral judgments and a substitution of unlimited compassion"? How applicable is this view to Bobbie, Buch, Grimm, Mr. McEachern, and Hines?

2. What evidence supports Waggoner's claim that Joe is "a man apparently capable of any violent and repulsive deed"? Which of Joe's acts, many of which are "violent," can also be considered "repulsive"?

3. Waggoner suggests that Joe Christmas is possibly "sado-masochistic." Longley has suggested that he suffers from an Oedipus complex. How effective do you find psychiatric approaches in understanding the character and comprehending the novel as a whole?

4. To what extent do you agree with Waggoner that *Light in August* is "deeply Christian in its meaning despite its excoriation of the exemplars of piety"? In terms of this essay and the novel, can one define "deeply Christian" or the phrase previously used, "religious profundity"?

5. How relevant is Waggoner's statement about Lena Grove that Faulkner had the Bible (Revised Standard Version) in mind in that she " 'bears all things, believes all things, hopes all things, endures all things' "? Does this, as Waggoner further comments, make her "saintly"? Is it possible that Faulkner is making a comparative study in religion whereby traditional dogma is set against the fertility myths, discussed by Sir James G. Frazer in *The Golden Bough*?

6. Is it accurate to suggest, as Waggoner does, that Joanna Burden is not often considered at length by critics? What is your reaction to his notion that "there is a real nobility in her that sets her quite apart from all the 'idealists' but Hightower. She pays the price of goodness unflinchingly"? What does her relationship with Joe Christmas do to this evaluation of her?

7. Do you agree with Waggoner that the only characters who are "approached wholly from outside" and of whom a "definite and single judgment is required" are McEachern, Hines, and Grimm? Should, for example, Mrs. McEachern or Bobbie Allen be included in the same list?

8. How far is it possible to use an author's sympathetic identification with his characters as an index to his theme and moral view?

9. Is Waggoner right in assuming that the street and corridor imagery in *Light in August* is "both banal and untrue"?

LONGLEY

1. Does Longley's essay imply any connections between Faulkner and James Joyce? How far can one profitably pursue parallels between

Joe Christmas and Stephen Dedalus of *A Portrait of the Artist as a Young Man?*

2. What comments would you make about Longley's statement that "Christmas is free to choose what he will be, and his freedom is infinite"? In what sense does Joe decide "he will simply be himself"? Is Joe's killing of Joanna Burden and his own death each connected with his quest for a definition of self?

3. What warrant do you find for Longley's claim that "Faulkner has used the subconscious fear of mutilation and distrust of miscegenation that lurks in all of us, the love of and response to violence and death, the simultaneous love and hate of the loved one, to arouse these emotions or their equivalents in us"? How valid is this statement as a way of viewing Joe Christmas or of establishing an analogy between him and Oedipus? Can the description be extended to other characters in the book?

ABEL

1. What do you understand to be the meaning of Abel's comments that "*Light in August* contains a *Divina Comedia*" and that a "*Comedie humaine* encompasses it?" Does such an analogy support either Waggoner's thesis or Howe's on the essential meaning of the novel?

2. How far would you agree with Abel that in a naturalistic cosmos Joe Christmas can be considered as Jesus Christ, Hightower as God Himself, Lena as a pagan generatrix? For which character can the best case be made in these terms? What relevance does such a reading have to the central theme of the novel?

3. Do you accept Abel's view that Hightower's story "is an exaggerated rendering of the truth that all men are directed by ancestral ghosts and do not possess their own realities"? What are the chief differences between "ancestral ghosts" and "realities"? How would you apply this dichotomy to Joe, Joanna Burden, Lena, Hightower, and Byron?

4. In what ways do you find helpful Abel's comments on Lena's confused identification of Joe Christmas with her own child? Do any other critics comment on this confusion? What do you think the scene reveals concerning the characters involved? Does it illuminate any of the central themes in the novel?

5. How far do you think it is possible to view Joe's career as a vain striving to emerge from the " 'lightless hot wet primogenitive Female' "? What actually is the role of the Woman in *Light in August?*

6. What chief points does Abel make about Faulkner's use of sound imagery in the novel? Is it possible to extend his evidence and his generalizations?

7. To what extent are Lena Grove and Byron Bunch participating in

a pastoral idyll? What do Abel and Brooks have to say about this view?

8. To what extent does Faulkner use the urn symbol as delineated by Keats in his poem "Ode on a Grecian Urn"?

9. What are the key aspects of Abel's discussion of the word "avatar"? What qualities of imagery, character, or theme would you single out in exploring this concept further?

LIND

1. What specific examples would you list in support of Lind's statement that repeatedly "we discover that Faulkner's seeming defects are failures of our own perception, which is not prepared for the new uses to which he applies his resources"?

2. To what extent are Joe Christmas and Joanna Burden explained as characters by Lind's suggestion that they are "the product of identical but conflicting impulses in the cultures which produced them"? How far can this comment be compared with Vickery's view?

3. Can Lind's statement that Mr. and Mrs. Hines are "cultural anachronisms" be extended to other characters in the book?

4. Do you agree with Lind's remark that Hines left the infant Joe Christmas "to enhance its opportunity to bring about evil"? What evidence supports such an interpretation?

5. Can we take as a key to Joe's character Lind's statement that "lacking self-acceptance, he cannot tolerate acceptance by others, even when it is tentatively offered"? To what extent could the interpretations of Joe by Howe, Vickery, and Longley be encompassed by this statement?

6. At one point Lind says: "Defiance and revolt, as the consequence of a too judicial early training, is no less a pattern in the Burden family than in the life of Joe Christmas." How close is the similarity Lind points out? Can it be extended to other characters?

7. To what extent is Joanna Burden's puritanism in her relationship with Joe wedded to Southern mores?

8. How far would you agree with Lind that "the Christmas-Burden narrative is a psychological horror story of unprecedented magnitude"? Does *Light in August* fit the Gothic tradition? Does Lind's use of the term "psychological" indicate a marked difference from the tradition?

9. Is Lind's statement that the church "is the strongest unified force in our Southern life since all Southerners are not white and are not Democrats, but all Southerners are religious and serve the same God" valid in terms of the novel? What light is thrown on this view by Hightower's perception of the church's involvement in Joe's death, Byron's disengagement, and Lena's possibly verbal acquiescence?

KAZIN

1. Is Kazin correct in feeling that, because Joe Christmas has "no background, no roots, no name of his own," he can be regarded as a "tabula rasa"? Would Howe or Lind agree with this view?
2. How far would you agree with Kazin that American writing in general is distinguished by "the fact that we are strangers to each other and each writer describes his own world to strangers living in the same land with himself"? In terms of this description, how would you compare Faulkner with F. Scott Fitzgerald, Ernest Hemingway, Thomas Wolfe, Willa Cather, or John Dos Passos?
3. How would you support Kazin's thesis that "as Lena is all fertility, so the others are all barrenness. . . . As soon as we get to Jefferson, we catch the typical dialectic of life and anti-life"? Most critics seem to interpret the novel as involving an antithesis between Lena and Joe Christmas. What other antitheses have been advanced besides Kazin's "life and anti-life"?
4. How accurate is Kazin in saying that Christmas is "only a thought in other people's minds"? How does this view square with Vickery's suggestion that he is continually interpenetrating with society?
5. Do you agree that "Joe Christmas is the most solitary character in American fiction"? What characters created by other writers might be so designated?
6. What scenes would you examine in evaluating Kazin's claim that Faulkner "both uses and parodies" Hightower? Is this combination of use and parody found also in the treatment of Joe Christmas or Joanna Burden?
7. Is Kazin correct in asserting that "everyone wants to play God to the orphan Joe Christmas"? Do they succeed? What sorts of God do they seek to be? How does Joe's treatment by other people compare with that given Lena or Byron Burch?
8. Would you agree that the "opening of *Light in August* is so beautiful that nothing after quite comes up to it"? Can the ending of the novel be considered as beautiful in the same sense?

HOLMAN

1. What three distinct bodies of material does Holman find in *Light in August*? Compare them with the groupings made by Vickery.
2. How successful is Holman in demonstrating that the three strands of action are "contrasting analogues of the Christ story"? Does the idea of analogues change our sense of the various narratives?
3. How far would you agree with Holman that *Light in August* expresses a "pervasive paralleling of character traits, actions and larger structural shapes to the story of Christ"? Does Faulkner's use

of Christ symbolism differ in *Light in August, The Sound and the Fury*, and *A Fable*?

4. What critics, other than those mentioned in Holman's footnote #2, have attempted to establish the unity of *Light in August*? How do they differ? Which do you regard as most successful?

5. What is Holman's main point about Joe Christmas's refusal of food? Are there other implications in those scenes where food is involved?

6. Is Joe's life shaped by "sexual distortions, perversions, and irregularities"? What events does Holman list that contribute to this pattern? How would you interpret their total impact on Joe? Could Holman's idea be extended to other characters such as Hightower, Byron Bunch, or Bobbie Allen? What is the function of sex in the novel as far as meaning and action are concerned?

7. Do you agree with Holman that Joe's death lacks any salvation? Is Joe "a futile and meaningless expiation of his 'guilt' "? What is the relationship between Joe's guilt and public guilt, especially in his death scene?

8. How would you define and explain the scene in which Mrs. Hines confuses Joe Christmas with Lena's new-born child?

SLATOFF

1. Is Slatoff correct in finding a "trivial side to Lena," evidenced by her desire to walk into town on foot and to believe that she has "et polite"? Does this triviality accord with Lena's character and the themes of the novel in general?

2. What evidence is there to corroborate or refute Slatoff's statement that Joe Christmas "comes to marry [Bobbie] after killing McEachern"?

3. To what extent can we agree with Slatoff that Joe's discovery that "Bobbie was a whore had much to do with determining his nature and fate"? How does this discovery compare with his recognition that Joanna Burden is, at least for a time, a nymphomaniac?

4. After the death of Joanna Burden, do you find Joe's pursuers being given a "satiric treatment," a "cops and robbers atmosphere," as Slatoff suggests? What methods of satire do you think are employed? To what ends are they directed?

5. Does Slatoff believe that Joe Christmas has "black blood"? Does his interpretation of the novel depend on his having assumed that Joe is indeed of mixed blood? What do other critics say on this issue? Why is it important for the novel?

6. Is it possible to conclude with Slatoff of Hightower that "we feel finally that we are viewing a pathological figure rather than a tragic one"? What evidence would you present for viewing him as either pathological or tragic? Is it possible to fuse the two views?

7. Does Slatoff's emphasis on the importance of recognizing the "am-

biguities and varied and conflicting emphases which provide the essential character" of *Light in August* lead to his conclusion that "they do not illuminate the book itself"?

MILLGATE

1. Would you agree with Millgate that Lena "seems not so much a character" as "a kind of impersonalized catalytic force"? What earlier critics have spoken in a similar way about Lena? Can she be regarded as a character in her own right? What specific scenes show her as an "impersonalized catalytic force"?
2. Is the structure of *Light in August* clarified by Millgate's comment that Faulkner was seeking to "incorporate within the structure of a conventional novel, the technique of multiple reflection"? How would you define the terms "conventional novel" and "multiple reflection"? Has Faulkner succeeded in unifying his two aims? What other critics make similar observations about the novel?
3. What light does Millgate throw on the relation between Percy Grimm's character and his and Jefferson's obsessions? Is Grimm the agent or a victim in the ritual pursuit and killing of Joe?
4. What does Millgate say about the use of parallelism in *Light in August*? What significance do you see in Joe's breaking into a Negro church, Hines' forays into Negro churches, and Hightower's expulsion from his own church?

SWIGGART

1. What comparisons does Swiggart suggest between Hines and Mc-Eachern as representatives of Calvinism and influences on Joe Christmas? How do these compare with the views of previous critics such as O'Connor and Lind?
2. After studying Joe's relations to the various women in his life, would you agree with Swiggart that he has "a guilty hatred of sex"?
3. Do you find plausible Swiggart's suggestion that Joanna Burden's function in the novel's structure is "first to reveal to Joe what he is, then to abandon him to his solitary path"? What other aspects of Joanna or her function in the novel need clarification or elaboration?
4. How valid or relevant do you find Swiggart's distinction between a "dark" world of nature and sex and a "white" world of puritanism and abstinence? Does such a distinction pertain to characters other than Joe and Joanna? Does it apply to Burch and Bobbie Allen or Bunch and Hightower?
5. Does the initial confusion of Bunch and Burch suggest that Faulkner may have had parallels in mind that have not been explained by critics? If such parallels are not demonstrable in terms of character, do they nevertheless illuminate theme and structure? How?

6. With what earlier critics is Swiggart aligning himself in saying that Joe's martyrdom is "a deliberate self-sacrifice"? Is it possible to distinguish stages in his progress toward martyrdom? Is the idea of Joe's self-sacrifice compatible with Swiggart's definition of him as a man who "assumes unwittingly the role of a sacrificial victim who accepts the white South's own burden of past sin and present injustice"?

BROOKS

1. Judging from the criticism you have read, is Brooks correct in suggesting that the "community" as it expresses itself in acts of kindness has not received just attention? What is the role of the community in its treatment of Joe, Joanna, Hightower, and Lena? Which other critics have most to say on this issue?
2. What specific scenes would you single out to support Brooks' idea that *Light in August* is in some respects "a bloody and violent pastoral"? How would you interpret the scenes of Joe's relationship to Bobbie Allen or his affair with Joanna Burden?
3. In your estimation, does the text of the novel support Brooks' suggestion that Percy Grimm was sincerely trying to prevent a lynching only to be overcome by his dammed-up sadism? What do you think Grimm's motives were with respect to the pursuit and killing of Joe? What is the kind and degree of his responsibility or guilt in comparison to that of the community?
4. According to Brooks, how important for Faulkner as a writer is his awareness of "an organic community"? How is this term defined in Brooks' essay? Can you relate it to your own reading of the novel?
5. To what extent do you support Brooks' suggestion that *Light in August* be read as a pastoral or a comedy? Can this view be worked out in specific detail?

ADAMS

1. In what sense is Lena's story "roughly analogous to the typical myth of the fertility goddess—Cybele, Aphrodite, Demeter-Persephone"?
2. What warrant is there for Adams' view that Lena is the protagonist of the novel while Joe is simply "the most direct foil and the most obvious antithesis" to her?
3. How probable is it that Faulkner did use the story of Buddha as a basis for his characterization of Hightower?
4. Are there grounds for regarding Byron Bunch as the protagonist?
5. Do you accept Adams' manner of using Faulkner as an authority on his own novels? How should an author's statements be regarded? What legitimate use can the critic make of them?

BRYLOWSKI

1. What does Brylowski mean by "the demonic imagery of sex"? What light is thrown on the phrase by close examination of the imagery in one or two scenes specifically involving sex?
2. Would you agree that Gavin Stevens' interpretation of Joe's actions at Hightower's house constitutes an example of the "scientific-empiric rationale"?
3. What similarities and differences do you see in Adams' and Brylowski's treatment of Joe as a Christ figure?
4. Do you agree with Brylowski that Faulkner focuses in a dual manner on both the rational and empiric and also on the mythic mode of consciousness? How would you classify the novel's minor characters in terms of this distinction?
5. How successfully does a mythic approach solve the problem of structure and tone, a problem recognized and commented on by most of Faulkner's critics? How would you distinguish between Adams' and Brylowski's use of the mythic approach?

A Selective Bibliography

This bibliography is restricted to articles dealing with *Light in August* that have not been incorporated into full-length studies of Faulkner or reprinted in this book. For a more detailed listing of Faulkner criticism, one should consult the bibliographies in F. J. Hoffman and Olga W. Vickery, eds., *William Faulkner: Three Decades of Criticism* (East Lansing: Michigan State University Press, 1960) and the Special William Faulkner Number of *Modern Fiction Studies*, XIII (Spring 1967).

Applewhite, Davis. "The South of 'Light in August,'" *Mississippi Quarterly*, XI (Fall 1958), 167–172.

Baldanza, Frank. "The Structure of 'Light in August,'" *Modern Fiction Studies*, XIII (Spring 1967), 67–78.

Benson, Carl. "Thematic Design in 'Light in August,'" *South Atlantic Quarterly*, 53 (October 1954), 540–555.

Berland, Alwyn. "'Light in August': The Calvinism of William Faulkner," *Modern Fiction Studies*, VIII (Summer 1962), 159–170.

Bernberg, Raymond E. "'Light in August': A Psychological View," *Mississippi Quarterly*, XI (Fall 1958), 173–176.

Cottrell, Beekman W. "Christian Symbols in 'Light in August,'" *Modern Fiction Studies*, II (Winter 1956), 207–213.

Frazier, David L. "Lucas Burch and the Polarity of 'Light in August,'" *Modern Language Notes*, LXXIII (June 1958), 417–419.

Gold, Joseph. "The Two Worlds of 'Light in August,'" *Mississippi Quarterly*, XVI (Summer 1963), 160–167.

Greenburg, Alvin. "Shaggy Dog in Mississippi," *Southern Folklore Quarterly*, XXIX (December 1965), 284–287.

Greer, Scott. "Joe Christmas and the 'Social Self,'" *Mississippi Quarterly*, XI (Fall 1958), 160–166.

Hirshleifer, Phyllis. "As Whirlwinds in the South: 'Light in August,'" *Perspective*, II (Summer 1949), 225–238.

Howell, Elmo. "A Note on Faulkner's Presbyterian Novel," *Papers on Language and Literature*, II (Spring 1966), 182–187.

————. "Reverend Hightower and the Uses of Southern Adversity," *College English*, XXIV (December 1962), 183–187.

Kimney, John L. "The Good Earth in 'Light in August,'" *Mississippi Quarterly*, XVII (Winter 1963), 1–8.

Kirk, Robert. "Faulkner's Lena Grove," *Georgia Review*, XXI (Spring 1967), 57–64.

Kunkel, Robert W. "Christ Symbolism in Faulkner: Prevalence of the Human," *Renascence*, XVII (Spring 1965), 148–156.

Langston, Beach. "The Meaning of Lena Grove and Gail Hightower in 'Light in August,'" *Boston University Studies in English*, V (Spring 1961), 46–63.

Leavis, F. R. "Dostoevsky or Dickens?" *Scrutiny*, II (June 1933), 91–93.

McCamy, Edward. "Byron Bunch," *Shenandoah*, III (Spring 1952), 8–12.

McElderry, B. R. "The Narrative Structure of 'Light in August,'" *College English*, XIX (February 1958), 200–207.

Morrison, Sister Kristen. "Faulkner's Joe Christmas: Character Through Voice," *Texas Studies in Literature and Language*, II (Winter 1964), 419–443.

Pearce, Richard. "Faulkner's One Ring Circus," *Wisconsin Studies in Contemporary Literature*, VII (Autumn 1966), 270–283.

Pearson, Norman Holmes. "Lena Grove," *Shenandoah*, III (Spring 1952), 3–7.

Pommer, Henry F. "'Light in August': A Letter by Faulkner," *English Language Notes*, IV (September 1966), 47–48.

Sandstrom, Glenn. "Identity Diffusion: Joe Christmas and Quentin Compson," *American Quarterly*, XIX (Summer 1967), 207–223.

Slabey, Robert M. "Faulkner's Geography and Hightower's House," *American Notes and Queries*, III (September 1964), 85–86.

—————. "Joe Christmas, Faulkner's Marginal Man," *Phylon*, XXI (Fall 1960), 266–277.

—————. "Myth and Ritual in 'Light in August,'" *Texas Studies in Literature and Language*, II (Autumn 1960), 328–349.

Smith, Hallet. "Summary of a Symposium on 'Light in August,'" *Mississippi Quarterly*, XI (Fall 1958), 188–190.

Sowder, William J. "Christmas as Existential Hero," *University Review*, XXX (June 1964), 279–284.

West, Ray B. "Faulkner's 'Light in August': A View of Tragedy," *Wisconsin Studies in Contemporary Literature*, I (Winter 1960), 5–12.

Williams, John S. "'The Final Copper Light of Afternoon': Hightower's Redemption," *Twentieth Century Literature*, XIII (January 1968), 205–215.